W9-AAB-633

Praise for *Embracing Israel/Palestine*

Embracing Israel/Palestine is a terrific book by a pioneer of global transformation. Out of love for both Israelis and Palestinians as equal creations of God, Rabbi Lerner offers us the deepest way out of the bloody conflict. Not just a political agreement, not a simple "real estate" and power sharing transaction, *Embracing Israel/Palestine* draws from a deep psychological and political understanding of the dynamics of the Middle East. Lerner's book is coming out of a loving heart and a powerful analytic mind. He offers us a strategy of trust that could heal and repair the mentalities of fear that limit the current perspectives that dominate our politics.

—**Avrum Burg**, *former chair of the Jewish Agency and World Zionist Organization, speaker of the Knesset, and interim president of Israel*

Rabbi Michael Lerner is one of America's most significant progressive intellectuals and political leaders, and *Embracing Israel/Palestine* is not only a great conceptual breakthrough in dealing with the Middle East but also demonstrates a methodology for how best to think about global and domestic U.S. politics. For many decades Muslims around the world have been cheered by Rabbi Lerner's challenge to the media's demeaning of our religion and dismissal of the rights of Palestinians, just as they have been challenged by his insistence that they recognize the importance of truly and deeply accepting Israel's right to exist in peace and security. I hope my colleagues on Capitol Hill, the cynical media, and leaders in Israel, Palestine, and throughout the world are pushed by ordinary readers to grapple with the brilliant path to peace and reconciliation put forward in this book. Rabbi Lerner's commitment to nonviolence and a path of love and generosity should not be dismissed as utopian. My experience in Congress leads me to believe, on the contrary, that it is precisely his way of thinking that is the only path that will give Israel, Palestine, and the United States the peace, security, and well-being all three deserve!

—*Rep. **Keith Ellison** (D-Minn.), the first elected Muslim to the U.S. Congress and chair of the seventy-member Progressive Caucus of the U.S. House of Representatives*

Rabbi Michael Lerner provides us with a brilliant and hopeful vision of how to transform the Middle East from a cauldron of violence to a vanguard of peace. For several decades Lerner has been a remarkably courageous rabbi, defying the orthodoxies of some in his own community to insist that Biblical teachings require recognizing the equal value to God of both Israelis and Palestinians. Challenging the extremists on all sides, Lerner insists on the practical and ethical necessity to embrace both Israel and Palestine with compassion and love. Lerner presents us with a path to peace that will require our replacing the strategy of domination and war with what Lerner appropriately describes as the far more effective path to homeland security: the strategy of generosity and genuine caring for the well-being of everyone involved. I hope every American will read this book and apply its lessons to change how we deal with the Middle East.

—*Jimmy **Carter**, 39th president of the United States of America*

Embracing Israel/Palestine is a must-read for those who care about peace in the Middle East. It is provocative, radical, persuasive, and, if given the attention it deserves, could make a major contribution to reconciliation. Please read this book!

—*Archbishop **Desmond Tutu***

Rabbi Michael Lerner is one of the great prophetic figures of our time. He inherited this mantle from his teacher and my hero, Rabbi Abraham Joshua Heschel. This book should be the indispensable work on the delicate and difficult effort to keep track of the precious humanity of Jews and Palestinians in the epic struggles for security and justice.

    —**Cornel West**, *author of* Race Matters *and professor of African American studies and religion at Princeton University*

Our sages tell us: words that come from the heart enter the heart. Michael Lerner's *Embracing Israel/Palestine* is not only a passionate book that comes from the heart, it also demands of us to use *our* hearts. Lerner suggests that a politics of generosity, a politics that begins with careful and compassionate listening to the stories of both Israelis and Palestinians, is the only way forward. The politics of greed and power that is once again on the rise in the United States can only be defeated by a politics that takes as its starting point the worth of all human beings. Lerner has sketched a path from here to there. Read the book. Take up the conversation. Change the world.

    —**Rabbi Aryeh Cohen**, *associate professor of rabbinic literature at American Jewish University and author of* Rereading Talmud

Rabbi Michael Lerner is one of the very few Jewish leaders in the Diaspora who has consistently challenged slavish Jewish pandering to right-wing Israeli chauvinism and messianism, opposed the Occupation of the West Bank and the crimes of many Israeli settlers, supported Palestinian rights and justice for the Palestinian people, called for an end to religious coercion and separation of state and synagogue in Israel, yet has simultaneously retained a strong commitment to the safety and well-being of Israel and the Jewish people. He has been a fierce critic of those who move from legitimate criticism of Israeli policies to illegitimate anti-Semitism or attempts to destroy Israel. His voice needs to be heard by Israelis, Palestinians, and all those who seek peace for the Middle East.

—*Uri Avnery, former member of the Knesset and current chair of the Israeli peace movement Gush Shalom*

This important book will be difficult for many people to read, and those who will find it off-putting are the ones who most need to read it. Some will want to reject it because Rabbi Lerner works so hard to compassionately present the narratives and fears of both "sides." How can he not take a "side"? Still others will seek to argue with one interpretation of a fact or another, or the omission that they deem critical, and will then be relieved that they can dismiss the entire book. These defensive strategies must be put aside, and this book must be read from cover to cover with an open mind, heart, and soul. If you dare to do so you may have a transformative experience.

—*Rabbi Arik W. Ascherman, former director of Rabbis for Human Rights in Israel for fifteen years*

Michael Lerner's passionate call to the Jewish community to heal the wounds of Jewish historical trauma is an indispensable element of peacemaking.

—*Rabbi Lynn Gottlieb*

Embracing Israel/Palestine is the nuanced, historically-balanced, psychologically astute, and spiritually resonant accounting of Israel/Palestine that we have been waiting for. A must-read for all who seek to deepen our understanding of, and our action around, Israel/Palestine.

—*Holly Taya Shere, co-founder of Kohenet Hebrew Priestess Institute*

Michael Lerner has been a national leader of the social change movements in the United States for the past forty-five years. The practical wisdom derived from that experience plus his analytic skills honed as a psychotherapist, philosopher, and theologian combine in this book to give Americans, Israelis, and Palestinians a brilliant path to heal the Middle East. This book is at once a major intellectual achievement, a practical guide for peacemakers, and a perspective on politics and social change that everyone needs to read. Share it with your most partisan friends on every side of this issue and on every side of America's political divisions, and watch how they begin to broaden and mellow their understanding of the world.
—**Michael Nagler**, *founder of Peace Studies at U.C. Berkeley and chair of the Metta Center for Nonviolence*

I've read dozens of books on the subject, but none has the potential this book has to inform wisely and fairly, mobilize good will effectively, and motivate action intelligently toward needed change. Rabbi Lerner's generous Jewish vision warms my Christian heart, and his deep integration of spirituality, theology, political philosophy, and human kindness serves as a model I hope many will join me in following.
—**Brian McLaren**, *Christian Evangelical Pastor and author of* A New Kind of Christianity

Rabbi Lerner writes from a deep and passionate framework of social justice within the Jewish tradition. Yet he is deeply sensitive to the humanity and moral imperative to find a solution that speaks to the needs of both Israel and Palestine— indeed, they are inextricably linked.
—**Aaron Back**, *director of Israel Social Justice Fund*

Embracing Israel/Palestine is a masterpiece among the myriads of studies dedicated to the numerous human catastrophes of our times. No matter how many books you've read on this subject, Rabbi Lerner will give you a new and powerfully insightful perspective that could empower you to play a significant and hopefully effective role in healing this conflict—and in doing so beginning to heal the world.

> —*Zygmunt Bauman, author of* Modernity and the Holocaust *and* Postmodernity and Its Discontents

Rabbi Lerner's penetrating analysis both grasps the complexities that polarize Israel and Palestine and lays out a stunningly clear potential for peace. Lerner's breathtaking insights challenge all of the assumptions of despair and cynicism and bring light and hope to one of the most difficult political conundrums of our time.

> — *Rabbi Dan Goldblatt*

Michael Lerner takes a courageous, enlightening position in *Embracing Israel/Palestine*, not only in speaking as an American Jewish rabbi who cares about both countries, but in his conviction that only real attention to the suffering and historical traumas of both sides can bring about peace. The intellectual clarity and psychological sophistication of his presentation is matched by his passionate plea for the transformation of religion from a tool for political partisanship to a basis for genuine renewal of commitment to justice and recognition of all peoples. His argument breaks the conventional splitting between the pragmatic and the idealistic, making a convincing case that only respect for the needs of all peoples will bring about the will and the possibility of resolution.

> —*Jessica Benjamin, psychoanalyst and author of* The Bonds of Love

Rabbi Lerner has been passionately advocating a new era of peace and reconciliation in the Holy Land utilizing the interfaith resources. We are confident that this spirit of mutual respect and cooperation can work in the Holy Land as well. There are enough resources in our scriptures, traditions, and history to make such solidarity legitimate. I hope that Muslims, Jews, and Christians will use *Embracing Israel/Palestine* as a jumping off point for discussing how our three faiths can work together to bring peace and justice to the Middle East.

—*Sayyid M. Syeed*, National Director at the Islamic Society of North America's Office for Interfaith & Community Alliances

This book would change the world if there were enough people who would open their eyes and read it. Lerner uses Israel/Palestine as a prism to look at the world as a whole—rife with conflicts of many kinds, a number of which involve the United States. He comes to the wildly "utopian" conclusion that the solution to these conflicts can only come by following the Biblical injunctions to love the stranger. Far from being utopian or unrealistic, Lerner shows that this will be the only practical way to keep the alliance of nationalism and capitalism that rules the world today from destroying the fabric of natural and social life. I hope this book will be used widely in courses in political science and sociology in our universities, not only in courses about the Middle East.

—*Robert Bellah*, Professor Emeritus, University of California, Berkeley, author of Religion in Human Evolution, and co-author of Habits of the Heart

There are good books and there are needed books. This book is both. It is good because Michael Lerner gives an insightful account of the history and politics of struggles between Israelis and Palestinians. It is needed because he grasps the religious underpinnings of this conflict and his spiritually progressive perspectives offer hope for peace. What Rabbi Lerner has to say will be especially helpful for my fellow Evangelicals who must balance their justifiable love for Israel with a cry for justice for the Palestinian people.

–*Tony Campolo*, *Evangelical pastor and professor of sociology at Eastern University*

Embracing
Israel/Palestine

Other Books by Rabbi Michael Lerner

Jewish Renewal:
A Path to Healing and Transformation

The Politics of Meaning:
Restoring Hope and Possibility in an Age of Cynicism

The Socialism of Fools:
Anti-Semitism on the Left

Spirit Matters:
Global Healing and the Wisdom of the Soul

Surplus Powerlessness:
The Psychodynamics of Everyday Life and the Psychology of
Individual and Social Transformation

Jews & Blacks:
A Dialogue on Race, Religion, and Culture in America
(with Cornel West)

Healing Israel/Palestine:
A Path to Peace and Reconciliation

The Left Hand of God:
Healing America's Political and Spiritual Crisis

Embracing Israel/Palestine

A Strategy to Heal

and Transform

the Middle East

Rabbi Michael Lerner

Tikkun Books

תיקון

North Atlantic Books
Berkeley, California

Copyright © 2012 by Tikkun Books. All rights reserved.

Published by Tikkun Books
2342 Shattuck Ave, Suite 1200
Berkeley, California 94704
www.tikkun.org • magazine@tikkun.org
and
North Atlantic Books
P.O. Box 12327
Berkeley, California 94712
www.northatlanticbooks.com

Printed in the United States of America

Cover art: No Exit by Samuel Bak. Courtesy of Pucker Gallery
www.puckergallery.com

Library of Congress Cataloging-in-Publication Data
Lerner, Michael, 1943–
 Embracing Israel/Palestine : a strategy to heal and transform the Middle
East / Michael Lerner.
    p. cm.
Includes index.
 "Some of this book first appeared in a Tikkun Books version called Healing
Israel/Palestine in 2003."—Intr.
 Summary: "Embracing Israel/Palestine presents Rabbi Michael Lerner's continuing
attempt to explain the current struggles between Israel and Palestine in a way that is
sympathetic to both sides and provides a strategy for building a lasting peace based on
overcoming the PTSD that shapes each side's perception of the Other, a recognition that
the well-being of each is intrinsically tied to the well-being of the Other, a spirit of generosity, and openhearted reconciliation"—Provided by publisher.
    ISBN 978-1-58394-307-6
    1. Arab-Israeli conflict—1993—Peace. 2. Jews—Palestine—History—20th
century. 3. American Foreign Policy 4. Refugees, Arab—Middle East—History—20th
century. 5 Pacific settlement of international disputes. 6. Reconciliation. 7. Conflict
management. 8. Arab-Israeli conflict. 9. Arab-Israeli conflict—Territorial questions.
10. Judaism I. Title.
 DS119.76.L467 2011
 956.05'4—dc23

                                        2011022037

            2 3 4 5 6 7 8 9 Malloy 17 16 15 14 13 12

This book is dedicated to my granddaughter
Ellie Lyla Lerner and my grandson
Jeremiah Jacob Lerner. May their generation
continue the work of *tikkun*.

And to my teacher and personal mentor at
the Jewish Theological Seminary,
Abraham Joshua Heschel.

Acknowledgments

I greatly appreciate the editing and production help I received from Alana Yu-lan Price, Robert Zeuner, David Sylvester, Phil Wolfson, Stephen Goldbart, David Glick, Kimmianne Webster, Mia Sullivan, Martha Woolverton, Mike Godbe, Ashley Bates, Sayaka Merriam, Laura Beckman, Natalie Rogers, Sabiha Basrai, Frank Paredes, and Emily Boyd, and the publishing support from Richard Grossinger and North Atlantic Books.

TABLE OF CONTENTS

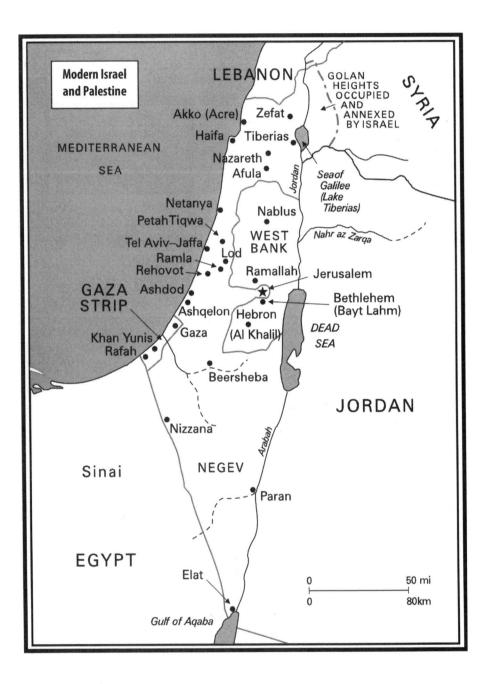

Introduction

The Challenge: The Historical Roots of Trauma

Jews did not return to their ancient homeland to oppress the Palestinian people, and Palestinians did not resist the creation of a Jewish state out of hatred of the Jews.

During the long history of propaganda battles between Zionists and Palestinians, each community has at times implied that the other has consistently done bad things for bad reasons. In fact, both sides have made and continue to make terrible mistakes. Yet the choices of both sides are also understandable, given their perceptions of their own and the other's situation. As long as each community clings to its own story, unable to acknowledge what is plausible in the story of the other side, peace will remain a distant hope. That clinging is a product of the trauma that both peoples have experienced in their history, including but not limited to the trauma of the Israeli-Palestinian conflict. One reason that I've chosen to refer to the Holy Land as Israel/Palestine is that I insist on the ultimate oneness of both peoples and believe that their fate is intrinsically linked.

In this book, I offer a more balanced perspective on this story—a perspective that explores how decent human beings in

1

each community could end up perceiving the other as an irreconcilable enemy. I also explore how, within their own frameworks, each became blind to the other's legitimate needs and the ways their own community contributed to the current mess. The eyes of both Israelis and Palestinians are so glazed over with the immediacy of painful historical memories that they have not been able to envision new possibilities in their relationship that might bring both communities the peace they actually desire.

Later on, I will outline what a final settlement could look like in light of the historical experiences and traumas of each community. But the first step in the process of healing is to tell the story of how we got where we are in a way that avoids demonization. We need to learn how two groups of human beings, each containing the usual range of people—from loving to hateful, rational to demented, idealistic to self-centered—could end up feeling so angry at each other.

Diplomats and politicians generally assume they can solve the problems of the Middle East with a new peace plan or a set of borders, paired with new security and trade agreements, but these measures alone will never be successful.

Huge traumas have constricted the ability of Israelis and Palestinians to see and act upon what is in their own best interests. For those of us who truly care about the well-being of both sides, or even of either side, the task is to heal the trauma. That healing is not just a political or psychological project but also a spiritual project.

THE FIRST STEP: LISTENING TO AND EMBRACING THE OTHER

A central task in reaching peace is for each community to embrace the other. Only after Palestinians and Israelis receive the emotional and spiritual nurturance they desperately need will they be able to develop an enlightened view of their own group's true self-interest. In this case, as in so many others, this necessarily involves the fulfillment of the legitimate needs of the other community's enlightened self-interest. It is by embracing each community in a spirit of genuine caring, openheartedness, and generosity that we can begin the process of transforming the Middle East. To be able to do that, we will need not only a new psychological orientation but also a spiritual transformation—one that allows us to let go of the idea that security requires domination of the other and instead to embrace the idea that lasting security can be better achieved through generosity and caring for others. This is the Strategy of Generosity.

We in the West could make a tremendous contribution to helping heal the strife between Israelis and Palestinians if we embraced the Strategy of Generosity ourselves and let it guide our foreign and domestic policies. Although the book is mostly about Israel and Palestine, it is really also about us and the path that our Western societies take. So far, under Democratic and Republican administrations the United States and its allies have taken the path based on the Strategy of Domination. It is unlikely that we are going to achieve any lasting healing in the Middle East until we ourselves can become embodiments of the Strategy of Generosity.

That won't happen in one single moment. It requires a process of consciousness transformation, toward which this book is intended to make a contribution. This may sound bookish or academic, so let me also translate it into ordinary language: the Strategy of Generosity is about empowering our most loving, kind, and generous instincts, honoring the spiritual wisdom of our traditions (both religious and secular) that teach us that every human being on the planet is equally precious and deserving of well-being and fulfillment. It's also about building political and economic arrangements that facilitate rather than undermine our capacity to care for each other across all religious, national, and ethnic lines. In policy terms, this means the launching of a Global Marshall Plan to end global poverty, hunger, inadequate education, and substandard health care and to repair the global physical environment. The first place to launch a Global Marshall Plan is the Middle East.

How can we begin this process of moving from domination to generosity in relation to the Middle East? By listening to the stories of each community and recognizing that each has a legitimate narrative, is in pain, and needs its pain acknowledged before it can move to a real *tikkun* (healing, repair). Such a reconciliation process depends on honestly confronting the wounds of each community. This does not mean making the wounds of the victim the same as the wounds of the oppressor—a reconciliation process does not need to equalize suffering—but it does involve the victims in both communities telling the stories of their oppressors. Palestinians whose homes were demolished or whose children were wounded, maimed, or killed need to tell their pain to the military planners in Israel, just as the residents of Sderot or mothers of children killed by suicide bombers need to describe their pain to the Hamas planners, with as many members of each society as possible listening to these testimonies.

It is only when people in both communities are able to open their minds to each other with real depth, compassion, openheartedness, and generosity that we can achieve the kind of reconciliation of the heart necessary to sustain any peace agreement.

As we listen to each other, we can recognize the mutual tragedy of both peoples. The Jews were people who jumped from the burning buildings in Europe onto the backs of the bystanders on the street below.

From 1880 to 1950, the Jewish people jumped from the burning buildings not because we wished to but because we were desperate to save ourselves from the hatred that would soon spawn the mass murder of Jews in Europe. Until the United States closed its doors to immigration in 1924, most Jews went to North and South America, South Africa, Australia, and England—not to colonize but to find refuge. Palestine was one of many such destinations, and by the 1930s, it was one of the very few places where many Jews could get in.

So we landed on the backs of Palestinians.

The Palestinians and the Arab people of the Middle East were in the midst of a struggle to free themselves from colonial powers and were afraid of the Zionist dream of creating a Jewish state on the very land where they were attempting to build their own fledgling Palestinian society. They viewed the Jews who came to Palestine not as desperate refugees but as Europeans introducing European cultural assumptions, economic and political arrangements, and thereby extending the dynamics of European domination to the Middle East. Therefore, the Arabs in general, and those who lived in Palestine in particular, were unwilling to give Jews a safe place to land.

The Palestinians used acts of violence and the influence of Arab states with the British to deny Jews a refuge. Their fearful rejection of the Jewish people and our needs helped create a dynamic in which Jews actually became what the Palestinians had feared: a group that would cause Palestinians to become refugees. Years later, Israelis responded in kind when they had gained power by refusing to provide a way for Palestinians to return to their homes.

As Jews established our state in our ancient homeland, we hurt many Palestinians and evicted many from their homes. When the Palestinian people cried out, we could not hear their pain—our ears were still ringing with the cries of family members who had been murdered and the cries of hundreds of thousands of Jews still stuck in refugee camps in Europe. We were only aware of the genocide we had barely survived. We believed that the scale of our own pain justified what we were doing to Palestinians as we sought to create a homeland and safe haven for ourselves, particularly in light of their violent resistance to Jews coming to Palestine.

Each community's denial of the pain that it inflicted on the other has made it impossible for each to talk honestly with the other and heal the wounds. Instead, they have continued to inflict new pains that intensify the old. For decades Israel has ruled over the Palestinian people, and Palestinians have responded to that Occupation with armed struggle and acts of terror against Israeli civilians. Israelis have increasingly secured the Occupation by using methods that violate international standards of human rights and make a mockery of the highest values of the Jewish tradition.

Each sides acts in ways that are cruel and insensitive to the other. As almost always happens in these situations, the most fearful feelings come to the fore, inciting ultranationalist or fundamentalist leaders to rise within the injured community and causing the opposing community to become equally as hard and harsh in order to protect itself. I'm writing this book as an attempt to aid those who wish to break this cycle of pain, mutual indifference, and cruelty.

THE NEXT STEP: A PEACE BASED ON COMPASSION AND HEALING

Later in the book, I will detail some of what a peace agreement might look like and how we in the West can help create the psychological, intellectual, and spiritual preconditions for an agreement that actually lasts. It is only when each side can genuinely understand and empathize with the other's history that we can create the kind of compassion that is needed to go beyond the narrow frame of political doctrines and demands and reach a reconciliation of the heart.

This is a great challenge, for the readers of this book and even more so for those in the societies that need this transformation of consciousness. You may well feel angry at me for even suggesting that we listen to both sides. Anyone who has visited the West Bank in the last few years knows that it can take three hours or more to get through one of the many checkpoints separating

Palestinian cities from each other and has watched the humiliating ways that Palestinians are often treated. Anyone who has participated in what was intended to be a nonviolent demonstration against the Occupation has seen how the demonstrators are fired upon with teargas and live ammunition and how younger Palestinians, frustrated with the discipline of nonviolence, pick up rocks to throw in self-defense only to find themselves or their friends getting shot. If you have actually witnessed the suffering of innocent Palestinians, listened to their heart-wrenching stories, you may find it offensive that this book asks you to also listen to the story of Israelis, particularly since you think you've heard it so many times before (though not with the framework presented here).

Similarly, anyone who has attended the funeral of children knifed to death by a Palestinian terrorist in early 2011, or who has visited Sderot in the Israeli Negev and talked to parents about the trauma their children have faced when they spend hours in underground shelters to escape shells from Gaza, may feel angry that I'm even trying to get them to imagine the story as understood by Palestinians.

It's even more difficult to think of an evenhanded account at moments like the one in which I'm writing. Israel has never had a more intransigent leadership and a population less interested in significant compromise. At the same time, Palestinians have a government more open to compromise and a population more anxious to achieve peace than ever. You may think I'm talking as though both sides were somehow equal when it's easy to see that for the moment, Israel has little interest in making any significant compromises for peace. And of course Israel has had overwhelming military power while Palestinians have virtually no capacity to withstand Israel's army, which enters and kills suspected "militants" at will in Gaza and the West Bank.

It is this inequality of power that has led a significant part of the Jewish world to reject the traditional story of Israel as the courageous David fighting an arrogant Goliath. Like many non-Jews, liberal and progressive Jews were outraged when, addressing the U.S. Congress in the spring of 2011, Prime Minister Netanyahu repeated empty formulas guaranteed to block any serious negotiations yet received twenty-nine standing ovations from Democrats and Republicans alike. Nor do I want to deny that I've met many Israelis and American Jews whose attitude could best be summed up as, "We won the wars, we have the military power to do what we want, the winners always get to define the terms, so let them complain as much as they want. Who cares as long as our army can beat them and their allies combined? Our Wall and secret service can stop most of their terrorists, and our ally in America can veto any negative resolutions proposed by the UN Security Council." This is the arrogance of the powerful, supported by the greatest superpower of the contemporary world: the United States.

I have been the editor of *Tikkun* magazine for the past twenty-five years, and every week for at least twenty of those years I get emails and phone calls from around the world, from people of every faith asking me to "do something" to end the horrible suffering of the Palestinian people. I also get calls from Jews who tell me how alienated they feel from their Jewishness because of what Israel is doing and angry letters denouncing me for being a self-hating Jew or an anti-Semite for even daring to present a Palestinian perspective. Yet I've also been subject to attack from many on the Left who see me as a sophisticated apologist for Israel and Zionism. I am a strong critic of those on the Left who have singled out Israel for special disdain. I cry when I hear of Israelis wounded or killed by terrorist violence, because they are my people, part of my extended family. But similarly, I find it extremely painful when I hear of acts of violence by Israeli settlers or by the Israeli Army (IDF) against Palestinian civilians including children, or when I read reports from various human rights organizations detailing torture or other atrocities committed in the name of Israel. So for me, these are very personal issues.

There is a great temptation, then, to rant and rave at the sins being committed by either or both sides. I think that articulating righteous indignation and confronting those who support oppressive or violent policies has a real and valuable place. The voice of the prophet is critical in waking people up to the realities and why they must be changed. Yet, I also believe that there is a temptation that must be avoided. We get mired in our own righteousness and avoid the more difficult question: how are we going to change things? *Tikkun* is the Hebrew word for healing and transformation, and our goal is not only to identify that which is evil, but to change it and transform it. And this next step sometimes requires us to modulate our cries of righteous indignation and to focus more on how we can change things.

It is my contention in this book that such change is going to require a healing of the pain and distortions in both Israel and Palestine and in their respective diaspora communities, and even a significant transformation in the consciousness of people throughout Western society regarding the best path to achieve homeland security. So, the challenge is to both affirm the righteous indignation and to simultaneously affirm the fundamental decency and humanity of people on the various sides of this conflict in a way that enables them to feel safe enough to open up their minds to the possibility of a new kind of relationship with each other and with the world. For that, we need to draw on the psychological and spiritual wisdom of the human race. And in so doing, we shall see that the issue of healing and transforming Israel and Palestine leads us directly into a way of thinking that is equally relevant to all the other struggles going on in the world today, including the struggles inside Western countries for peace, justice, and environmental sanity.

L PATH TO HEALING

of Judaism, Christianity, and Islam requires oples in Israel/Palestine. The task is not to determine whᴏ ᴏght" but to build a path that will be best for both peoples. Although Israel has superior strength at this historical moment, that may not always be the case in the future. However, the more immediate risk is to Judaism. As it continues the Occupation of the West Bank, Israel risks losing its moral authority and the right to claim itself as an inheritor of the Jewish tradition. Its current policies put Israel in danger of becoming a globally despised state, not because of anti-Semitism but because of its actual policies toward Palestinians. And this would obscure for many the tremendous beauty of Israeli society and its already significant contributions to health, scientific and technological knowledge, and the well-being of many on this planet.

Instead, Jews must revitalize Israel as a moral community in order to achieve a positive outcome for Jewish identity itself. One need not be a believer in God or a practitioner of Judaism or any other religion in order to respond to my call for a morally rooted Judaism—what I call Emancipatory Judaism. I describe later in this book what a love-oriented Judaism has been and can be again—based on the history of the formation of Jewish identity during oppression, slavery, suffering, idealism, hope, and the ultimate perception of the universal goodness in humanity and the way that the arc of the universe tilts toward love and generosity. That same kind of transformation is needed in Christianity and Islam, and even in some of the assumptions of atheists and secular individuals, if we are ever to build a sane and environmentally sustainable global human society.

Although the meaning of this moral dimension is expressed for me and for many others through the transcendent religious discourse of God, this concern can be just as powerful for secular

Jews and non-Jews who grasp the moral dimension of reality and the importance of a spiritualizing awareness but don't reach that moral dimension through God language. I'm hoping that the many secular Jews and non-Jews will not lose interest because at points, particularly in the last chapter, I present my moral commitments in a religious framework and call for a significant change in Judaism (and by implication, in all religious communities).

To those readers who are Jewish, my message is simple: we need to reclaim Judaism from the hands of those who have mistakenly identified it with policies of ultra-nationalism, fundamentalism, and ethnic chauvinism. What I call "Settler Judaism" is actually an unconscious rebellion against God and against that which has been most sacred and valuable about the Jewish tradition, led by people who go through all the motions of a religious life but who have totally abandoned a belief that the world could actually be based on central principles of Judaism like "love your neighbor," "love the stranger," or "justice, justice shalt thou pursue." Young Jews whom I meet when I'm invited to speak on college campuses often tell me that they want nothing to do with Judaism because they have been told by parents, by teachers at their religious school, or by leaders of the Jewish community that to be a "good Jew" one must support the current policies of the State of Israel. Many respond in their hearts by saying, "If this is the precondition for being Jewish, I can't be Jewish anymore."

Yet I know that there is a very different path to being Jewish, a path that embraces love, kindness, and a generosity of spirit. That path, which I'll discuss in the latter part of this book, is an alternative that could save Judaism and the Jewish people from the damage being done by those who have hijacked our religion and turned it into a public relations arm of a particular government of the State of Israel.

However, I did not write this book only for Jews. I've met many Christians and Muslims, Hindus and Buddhists, who have watched with pain as their own religions have been hijacked by the chauvinists, fundamentalists, and ultra-nationalists as well. And I know many secular humanists—people who reject religion as the basis for morality and espouse a philosophy based on human reason and ethical justice—who have watched with great pain as the best ideals of democracy and human rights have been appropriated by powerful elites to justify global imperialism and the domination of others. Many of these people are central to building a world of love, justice, peace, environmental sanity, and mutual caring. Yet when they look at the Middle East they often feel despair. Some have said to me, "If even in the Holy Land, the place where the world heard the vision of peace and justice first articulated, we now see the very people who articulated those ideals at each other's throats, what chance do we have to build peace and justice on this planet?"

We must take seriously the words of the Prophet Isaiah: "Nation shall not lift up sword against nation, neither shall they learn war anymore." The path to peace is a path of peace, and it is also a path of forgiveness, love, and generosity. Before you dismiss this as a utopian fantasy, please read this book and share it with others.

My Personal Journey

At the same time, those who are familiar with the Palestinian experience will likely feel that the way I tell the story is inadequate—a story told by a Jew who doesn't fully understand or know the psychodynamics and realities of Palestinian and Arab history and society and hence will not give adequate weight to all the outrages of Israeli behavior. I acknowledge the validity of this criticism about the limits of what I can see and hence of what this book can present. Some readers of this book may also come away with the mistaken impression that Palestinian life is only about suffering and not realize that even within the context of oppression and expulsion, Palestinians have developed a rich cultural community, in part drawing upon the rich spiritual and intellectual heritage of Arab, Muslim, and Christian life of the past 1400 years. Many are able to build joyous and fulfilling lives for themselves, and some have developed fulfilling friendships on a personal basis with some Israelis.

I can understand why each side would feel uncomfortable with my attempt to tell the story in ways that give the other side's narrative more validity than perhaps they have ever considered giving it in the past. And they will be right to point to the limits of my perspective, inevitably shaped as it is by my own background and assumptions.

I am Jewish and the rabbi of Beyt Tikkun Synagogue-Without-Walls in Berkeley, California (www.beyttikkun.org). I grew up in a Zionist household. My father was national vice president of the Zionist Organization of America. As a result, I was able to hear the Zionist account from the inside. David Ben Gurion, Abba Eban, Golda Meir, and Abba Hillel Silver visited our family home while I was growing up, and their perceptions of the world shaped the discourse in my family. My parents believed that their own role as political forces inside the Democratic Party (my father was a judge, my mother a political advisor to a U.S. senator and to several governors) made it possible for them to do more for Israel from the United States than they could by making aliyah (moving to Israel). But I also learned of a less appealing discourse about Israel when former President Truman and soon-to-be U.S. Representative to the United Nations Adlai Stevenson visited my home and talked about their support for Israel in terms of its value in the Cold War. I also heard this discourse in my visits to soon-to-be-President John F. Kennedy in his Senate offices. Even then, I was not a big fan of wars; I was well aware that the United States was using the excuse of the Cold War to extend its military power around the world. American Zionists told themselves that they had organized and successfully pushed elected representatives away from the State Department's tilt toward the Arabs, so they found it hard to acknowledge how much the United States' shift toward Israeli interests was a product of American military and strategic thinking that emerged during and after the 1970s.

Israel was not a huge issue in public consciousness during my years at the Jewish Theological Seminary in New York, nor was it a central issue in Jewish thought. I shared with my mentor Abraham Joshua Heschel a clear commitment to Israel's well-being and an understanding that the central issue on the Jewish agenda must move from "security" and "defense" to the spiritual need to serve God and heal the world.

I waited until I was twenty-two to embark on my first extended stay on a kibbutz, and I loved it. Yet I was stunned by the lack of strong commitment to the socialist ideals that had originally motivated it—the ideals of equality and social justice that the early kibbutzniks believed would infuse the life of the kibbutz and eventually shape the larger Israeli society. It was only when I began to ask about the origins of this particular kibbutz in the struggle against the Palestinian Arabs that I stumbled upon a terrible truth: the land on which I was working had been owned by Palestinians who had been displaced by the Zionist enterprise. In the course of that struggle, most kibbutzniks picked nationalist loyalties over internationalist commitments, a choice that played a powerful role in undermining the larger socialist commitments that had led the founders of this kibbutz to start the enterprise in the first place.

Still, at the time, those issues stayed abstract and academic to me, since I had not met any Palestinians. I loved the kibbutz and loved the people I met on it. During the Six Day War of 1967, I cheered Israel's victories and defended it to some of my friends in the anti-Vietnam War movement who were hostile toward Zionism. At the time, I had no hesitation in identifying with the State of Israel.

The next year, in response to challenges to Israel from leftists on the campus at the University of California, Berkeley, where I was earning my Ph.D. and organizing against the Vietnam War, I started an organization called the Committee for Peace in the Middle East, together with Mario Savio. He had been the fiery orator of the Free Speech Movement and an activist in the Student Nonviolent Coordinating Committee (SNCC). We spoke out for a position that validated both the Zionist state and Palestinians' right to national self-determination. Even then, the Jewish world was outraged that we dared to criticize Israeli policies and the American Jewish institutions that supported it. The Jewish world became steadily more repressive toward dissenters who criticized Israeli policy toward Palestinians. The next year, the American Jewish Congress fired the editor of *Judaism* magazine, Steven Schwarzschild. He had committed the "sin" of reprinting a section of the founding statement of our Committee for Peace in the Middle East and my personal statement of critique in which I used prophetic tones that now seem to me overly harsh toward the Jewish community that I loved. Yet many were shocked that the American Jewish Congress, once a bastion of civil liberties, had moved so far from its founding commitments to free speech in order to do what they felt was necessary to protect Israel from its critics.

As I write this, the denial of free speech has gone much further and permeates many institutions of the organized diaspora Jewish community. In the West, people who criticize Israeli policies are often denounced for "delegitimizing" Israel, even though many of these people are overt supporters of Israel. Similarly, in Palestine and in other parts of the Arab world, Arabs who criticize Hamas or advocate nonviolence—as a growing number of Palestinians are now doing—face angry and hostile criticism, and in some cases overt violence, from members of their own community. The split between fundamentalist Muslims and more accommodationist Palestinians (both Muslim and Christian) has sometimes led to deadly conflict. In the West and the Middle East, it is economically and politically risky to criticize either side. Each side interprets all criticism as reflective of a deeper irrational hostility that confirms its members' feeling of being abandoned by the rest of the world. Many people in each community will strike out at the critics rather than reflect on what in their own activities might have legitimately drawn criticism.

In the West, many people refuse to criticize Israeli policy even vaguely unless they are willing to face loss of jobs or promotions, isolation from many parts of the Jewish community, and outright slander and abuse. There are few Jewish families in the United States in which some member has not been accused of being a "self-hating Jew" because she or he questioned certain Israeli policies toward Palestinians. As a rabbi, I find that one of my most difficult tasks is to bring people back into the Jewish world who felt they had to leave Judaism altogether in order to maintain their own ethical and spiritual integrity, since their previous Jewish communities were so hostile to their independent moral judgments.

My study of the history of the conflict in Israel/Palestine has led me to a deeper understanding of some of the pathologies and violence that have been perpetrated by people on both sides. That understanding has reinforced my view that both sides have legitimate claims, each side has legitimate grievances against the other, and both sides have made terrible errors.

In my study of the history of past societies and their conflicts, it is very rare that one party to a struggle is "right" and the other "wrong." There are instances in anti-colonial or anti-imperialist struggles in which one side seems to be interested only in grabbing the land and resources of another for no reason beyond self-aggrandizement and material gain, but most struggles are far more complex. For example, people without adequate food and agricultural land migrate to lands where there is more food. However, the people who live on that land, themselves descendents of previous migrants, decide they cannot afford to share and so they try to repel the new migrants. Is the group who got there first more right than the second group, who needs food, even if the first group got their land by fighting against some previous group? Many of the more famous wars in history were motivated by greed and the desire for more, yet not all such struggles can be reduced to colonial or imperial lust.

In fact, most people who engage in discourse about the Middle East know this. In the rest of their lives they are far more sophisticated, and they look for economic, social, and psychological factors to explain the realities that they encounter. But when it comes to the Middle East, their prejudices require that they suspend their own intellectual and psychological sophistication to weave tales that "prove" that their side is right and the other is wrong.

They justify this failure of nerve by saying: "The Middle East is different. The people there are unlike other people, so you can't apply what you know to this reality." What they are really saying is, "The people I disagree with there are evil or primitive and you are naïve to believe otherwise." Some have even adopted various schemas of psychological, ethical, or spiritual development to indicate that the people they support (usually of European origin) are on a higher stage of evolution than those whom they oppose; therefore it would be a mistake to reason with them the way you'd reason with someone at a higher stage of development.

I see this dehumanization of the Other as something akin to racism. Instead of recognizing their shared humanity, many people treat those perceived as the Other as though they didn't share the same emotional, physical, spiritual, and ethical needs and desires as members of their own community. This is racism in its broadest sense: the systematic denial of an entire group's fundamental humanity.

I'm aware of atrocities and racist actions on all sides of this conflict, and I regularly receive information from partisans on both sides who point out ethically outrageous words and actions of the other side.

A major contribution to the needed healing can occur when people begin to tell the story of the Middle East in ways that validate both sides' truth, pain, and suffering and affirm the fundamental decency of the people caught in this struggle. In this way, I am both pro-Israel and pro-Palestine, and this book will show you how that can be possible.

Peace can be achieved in the Middle East. The difficult news is this: it depends on ordinary people like you and me to make it happen. One reason I've written this book is to give you tools to help you talk effectively with others. Please use this book as a basis for a small study group to discuss the issues raised here and explore further readings, study, and action. Please get it into the hands of others and encourage them to read it as well. You'll find that many people have never heard a balanced perspective, have never really tried to empathize with those with whom they disagree. Even if they still disagree after reading this book, they may have less anger and be less willing to dismiss the other side as "evil." And they may learn from this book how to use the strategy of empathizing with those with whom they disagree as a key to developing social change.

If you allow yourself to perceive the world through the framework I develop in this book, you will become a boundary spanner, one who seeks to mend deep wounds with an ethos of compassion and openhearted spirit of generosity toward the Other. And that is the very meaning of the word "Hebrew," derived from the Semitic root for the notion of crossing over a boundary. The Hebrews were ancient boundary crossers, and through the history of Judaism, Christianity, and Islam, the children of Abraham have been noted precisely for this capacity to cross existing boundaries and popularize boundary-shattering ideas. So I invite you to be this kind of Hebrew, to read this book not primarily in order to find where you disagree, but rather to suspend your disagreements for a moment and to look at the world through a framework of genuine openheartedness.

Some of you reading this book may already know that too many people in the Israeli and Palestinian communities and in their Diaspora, and their supporters around the world, hold a belief that they are righteous victims. You know that this narrative is fundamentally mistaken, because each community has been unnecessarily insensitive and at times cruel toward the Other. You may also think you know enough about the historical details, or feel that you simply don't need to, in order to want to heal and transform the psychological and spiritual dynamics that keep people attached to this process of demonizing the Other. In that case, you may simply skip to the last part of this book, starting with Chapter Seven. You have my permission.

In the final four chapters of the book, you will find a psychological and spiritual vision and an explanation of how it ties to a specific political program for resolving the Middle East conflict. More than that, you'll find ideas on how to deal with Post-Traumatic Stress Disorders (PTSDs) when they manifest for an entire society, not just for Israeli and Palestinian societies, but also for the United States and other Western societies. It is my contention that we cannot save the United States from various forms of Tea Party or other pre-fascist developments in the West unless we can address the PTSD elements in our collective consciousness. And, speaking as a Jewish spiritual leader, I'll also present what I'm calling a love-oriented Emancipatory Judaism that can become an effective counter to the kind of Settler Judaism that increasingly dominates most of the existing denominations of Jewish life in the United States and Israel. I also believe that there are growing numbers of Christians, Muslims, Buddhists, Hindus, secular humanists, and atheists who are recognizing the need for a love-oriented emancipatory vision for their own communities. I hope they will find the analysis I've presented of considerable use in their own activities.

However, a cautionary note: if you actually want to become involved in actively changing the situation in the Middle East, you would do best not to skip but to review the historical analysis. You may know many of the facts, but it is unlikely you've found many other sources that attempt to present the history in a framework that seeks to develop our compassion for both Israelis and Palestinians.

A Framework to Understand, Not a History

This is not meant to be a new work of scholarship but rather a way to understand contemporary reality in order to have the tools to change it. This is not a book of history but a framework through which one can understand history. I don't use footnotes because I don't want to interrupt the flow of the argument to "prove" my historical reading. I'm not claiming to have unearthed new historical facts. I'm not an academic seeking to use this to prove my credentials. After earning two Ph.D.s and serving on the faculty of four institutions of higher learning, I retired from academia and took a different path, seeking not only to understand the world but also to change it. So what is unusual about the book is its perspective, not its facts.

This book is heavily dependent on the works of many other historians and Middle East scholars, social theorists, political activists, psychologists, poets, novelists, and philosophers. In some places I've merely summarized and synthesized the writing of these scholars. I encourage you to read the books listed in the appendix that provided some of the empirical basis for my thinking. The original contribution that I seek to make through this book is a way of thinking about the facts that tells the story of both sides in a compassionate way—something you won't find in many history books.

I rely particularly on the work of Benny Morris and Samih K. Farsoun, whose writings are sometimes taken into this text without direct attribution. Yet my perspective is also influenced by the writings of or the personal conversations (and sometimes intense arguments) I had over the years with Shulamit Aloni, Daniel Ben-Ami, Yehuda Amichai, Hanan Ashrawi, Shlomo Avineri, Uri Avnery, Mubarak Awad, Ariella Azoulay, Aaron Back, Uzi Baram, Mustafa Barghouti, Mordechai Bar-On, Zygmunt Bauman, Yossi Beilin, David Biale, Ian J. Bickerton, Azmi Bishara, Tsvi Blanchard, Cherie Brown, Avrum Burg, Noam Chomsky, Hillel Cohen, Yael Dayan, Abba Eban, Bassem Eid, Akiva Eldar, Sidra DeKoven Ezrahi, Yarom Ezrahi, Jacob Feldt, Eitan Felner, Yaakov Fogelman, Yitzhak Frankenthal, Tom Friedman, Mordecai Gafni, Daphna Golan, Galia Golan, Marc Gopin, Neve Gordon, Yosef Gorny, Yitz Greenberg, David Grossman, Bonna Devora Haberman, Moshe Halbertal, Jeff Halper, David Hartman, Geoffrey Hartman, Amira Hass, Naomi Hazan, Yoram Hazony, Tamar Hermann, Arthur Hertzberg, Hannan Hever, Anat Hoffman, Faisal Husseini, Rashid Khalidi, Baruch Kimmerling, Michael Kleiner, David Kretzmer, Irwin Kula, Daoud Kuttab, Daniel Landes, Yitzhak Laor, Yeshayahu

Leibowitz, Akiba Lerner, Debora Kohn Lerner, Joseph Lerner, Mark LeVine, Ian Lustick, Jonathan Mark, Tzvi Marx, Uri Milstein, Jessica Montell, David Newman, Micha Odenheimer, Adi Ophir, Wendy Orange, Amos Oz, Ilan Pappé, Pinchas Peli, Shimon Peres, Letty Cottin Pogrebin, Yehoshua Porath, Yitzhak Rabin, Avi Ravitsky, Amnon Raz-Krakotzkin, Michael Rosenak, Mordechai Rotenberg, Sara Roy, Edward Said, David Saperstein, Yossi Sarid, Uri Savir, Ze'ev Schiff, Jonathan Schorsch, Jerome M. Segal, Tom Segev, Gershon Shafir, Alice Shalvi, Anita Shapira, Raja Shehadeh, Avi Shlaim, Uri Simon, Ehud Sprinzak, Zeev Sternhell, Shabtai Teveth, David Vital, Michael Walzer, Arthur Waskow, Avi Weiss, A.B. Yehoshua, Oren Yiftachel, Eric Yoffie, Yossi Yonah, and Idith Zertal.

I would be surprised if any of these thinkers fully agree with me, and I suspect some (like Benny Morris) will probably be upset that I have used their research to arrive at very different conclusions. Needless to say, these historians and thinkers bear no responsibility for any of my conclusions.

More than any of the reading and thinking I have done, I have learned the most about Israel/Palestine from the thirty-two months I have spent there since 1984. I've learned from conversations with Palestinians in the West Bank and Gaza; from interviews with Israeli government leaders (some of whom have appeared in *Tikkun* magazine); from meetings with various Israeli peace organizations; from visits to West Bank settlements; from study sessions at the Hartman Institute in Jerusalem; from the time I spent studying in the *yeshivot* (religious schools) and *davening* (praying) at Kehillat Yedidya and many other Orthodox synagogues in Jerusalem and Tel Aviv; and from the many pleasant, and sometimes upsetting, Shabbat afternoons spent in the homes of Orthodox Jews and labor Zionist secularists, talking about what had happened and what could yet be.

From all my experiences, I have realized that there are many perspectives on the same facts and that many of them make sense. In all humility, I offer up the deepest truths that I have been able to learn from the combination of books, study, conversations, firsthand experience, and training as a psychologist, philosopher, and rabbi. I offer my perspective not as "the truth" but as "a truth," rooted in the worldview of the prophets of Israel and their teachings as transmitted to me in person by Abraham Joshua Heschel, Zalman Schachter-Shalomi, Joachim Prinz, and Emmanuel Levinas, and, in secularized form, by the writings of Erich Fromm, Wilhelm Reich, Herbert Marcuse, and Martin Buber. And I have greatly benefited from the wisdom I learned from my son Akiba, who often disagrees with me in a spirited and intellectually sophisticated way; from my colleague and friend of the past 36 years Peter Gabel, who has been the co-shaper with me of the *Tikkun* vision; and from my wife, Debora, who made aliyah and spent 18 years in Israel and who has been a true challenger, critic, supporter, playmate, and partner in the sense described in Genesis—*ezer ke'neg'doe. Hamayveen yaveen.* Her beautiful soul is both an inspiration and a joy to me and, in the past decade that she has been a rabbi, also to all who have the privilege of dealing with her or receiving her wisdom and goodness.

Some of this book first appeared in 2003 in a Tikkun Books version called *Healing Israel/Palestine.* I have decided to change the title of this revised version because the framework I am now using has shifted significantly and my conclusions are very different. This is really a different book, not merely an update but rather a new formulation that could lead in different directions.

I am, like everyone else, a flawed and limited human being. I speak the deepest truths I can access, and I've been blessed with incredible teachers and the opportunity to meet and learn from many wise people. I urge you not to rely on my perspective but to use your own intelligence, creativity, moral sensitivity, and connection to God or Spirit or whatever transcendent connection you have—and then apply that to the reality of building peace and reconciliation between Israel and Palestine. Go and learn. Spend time in Israel but also spend equal time in Palestine, and then go and make tikkun. You don't have to do this by yourself. I invite you to start reading *Tikkun* magazine (www.tikkun.org) and join me in our interfaith Network of Spiritual Progressives (www.spiritualprogressives.org), which is also welcoming to secularists and atheists. You can read more about this in the Resources section at the end of the book.

I invite you to take the perspective in this book, build upon it, refine it, correct my mistakes and overcome my limitations, share it with friends, and use this book to help build peace and reconciliation in the Middle East. If you find others are reluctant to read it because they have me pegged as "too" something (too pro-Israel or too pro-Palestine or whatever), I hereby give you permission to take any part of this book or the whole of it and reprint under your own name. I didn't write this book for money or ego gratification, but to get its message read as widely as possible; if that can best be done under some other name, please feel free to do so or take whatever other nonviolent steps you can to make its message known. And if you want to help me and *Tikkun* continue to do this kind of work, please make a tax-deductible contribution to *Tikkun* at www.tikkun.org, or come volunteer as an intern at our publishing office near the University of California in Berkeley, California. In the past, we've had interns from colleges and graduate schools, many of whom have used their experience with us as a stepping stone to careers in academia, media, community organizing, religious life, publishing, government, or electoral politics, or simply to deepen their own understanding of the world or their own spiritual lives. We've also had retirees or sabbatical year volunteers who were college professors, newspaper editors, writers, poets, lawyers, social workers, teachers, tech-workers, researchers, carpenters, computer experts, social media people, artists, designers, public relations people, grant writers, fundraisers, mystics, and prophets.

Many blessings to you as you read this book and share its message.

—Rabbi Michael Lerner
rabbilerner@tikkun.org
September 2011

Chapter One

Peoples of the Land

The Ancient World: Liberation from Slavery

FROM OUR EARLIEST RECORDED HISTORY, the Jewish people have been objects of both respect and hatred, admiration and fear. Non-Jewish intellectuals have sometimes praised the Jews for having an advanced concept of God and highly developed moral and legal codes. Jews have often been denigrated, however, by those most closely aligned with the ruling elites. This was particularly true in the ancient world.

It is no wonder that rulers of the ancient world felt threatened by the Jewish people and thus hoped to provoke anger between the Jews and others in their kingdoms or empires—just look at the way Jews have told their own story. Although the origins of the Jewish people are clouded in historical debate, the Jews emerged into history with a conception of themselves as having been enslaved in Egypt and as having subsequently broken out of slavery and created a free and self-governing existence for themselves in the area they eventually called Eretz Yisrael, the land of Israel. (The word Yisrael was the name given to their patriarch the biblical Jacob and literally means "one who wrestles with God," and the people called themselves bney Yisrael, the children of Israel.) At a moment in the ancient world when slavery was becoming more and more pervasive, the Jews told of the ways they had broken out of slavery.

Elites in the ancient world tended to rule through a combination of brute force and the imposition of various ideologies based on the central theme that existing class distinctions were sanctified by an unchanging natural and sacred order. Whether through ancient myths about the gods who ruled nature or through the more sophisticated formulation offered by Plato in *The Republic*, elite ideology taught that society was destined to remain divided by class, either by virtue of some inherent feature of each class itself (based on the ontological nature of human beings) or by will of the gods.

The Jewish story was a living testimony that these myths and ideologies were untrue. Jews had managed to break out of slavery, the most degrading position on the class ladder, and had gone on to run their own society successfully as a free people. Most ancient people traced their lineage back to heroes in the past. Here were people who proudly identified instead with the most oppressed and demeaned. Theirs was, and continues to be, a revolutionary story, which insists that the world can change and that slaves can rule themselves, and which warns them against having kings and about the potential of kings to engage in wars and self-enrichment. To the intellectuals and power elites of the ancient world, the very existence of such a people was a scandal, a *shanda* (outrage), with profoundly disturbing and potentially world-upsetting implications.

The account of the Israelite or Jewish liberation struggle was the main focus of the Torah. In fact, the Torah mandates that one day of the week be set aside as a Sabbath (Shabbat) "in commemoration of the exodus from Egypt." On this day, from Friday night slightly before dark to Saturday night slightly after dark, no one can make Jews work; instead, each week throughout the year Jews are enjoined to celebrate the creation of the world, immerse themselves in spiritual reality, have pleasure in food and sex, sing, dance, rest, sleep, pray, and meditate. In their synagogues on the Sabbath each week they read successive sections of the Torah that focus on telling this story and what Jews learned from it. When they finish reading it, they begin anew in a continuous annual cycle.

The very idea that the oppressed could hold on to a weekly Sabbath, set a day aside to celebrate the freedoms they had won in the past, and thereby limit how much work those with power could demand from them—even if the oppressors threatened to kill them for not working on that day—was itself a revolutionary reform. It was the first real victory in the class struggle against the oppressors. The Sabbath thus served as an enduring, weekly reminder that oppression could be overcome. In this way, Jews created the "weekend."

Even Judaism's essential concept of God is revolutionary. God described her/himself to Moses as *ehyeh asher ehyeh*. This is often translated in English as "I am that I am" but is more accurately rendered as "I shall be who I shall be." That is, the God of the universe is the force of emancipation and transformation. It is not the gods of nature with its fixed cyclical patterns that rule the universe in the Jewish cosmology but rather the force of possibility for healing and transformation who has created nature. Here is a god, the creator of the universe, who ensures everything can be changed, including the social order of oppression, and even nature itself. Human life can embody a higher level of love and caring for one another than currently exists, and the task of human beings is to recreate their world in ways that embody this possibility.

This, of course, isn't the only message of the Torah. The Torah is a record of how human beings hear God's voice, and sometimes the voice they hear is not the God of possibility, a

God who has commanded that people seek justice and love their neighbors and manifest compassion and generosity, but an angry, vengeful God. (I detail the struggle between these two ways of hearing God's voice in my book *Jewish Renewal: A Path to Healing and Transformation*.)

The vengeful voice in Torah implicitly validates a despairing view of human beings; it speaks of a world in which anger and hatred prevail, rule-breakers are cruelly punished, and the children of Israel will always dwell alone. It directs the children of Israel to conquer the Land of Israel and exterminate all of its inhabitants. The loving and compassionate voice in Torah validates a hopeful vision of a world that can be transformed into an embodiment of justice, love, and communal welfare. It calls for radical redistribution of the land every fifty years (the Jubilee); for a sabbatical year every seventh year, when the land is to lie fallow and debts are eliminated; for a society based on generosity (loaning for interest is forbidden); and for all members of the society to fight against oppression and to "love the stranger."

Both voices are there, both identified as the voice of God, and sometimes both are subtly intermixed, because both voices are inside most of us. Each of us hears a voice of what I call the Left Hand of God—a voice of hope, trust, and caring for others that says the world can be based on love and generosity. But we also each hear another voice of despair that I call the Right Hand of God—the voice that leads toward rigid boundaries, doing to others what we suspect they might want to do to us, and protecting ourselves from a world we believe to be essentially filled with evil and hatred. From this second voice we get the notion that homeland security can be achieved only through domination and control of the Other, and that responding to strangers as human beings equally created in the image of God is naïve and potentially self-destructive.

The voice that predominates in each of us at any moment shapes how we view one another, our society, and those we are told are "our enemies." These judgments are never simply matters of "fact," but are always shaped by the framework we bring to our experiences and to our reading of the "facts."

Whether the vengeful or the caring voice predominates at any given time in history depends on how much hope people are feeling at the time. The less hope, the more people gravitate to accounts of the world (including approaches to psychology, history, philosophy, sociology, political science, economics, literature, religion, and interpretations of the Bible) based on a belief in evil and a certainty that selfishness and cruelty will predominate. The more hope, the more people gravitate to accounts of the world that highlight our capacity to break the repetition compulsion (the tendency to act out on others what was done to us) and to focus on the possibilities for transformation in even the most discouraging of circumstances.

Any set of circumstances, contemporary or historical, can be read from within either of these two frameworks. It is a matter of belief. Those who see the world primarily through the framework of hope are seeing the world through the lens that Jews call God, or at least what I described as the Left Hand of God in my 2006 book of that title. I understand full well that there are other possible and legitimate readings of our tradition and holy texts that arrive at a very different framework.

I start from this point, that Judaism, in my reading of the texts and the tradition that evolved from them, is based in a liberation struggle and embraces the revolutionary belief in God as the force for transformation and healing. This does not mean, however, that I want to romanticize the realities of Jewish society or Judaism. Alongside the revolutionary ethos, and sometimes even within the same people who express this revolutionary yearning, there remain deep ethical distortions.

This is not surprising, since similar distortions exist in almost everyone on the planet. How we read sacred texts, just as how we read and understand the realities around us in daily life, is a reflection of who we are at any given moment in our lives as individuals. It is also a reflection of how we respond to and to some extent internalize the social realities in which we find ourselves and that shape our imagination of what is possible and what is not.

The manner in which the Jews actually established a Jewish society in the land of Israel is typical of the ethical dilemmas that Jewish history raises. According to the Torah account, the Jews ended forty years of wandering in the desert by conquering the land of Canaan and killing its inhabitants.

Many contemporary anthropologists question whether there ever was a conquest (or, for that matter, whether there ever was a Moses). There is no way to know which will be firmly established, the biblical stories of conquest or more recent anthropological and historical accounts.

What we know as hard fact is that at least some 2,300 years ago a group we now call the Jews created religious and cultural institutions in some part of the area we now call Israel/Palestine. We know that some in this group embraced the version of history that celebrates Jewish conquest of Canaan and the annihilation of its residents, described in the biblical book of Joshua. We also know that a group of rabbis and teachers emerged who preached a religion of love and justice and read the Torah as a story of emancipation and revolutionary transformation from slavery to freedom—a transformation that became the object of hatred and ridicule by Greek and Roman imperialists and those who were influenced by the worldview of those who dominated them. Both the voice of despair and the voice of hope were already present in the Jewish holy texts some 2,300 years ago (if not even longer ago).

The sexism and xenophobia built into Torah-based religious practices, the stories of conquering and annihilating the residents of Canaan, and the compromises that allowed slavery to persist—all these were part of the reality of ancient Israel. I could say that they were all the manifestations of the Right Hand of God and its domination consciousness, a manifestation of Settler Judaism that has persisted as one theme in Judaism for the past several thousand years, alongside the Left Hand of God and a love-oriented Emancipatory Judaism that has commanded us to "love the stranger" and pursue justice. Both strands have been there since the earliest records we have of Jewish life and thought. Yet it's important to remember that Judaism emerged among those Israelites who had been exiled to Babylon by the Babylonian conquerors. It was the religion of the homeless, the disempowered, the exiles of Babylonia who in remembering Zion also sought ways to build mythologies that would empower them to believe that they could once again regain their independence as a people. In that context, the Right Hand of God, the vision of Jews as having once had the power to conquer the land, was an empowerment that felt necessary to convince some of the Jews to return to their holy land once the Persian conqueror of Babylonia had issued an edict permitting and even encouraging that return.

However, I do not mean to provide a defense of the stories of conquest, but only to understand their psychological function for the Jews in exile. A sad reality: it is often typical of those who have been oppressed that they adopt the language and thought patterns of the oppressor. For this reason, it's no surprise to me that Jews copied some of the most oppressive practices of the societies that surrounded them while they developed as a people. It's no surprise that the Torah at times calls for cruelty or genocide of the Other, because all religious traditions in the ancient Near East expressed a similar bloodlust. These sentiments pop up constantly in American politics a few thousand years later and shape our approach to criminal justice and the death penalty, and to "national defense" and "homeland security," though camouflaged by more carefully shaped public relations words to legitimate our mass murder of others as "war." What is surprising is the transcendent voice that one also finds in the Torah along with the other voice of cruelty. The transcendent voice calls for a world of love and justice, compassion, and support for the most oppressed; it's an explicit challenge to oppressive norms. That voice is more prominent in the Torah than it is in contemporary American politics.

Reading back into the Bible from a modern perspective, many people are dismayed by the inconsistencies of message in moments when the call for justice, love, kindness, and generosity are belied by stories that fail to embody those values. However, even these inconsistencies are not present in many other texts from that time for a simple reason: the call for compassion, peace, and love of the stranger was mostly absent from the official ideologies and religious teachings of the Egyptian, Assyrian, Babylonian, Greek, and Roman empires.

Such inconsistencies are a reflection of the times when the voice of love and generosity, the Left Hand of God, has become manifest, even if only in the voices of scorned prophets of Israel. When the prophets talked of radical transformation and insisted on taking seriously the most revolutionary messages of the tradition—the call for justice for the least powerful elements of the society, for a sabbatical year, and for the Jubilee with its radical redistribution of wealth—they highlighted the aspects of the Torah that insisted on the possibility of an ethical order that other societies saw as impossible or undesirable. That those prophetic voices were included in the canon—and incorporated into the sacred tradition read in synagogues ever since—is an indication that Jews eventually responded to this prophetic consciousness and felt obligated to honor it.

Jews were a threat to ruling elites because the dominant Jewish story taught them that God made it both wrong and unnecessary to accept reality and subordinate themselves to the logic of imperial regimes or to a world based on injustice and lack of love. So ruling elites sought to instill a hatred of Jews in their own peoples, hoping to inoculate them against the subversive potential of an encounter with Jews and their liberation story.

I am not suggesting that Jews were a self-conscious revolutionary vanguard plotting to overthrow empires, an ancient-world version of Che Guevara. For the most part, Jews did not consciously say to themselves that their very existence threatened existing systems of domination around the world (although the biblical language of Jews as a chosen people and the prophetic language urging Jews to become a "light unto the nations" contained this element of a world-transforming vanguard). Nor did ruling elites explicitly articulate their opposition to the Jews in this kind of nineteenth-century language. Yet, as the biblical book of Esther makes clear, even in the ancient world, Jews understood that their refusal to act in a subordinate way infuriated ruling elites and provoked anti-Semitic attacks.

This confrontational attitude and refusal to play along as obedient clients within the state eventually led to the Hasmonean rebellion against Greek rule in 167-160 BCE (sanctified by later Jews in the celebration of Chanukah) and to a whole series of later rebellions against Roman rule. These uprisings, in turn, led Rome to repress Judaism brutally, forbid the study of the Torah, rename the country "Palestine," and destroy the Temple in Jerusalem in 70 CE. But it was only the massive and militarily futile uprising of Bar Kochba and Rabbi Akiba from 132–135 CE that finally provoked the Romans to realize that the Jewish spirit of freedom must be suppressed if the Roman Empire was to survive. Hundreds of thousands of Jews were murdered, and tens of thousands were taken as slaves to Rome. Some remained in the land under Roman rule, while many others moved to other parts of the Roman Empire or to Babylonia and Persia. Momentarily, Roman imperialism triumphed.

What is certain is that from the time the Mishnah (a codification of post-Torah Jewish law circa 200 CE) was written, religious Jews prayed three times a day for the rebuilding of Zion and included at the end of every meal similar prayers, such as, "Rebuild Jerusalem, the Holy City, quickly and in our days. Be Blessed, You, the Transformative Power, Yud Hey Vav Hey (YHVH), who rebuilds Jerusalem with great compassion." The attachment to Zion was no nineteenth-century creation of European nationalism, but rather an integral part of Jewish consciousness long before either Christians or Muslims had conquered the region.

Jewish Reality: The Christian Role in Generating Hatred of Jews

Though many early Christians also practiced Judaism, there were other converts to Christianity who felt antagonism toward the Jews. In those early centuries after Jesus's death, many Christians competed with Jews for converts in the Roman Empire, and they had great difficulty explaining why people who had known this Jewish man from Galilee, not far from the centers of Jewish life in ancient Judaea, had failed to see him as either the Messiah or the Son of God. The elaborate stories of miracles and resurrection made a bigger impression on non-Jews than on most Jews.

One way that Christians could account for their failure to convince many Jews was to say that the Jews had at one point been chosen, but had lost that status and become outcasts because they had rejected Jesus. They interpreted the Romans' success in destroying the Temple and exiling the Jews as a sign that God had rejected Judaism, which would now be superseded by Christianity. The Jews deserved punishment and denigration, these Christians argued, because they had rejected the Messiah.

In the very early years after Jesus's death, this kind of teaching had only limited impact. The Christians were themselves being persecuted, so it did not work well to claim that one could read God's intentions or the objective worth of one's religion by how well its followers were received by the ruling elites of Roman society. But once the Christian church merged with state power in the fourth century, Christian triumphalism was widely accepted and led to an intensification of the persecution of the Jews.

Jewish proselytism was outlawed in 329 CE, and soon thereafter, the demonization of Jews began. As Catholic priest Edward H. Flannery describes it in his classic work *The Anguish of the Jews: Twenty-Three Centuries of Anti-Semitism*, at the end of the third century and before the triumph of Christianity in the Roman world, the Jew "was no more than a special type of unbeliever." However, one century later, the Jew had become "a semi-satanic figure, cursed by God, and marked off by the State."

It was this Christian institutionalization of hatred against Jews that evolved eventually into the systematic genocide of the Holocaust.

A full-scale attack on Jews as "inveterate murderers, destroyers," and "lustful, rapacious, greedy, perfidious bandits" whose synagogues were "the house of the devil" and filled with prostitution (the words of St. John Chrysostom, ca. 344–407 CE) helped generate a popular culture of hatred toward Jews that Church teachings sustained for the next fifteen hundred years. During the centuries of "Christian Europe," anti-Jewish legislation adopted by the Church became the law of the land. Jewish-Christian marriages were forbidden, except in the case of conversion by the Jewish party. Christians were forbidden to celebrate

Passover with Jews. Jewish property rights were restricted. Jews were barred from public functions and from practicing law. Jews were prevented from testifying against Christians. The Mishnah, and later the entire Talmud, were banned (and in some places burned). Jews were forcibly baptized and their property expropriated. Eventually, many countries expelled their Jews, including England, France, Spain, and Portugal. All this happened with the full backing of the Church, though sometimes the royal authorities would seek to protect the Jews in their dominion from the decrees of Church officials.

There were some counter-tendencies. Sometimes a particular bishop or pope would come along with feelings of compassion or at least lower levels of hostility toward Jews. Augustine taught that it was important to keep Jews alive as living testimony to the degraded status of those who did not accept Jesus (thereby saving Jews from the genocide faced by many other "pagans"). From time to time, there were humane Church leaders who did not wish to see Jews suffer and would, in their own regions, temporarily ban attacks on Jews or protect Jews from the bloody *pogroms* (armed attacks on Jews). These often followed the readings in church on Good Friday and Easter when the populace was reminded of "the perfidious Jews" who, according to the New Testament, were responsible for the killing of the world's Messiah and Son of God.

But overall, throughout the more than 1,500 years in which the Church had a huge influence over the fate of the Jews, the Christian world was permeated by teachings of hatred in nearly every branch of the Church. Even Protestant reformer Martin Luther's hatred of Jews became particularly vicious and set the tone for hatred of Jews in the Protestant communities of Europe.

KILLING OF JEWS BY CHRISTIANS

The first massive slaying of Jews by Christians took place during the Crusades. As tens of thousands of West European Christians mobilized to take back Palestine from the hands of the Muslims who had conquered it, they swept through the Rhineland murdering Jews wherever they could find them. The arrogant and racist attitude toward the Other—already a legacy from Greek and Roman imperialism—would later manifest in Western colonialism and its re-conquest of the Middle East from Arab Muslims in the nineteenth and twentieth centuries. But it found its first Christian expression in this attempted destruction of Jews.

The Crusades proved traumatic for both Jews and Muslims and shaped the historical memory of both peoples, placing the question of "who owns Jerusalem" at the center of their consciousness. Some believed that whoever controlled Jerusalem had proof that God was on their side. It is important to recall that the Crusades put Muslims on alert to the dangers of Westerners trying to control the holy lands of Islam.

Not every outburst of anti-Semitism in Europe was the direct result of an intentional act by Christian leaders. Once anti-Semitism had been deeply ingrained in the culture of European life, it took on a life of its own and was passed from parents to children in every generation. Stories and prejudices about Jews became part of "shared wisdom," part of the socialization of people in European societies in much the same way that similar stories about African Americans became the shared legacy among whites in America.

Oppression forced Jews living in the West to band together tightly, to define rigid boundaries around their communities and lifestyles, and to develop compensatory fantasies about being "special" or "chosen" in contrast to non-Jews, whom they frequently perceived as being unintelligent and morally bankrupt.

This clannishness and separateness, which was later used by non-Jews as an excuse for anti-Semitism, first began as a response to Greek and Roman imperialism: back then Jews developed customs such as declining to consume non-Jews' food or wine and refusing to marry into their families as a sort of "boycott" of the culture of the oppressor. Later, Jews maintained their separateness as a response to the more lasting and devastating forms of Christian oppression—a defensive response to legal arrangements that prescribed where Jews could live and travel and what Jews could do to make a living.

The idea that this alleged "clannishness" was built into the psychology of Jews was disproved once Jews believed it was safe for them to mix with non-Jews. The moment that legal restrictions on Jews were removed after the French Revolution, Jews poured out of the ghettos and into the mainstream of European life, many attempting to leave behind all of the separateness and clannish behavior. Many rushed to assimilate in one way or another. In fact, it was the sudden infusion of Jews into European economic and social life in the nineteenth century that inspired a new wave of anti-Semitism based on the fear that Jews were taking over European society.

While medieval Jews erected powerful psychological defenses to protect themselves, the economic and political degradation of their daily lives, coupled with the constant feeling of being rejected and treated as pariahs, predictably generated a deep level of isolation, pain, and humiliation that scarred the Jewish psyche. The fierce barriers Jews erected to prevent social contact with non-Jews, the fantasies of revenge on those who had spilled Jewish blood, and the cultural denigration of the intelligence and moral sensibility of non-Jews were the flip side of this pain.

It was no wonder, then, that Jews rejoiced at the demise of the feudal order and the official power of Christianity. Jews championed the new capitalist order with its promise of liberty, equality, and fraternity. Finally, Jews expected that they would be able to participate in society as equals.

Imagine, then, the deep disappointment and despair that swept the Jewish people when the emancipation of European Jews from legal restrictions between 1789 and 1871 did not, in fact, eliminate anti-Semitism.

Catholic theologian Rosemary Radford Ruether, the Rev. John Pawlikowski, professor of social ethics at the Catholic Theological Union, and other contemporary Christian theologians and historians now agree that centuries of Church-sponsored indoctrination against the Jews led to a popular anti-Semitism that flourished throughout most of the nineteenth and twentieth centuries. (This was assisted by Christian teachings that still denigrated Jews or blamed all living Jews for the alleged killing of Jesus by some Jews some 1,800 years before, which exonerated the Romans who carried out the crucifixion depicted in the New Testament.)

JEWS TAKE THE RAP FOR CAPITALISM

It was not only the Church that helped sustain the popular Jew-hatred that it had inculcated centuries before into mass culture. New economic elites exploited anti-Semitic fantasies and used the Jews as a public target whenever resentment of the existing social order grew to threatening proportions.

Jews took the rap for the distortions in daily life that were rooted in the experience of alienation from living in a capitalist society. To ordinary citizens who had little contact with the real owners of wealth and power—but had daily contact with Jews who were disproportionately prominent as the public representatives of "the system" in the courts, schools, welfare bureaucracies, media, and medical system—the Jews appeared to be the ones with real power. It didn't help that when Jews were finally able to compete for these kinds of professional positions (after having been legally banned from them during the feudal period), they often adopted the ideologies and orientations of the ruling elites whom these professions served. Having been denied a place in the societies of Europe for hundreds of years, many Jews were all too willing to become spokespeople and public representatives of the newly emerging capitalist economy, just as many had served as tax-collectors, bankers, traders, and in other despised professions of the Middle Ages. Because of this, it wasn't hard for the elites to displace common people's anger onto the Jews.

No wonder, then, that as the hope that capitalism could provide equally for everyone began to disappear in the mid-nineteenth century, ruling elites began to finance anti-Semitic political parties to counter the appeal of socialist movements by deflecting anger away from the system and onto the Jews. The Jews were the group that most consistently and enthusiastically opposed the old feudal order, but they were sometimes blind to the ways that village life in the old order had offered many Christian peasants comfort, community, and security in spite of its hardships, oppression, and injustices.

As Zygmunt Bauman argues persuasively in *Modernity and the Holocaust*, even though the new capitalist order worked for some, including many Jews, many ordinary citizens and non-Jews felt bereft of the traditional supports that the old order had provided for those most in need. The sense of a community connected through the dominant religious sensibility, the sharing of resources in the forms of "commons" (collectively owned areas where farmers could feed or water their animals), the ethos of everyone having a place (however meager) in the social order—none of these had done much for the Jews during feudalism but had given something real and valuable to everyone else.

Overcoming the oppression they faced in feudal society seemed an unequivocally good thing for most Jews. The old feudal order treated people differently according to the caste, class, or religion into which they had been born and in which they were fated to live their lives. To transcend these categories, to be treated as a human being rather than as "a carpenter" or "a serf" or "a Jew" was the great allure of the individualism that the new capitalist order promised to deliver. No wonder, then, that many Jews were intellectual cheerleaders for undermining the old form of community and replacing it with the rule of the individual. They also supported efforts to undermine the regulated feudal and mercantile-trade economy and replace it with unlimited competition in the marketplace. In this competition, Jews started with many cultural advantages derived from Jewish traditions that refined their capacities, skills, and intellectual prowess.

Capitalist liberation from feudalism also wasn't quite as one-sidedly good for many non-Jews as they streamed into the emerging factory-dominated cities for work in sweatshops, mines, or health-polluting factories. For many non-Jews in industrializing Europe, the new freedom of opportunity was experienced primarily as the freedom to sell their labor power to one exploiting capitalist firm or another. Although some of these non-Jews joined (often Jewish-led) socialist movements, many others responded to the appeal of "returning to the good old days" of village life and communal solidarity (often wildly romanticized). This was often part of the appeal of anti-Semitic nationalist movements.

Resentment against the social and economic realities of capitalist societies began to be directed not at the elites but at the Jews who, as a whole, seemed to be benefiting disproportionately in an economic system that rewarded skills and pretended to be even-handed and free of religious prejudice.

Imagine the Jews' surprise when they found themselves facing the emergence of anti-Semitic parties and movements at the end of the nineteenth century in European societies that had only years before proclaimed themselves committed to values of rationalism, science, humanism, and enlightenment. Imagine their surprise when scientific enterprises emerged to demonstrate the racial characteristics and defects of the Jews.

All of this came to a head with the Dreyfus Affair in France in the 1890s, in which a Jewish army officer was falsely charged with treason. Suddenly, what had seemed to be an enlightened French society was filled with anti-Semitic outbursts. The Jewish people were forced to confront a frightening reality: they had been too optimistic in hoping that capitalism and legal equality would bring an end to Jew-hating. European Christians politely dubbed this "anti-Semitism" in flagrant disregard of the fact that millions of Muslims were also Semites, though such racial groupings are themselves a questionable construct of the racist imagination.

JEWISH RESPONSES TO MODERN EUROPEAN ANTI-SEMITISM

The reemergence of anti-Semitism in supposedly enlightened European societies in the late nineteenth and early twentieth centuries led many Jews to the conclusion that anti-Semitism was an irreversible aspect of non-Jewish societies, built into the structure of the non-Jewish mind. Jews responded to this conclusion in a variety of ways:

1. Zionists believed that the only solution was to recognize that in a historical period when most people were finding their sense of mission and higher purpose through national identity, the Jews needed their own state for self-defense. Zionism

became the name of the national liberation struggle of the Jewish people, a struggle based on the assumption that Jews must have the same national rights as every other people. But since those rights could not be exercised in Christian Europe or Islamic North Africa, many Jews began to turn toward what they believed to be their ancient homeland as the place where this Jewish national destiny could be fulfilled. Just like other national liberation struggles in the late nineteenth and twentieth centuries, the Zionist movement contained within it people of many different political persuasions, from right-wing ultra-nationalists to socialist and even communist groups.

2. Some religious Jews tended to see contemporary anti-Semitism as further proof of the degraded status of the non-Jew and of the need to avoid or protect oneself against non-Jewish culture and thought. Moreover, they saw Jewish attempts to assimilate into Christian societies as an illusory path and a tragic abandonment of Judaism. Thus, the ultra-Orthodox built even deeper walls of restrictions around their communities. They hoped that the repression of alternatives might protect the core of Judaism from pollution by the non-Jews and those who were assimilating or attempting to build non-Orthodox versions of Judaism that the Orthodox perceived as a slippery slope toward full assimilation.

3. The modernizing religious Jews, now identified as the modern Orthodox, made accommodations to the new social world and sought to function within it. In sharp counter distinction to the ultra-Orthodox, they increasingly turned to Zionist solutions and articulated the notion that the (mostly secular and anti-religious) Zionist movement was actually a manifestation of God's will working through human beings who did not think of themselves as serving God (a version of Adam Smith's "invisible hand" in a different realm). Rabbi Kook, a respected leader of the orthodox community living in Jerusalem in the early twentieth

century, pioneered this approach later adopted by his son as a foundational idea of post-1967 modern Orthodoxy. Conservative Judaism emerged in Germany and later in the United States as a similar attempt to speak to modern sensibilities without totally abandoning Judaism, and Reform Judaism went even further. In some cases, Reform Jews put organs and choirs in their synagogues, abandoned the kosher laws that restricted what Jews could eat, cut their beards and eliminated the head coverings for both men and women that had been traditional signs of modesty, and abandoned daily prayer and many of the ritual laws of Judaism. A few even switched the observance of the Sabbath to Sunday. Embracing the autonomy that had become a central tenet of capitalist societies, the Reform movement encouraged individuals to make their own decisions about how much of the religious tradition they wished to keep in their personal lives.

4. Assimilationists thought that if Jews would convert or at least become as non-Jewish as possible (adopt Western forms of dress, cut our beards, get rid of our skullcaps, straighten our hair, get nose jobs, lower our voices, be more polite, and adopt Western table manners), we would be safer from anti-Semitism. However, assimilationist strategies seemed to have little impact on non-Jews. The German Jewish community appeared to be the most highly assimilated in the world, yet Nazis made a conscious effort to find "Jewish blood" that went back several generations. No matter how polite or goyish individual Jews acted, they still ended up in concentration camps.

5. Internationalists thought the best way to overcome anti-Semitism was for Jews to reject their national or particularistic identity. They reasoned that Jews should count on solidarity from members of the international working class, who would soon recognize that their real interests were to oppose every form of national chauvinism and racism.

FAILURE OF INTERNATIONALISM AND ANTI-SEMITISM IN THE LEFT

The internationalists may seem to us today to have hit on the most progressive solution. The problem is that many of their non-Jewish comrades didn't join them in a true spirit of equality and fraternity. Though many Jewish socialists could "prove" that the "objective interest" of the working class was in international solidarity, the non-Jewish working classes of Europe too frequently responded to nationalism and anti-Semitism and passively or actively supported fascist regimes.

All too often, the Jews inside the labor movement, the socialist movement, and the communist movement failed to make anti-Semitism a central issue of concern. Many feared that doing so would only make them appear self-interested, thereby proving a point frequently made by anti-Semites who argued that Jews cared only for themselves. So Jews played down the struggle against anti-Semitism to prove how internationalist they really were, and thus never really attempted a large-scale effort to challenge anti-Semitism within the Left.

Imagine the sense of betrayal these Jewish leftists experienced when communist or socialist groups that were involved in resisting the fascists were simultaneously filled with anti-Semites; when groups of partisans fighting Nazi rule rejected or turned on Jewish escapees from concentration camps; when the Soviet Union began to discriminate against Jews; and when postwar Soviet regimes in Eastern Europe resorted to anti-Semitic purges of their own ranks in order to deflect the rising anti-communist sentiments. Since a large number of the progressive Christians and humane nationalists had been killed off by the Nazis or by the invading Red Army during the war, these countries conquered and ruled by the Soviet Union were full of the most anti-Semitic Eastern European Christians and reactionary nationalists.

The silence of most leftists around the world in the face of all this, and the refusal of leftist Jews to acknowledge the problem of anti-Semitism within the Left made many formerly liberal and progressive Jews deeply suspicious of a Left solution to the problem of anti-Semitism. By the early 1950s, many of these former Jewish leftists had turned to Zionism out of disgust at the way they were betrayed by the global communist movement. Many more turned away from the Left in the 1960s when they felt that Jewish concerns were either belittled or ignored by young radicals who championed the needs of other minority groups but not those of the Jewish people only two decades after the Holocaust.

PALESTINIAN REALITY: A LAND WITH A PEOPLE

Jews were not the only inhabitants of ancient Palestine. After the Romans succeeded in crushing Jewish political independence in 70 CE and the locus of Jewish life moved to Babylonia, the land continued to be worked by people who remained there for the ensuing centuries. Many were descendents of the Israelites who had lived there a thousand years before, or tribes the Israelites had conquered or assimilated into life in ancient Israel. Others had lived there before the Israelites or had been brought there as slaves by the various imperial regimes that conquered the Israelites and Judaea during the period from 586 BCE to 500 CE.

After repeated conquests by Islamic, Christian, and then Ottoman powers, the region's population decreased so that by the end of the eighteenth century there were probably fewer than 300,000 people living on the land, including Muslims, Christians, and Jews. (By 1978, that figure had increased to 500,000, and to over 700,000 between 1880 and 1913.)

Arabs from all over the Arab world have a very special and long-lasting relationship to the Land of Israel. From the very first days of Islam and the subsequent Islamic conquest of Palestine, all Muslims (not only Arab Muslims) have treasured Jerusalem as a site of special religious significance. That attachment arose not in response to the Zionist movement or even to the Crusades, but to a long history in the Islamic faith. The Al-Aqsa Mosque, built in triumphalist fervor atop the place that Jews believe to have been the site of the ancient Temple, is one of the three most sacred spots in Islam and has been a popular pilgrimage site for centuries. Arab Christians as well have long valued much of ancient Palestine as the Holy Land where Jesus and his disciples lived and taught. To claim that these ties were suddenly created in the last hundred years only to stifle Jews is to deny a well-documented history of Arab attachment to this land.

The exact lineage of the Palestinian people is murkier. Most of the inhabitants of Palestine in the eighteenth and nineteenth centuries were Arabs. Many of their families had worked the land for hundreds of years; many others had returned to the area in two immigrant waves—one after the 1832 invasion and subsequent rule of Palestine by Muhammad Ali's son Ibrahim Pasha, and the second as Western colonial forces started to show greater interest and create new economic opportunities. By the end of the nineteenth century, most people living in the area thought of themselves as Arabs but not particularly as part of a Palestinian nation. In other words, they could be called Palestinian because they lived in the area once designated "Palestine" by the Romans, but they did not self-consciously identify themselves as part of a nationality called the "Palestinian people."

It is hard for us today to grasp that nationality is a new idea. When visionaries today suggest the possibility of a post-nationalist world to deal with the environmental crisis facing humanity, they are often dismissed as utopians by those in the majority who have come to think of nation-states as an almost immutable fact of nature. Yet, before the eighteenth century, most people thought of themselves as belonging to religious groups or tribes or ethnic groups, or they identified themselves as citizens of cities and states. Few thought of themselves as belonging to a nation.

This was true of the Jews as well. Before they became enamored of nineteenth-century nationalism, most Jews did not identify themselves as part of a nation currently living in Palestine, but as the *am yisrael* (people of Israel), a globally scattered religious people whose return to the Holy Land would take place after the Messiah arrived and not sooner. While small groups of Jews did in fact move to Tsfat, Hebron, Jerusalem, and Jaffa, they did so as religious Jews and had no conception that am yisrael would be interpreted later in nationalist terms.

Contemporary Jewish national (as opposed to religious) identity was in large part formed by (or in reaction to) the modern Zionist movement. Before that, for example, Jews in Persia and Jews in Poland may have shared the same prayers and religious festivals, but they otherwise had little in common, had little contact, and showed little concern for each other's political situation. The religious references to "the people of Israel" had little to do with the notion of national identity or self-determination that emerged in the late nineteenth century.

Similarly, most Arabs living in what had been called by the Romans "Palestine" thought of themselves as part of the *ummah*, the larger Arab nation. It was only through struggle with the Ottoman Empire in the late nineteenth century, and then with the subsequent divisions of the Middle East into distinct states by European colonialists, that the people living in Palestine started to define themselves as Palestinian.

Both Jewish and Palestinian nationalism originally emerged for reasons pertaining to the specific historical, cultural, and geographic situations these peoples faced. But once Zionism hit

Wikimedia Commons

Two residents converse in the ancient city of Ramallah, which was founded in the mid-1500s and is now the headquarters of the Palestinian Authority.

the ground in Palestine in the 1880s, at the earliest stages in the development of the nationalist consciousness of each people, both movements inevitably developed through their mutually formative, often mutually hostile, impact on each other.

Before the arrival of the Zionists, the people who would later call themselves Palestinians had lived in peace in spite of their religious divisions; the Islamic majority lived alongside minority Christian and ultra-Orthodox Jewish Palestinians. Though subject to a special poll tax under Ottoman rule, Christians and Jews had autonomous authority to run their own family and

Noura Ballouk

Palestinian Arab communities like Jaffa, shown here in 1900, existed for many centuries.

religious affairs as well as their own courts. As the Ottoman Empire dissolved, Greek Orthodox Palestinians played an important social role, as local Christians created hospitals, schools, and orphanages while affirming their connection with the Arab world in general and with the Palestinian people in particular.

At the same time, a popular nationalist movement began to spring up, emphasizing Palestinian consciousness as a common thread that transcended specific religious traditions. A revival of Arabic language and literacy became a weapon of resistance to Ottoman Turkish ways and intensified Palestinian identity.

Yet it was only after the arrival of a new breed of Jew—a Jew no longer waiting for the Messiah but instead intent on recreating a national homeland for Jews around the world in Palestine—that significant numbers of Palestinians began to exhibit a special awareness, and then a hostility, toward Jews. The more passive Orthodox Jews whose communities had lived in the Holy Land continually since the days of the Second Temple had accepted their political powerlessness with docility and disinterest. They usually lived in harmony and even friendship with their Arab neighbors. These Jews were absorbed in a life of study and Jewish mysticism and had no particular interest in equal political power with the Arabs, who didn't have that much political power themselves. All this changed when Zionist Jews began to arrive in Palestine in the 1880s.

At first, Palestinian hostility was confined specifically to Zionist Jews. In the early decades of the Zionist enterprise, this hostility did not poison long-established relationships between the centuries-old religious Palestinian Jewish communities and Palestinian Arabs.

The hostility that did emerge toward Jewish newcomers was in part a product of a larger resistance Palestinians felt toward the ways of European societies that had been encroaching on Palestine for much of the nineteenth century. In previous centuries, most Palestinians were peasants "organized in patrilineal clans, surviving by farming small plots of land, and living by norms, customs and values anchored in their Islamic civilization," as Samih K. Farsoun and Christina E. Zacharia wrote in *Palestine and the Palestinians.* The *hamulas* (clans) gave life stability and safety, protecting the individual and kin and providing access to land. The *shayks* (hamula chiefs) were responsible for collecting taxes for the Ottoman authorities, who in turn appointed shayks and often helped foster competition between them.

It was a combination of local economic development (citrus and soap, for example), tourism from Europe, and Ottoman centralization and modernization policies that led to growing trade with Europe—a trade that involved exchanging Arab agricultural commodities for European manufactured goods. Europeans began to settle in Palestine, and the Roman Catholic and Eastern Orthodox populations swelled during the nineteenth century. As the Ottoman Empire declined in power, European states began to claim special rights in the Middle East as "protectors" of the Europeans who were living there.

The process of undermining local economies had already begun before Zionist immigration became a factor. Nablus merchants played an important role in the monetization of the economy, and money lending led to massive indebtedness throughout the rural population. Again Farsoun and Zacharia paint the picture for us:

> By the second half of the [nineteenth] century,
> a growing number of peasants lost their land
> and became sharecroppers and tenant farmers
> on land that their ancestors had tilled for
> centuries.... Usurious merchants transformed
> themselves into large landlords.

Moreover, a growing stratification produced both landless and rich peasants. By the last half of the nineteenth century, there was a marked decline in small and medium-sized properties, a rise in huge estates, and an increase in land prices. Farsoun and Zacharia write:

> The decline of village work led many Palestinian
> peasants (*fellahin*) to seek work as wage
> laborers, either as free laborers in the fields or
> in unskilled construction jobs in the towns. In
> the towns a new class structure was emerging,
> comprised of a respected nobility tracing their

roots to the days of Islamic conquest in the
seventh century, a new commercial bourgeoisie
(often Christian Palestinians who were favored
by European powers), and Islamic merchants,
artisans and a nascent working class.

From the standpoint of the Palestinians, the Jews who were
arriving in Palestine at the end of the nineteenth and beginning
of the twentieth century seemed to be part of the major changes
in ordinary life brought on largely by European colonialism and
trade. Arab Jews (often referred to as Sephardim or Mizrachim)
were well accepted by Palestinian society and tended to be seen
as part of their cultural landscape, not as a manifestation of a
threatening colonial invasion. This was true in part because
these Jews accepted their lesser status in the political hierarchy
of the country and did not bring with them expectations of democratic equality. In contrast, Ashkenazi Jews—primarily from
Eastern and Central Europe, but also from France, England,
and Germany (some with backgrounds in European imperial
and colonial enterprises)—brought with them the culture of
the West and the economic and political assumptions that went
with it. So when the Ashkenazi Jewish population jumped dramatically between 1882 and 1914, so too did the concerns of
Palestinians that these people were becoming the vanguard of
European penetration of their land.

The decline of Palestine and the reduction of the fellahin to
penury and sharecropping, as well as the overall degeneration of
the land, began considerably before the resettlement of Palestine
by the Zionists. But it was accelerated by Jewish resettlement, a
fact that Arab elites capitalized on to deflect toward Jews resentment that might have otherwise been directed at them. The
Jews thus became the embodiment for many Palestinians of the
worst impacts of the global capitalist market, and opposition to

their presence in Palestine was a way of expressing the anger that people were feeling at the changes imposed by the new global order. No surprise, then, that many Palestinians were opposed to and deeply resented the increased presence of Jews in Palestine.

That opposition existed even before the Zionist movement's founding conferences, but it greatly increased after the Zionist movement declared its intention to form a home for the Jewish people in Palestine.

Chapter Two

ZIONISM COMES TO THE LAND

EVER SINCE THE DESTRUCTION of the temple by the Romans (70 CE) and the subsequent defeat of the Bar Kokhba Rebellion (135 CE), Jews have perceived themselves as in exile from their homeland. Through most of the two thousand years before the founding of the State of Israel, observant Jews would turn three times a day toward Jerusalem and pray for God's help in returning to Zion. After every meal they would call for the rebuilding of Jerusalem and pray for God to "lift the bonds of our oppression from our necks and lead us speedily back to our land."

The phrase "Next year in Jerusalem" (the words sung at the end of the Passover Seder, at which Jews retell the story of the exodus from Egypt) was so deeply inscribed in Jewish consciousness that it is somewhat surprising that Jews in larger numbers did not seek to return. Part of the reason is that, according to religious interpretations of the Exile, the time of return is God's will, so it would violate God's will to return to Zion before the Messiah arrives. Thus most religious Jews did not make any actual efforts to return to Zion.

As always, there were counter tendencies. In Europe, both the followers of the Vilna Gaon and leaders of the early Hasidic movement in the eighteenth century sent some of their followers to live in Israel and to join Kabbalists and other Jews who had continued to live in Jerusalem, Hebron, Tsfat, and Jaffa through much of the Middle Ages. This was partly in response to millennial messianic awakenings that periodically reverberated through Jewish society in the centuries before the creation of Zionism. Crucial works of Jewish religious thought and law such as the Schulchan Aruch, the Lurianic Kabbalah, and the Shnei Luchot Habrit were composed there (in the sixteenth and seventeenth centuries). Yet the majority of Jews lived elsewhere, and most of them saw living in Israel as an ideal rather than as a realistic or religiously acceptable choice for the Jewish majority. Not only did the Jews living in the Land of Israel depend on charity from Jewish communities around the world—an economic reality that made it impossible to expand those communities with new immigrants—but moving to the Land of Israel was also seen as an appropriate development only once the Messiah had arrived.

It took a powerful break from this traditional Jewish understanding of the Holy Land to take seriously the call for secular nationalism that fueled the early Zionists. Because Israel had become a religious ideal more than a geographic location for a state, the religious traditionalists, and even more so the fundamentalists, wanted nothing to do with the Zionist movement, seeing it as "a rebellion against God" (the Messiah had not yet arrived, after all).

Yet Zionism spoke to a yearning that had persisted in Jewish consciousness for two thousand years—a desire to return to the homeland and live a normal life as a people with a land.

Zionism took this yearning and gave it concrete political expression. The Zionists were overwhelmingly secular, and the dominant forces in the early Zionist movement were socialists who hoped to create a socialist reality in the context of a Jewish state. They were particularly hostile to what they saw as the passivity and powerlessness in Jewish life in the Diaspora, believing that Jews would be able to achieve real dignity and empowerment only when they transferred their messianic yearnings from the realm of religious mysticism to the realm of practical politics.

While it is probably true, as David Biale argues in *Power and Powerlessness in Jewish History*, that Zionists exaggerated the degree of Jewish powerlessness throughout the centuries of Diaspora, for many Jews the Zionist notion of creating a Jewish state in the land of their ancestors provided their first experience of healthy self-affirmation. During their 1,800 years in a larger society that increasingly demeaned Jews, Judaism itself had adopted a theology of self-blame. Religious Jews recited a prayer that proclaimed, "Because of our sins we were exiled from our land." Jewish communists and socialists in the nineteenth century secularized this self-denigration and the forthright renunciation of Jewish interests by blaming Jews for adopting the personality traits and interests that their oppression had forced upon them. (Marx's writing on "the Jewish question" went so far as to essentialize these oppression-generated behaviors by labeling some of the worst practices of capitalist society "Jewish.")

In this environment, Zionism was an affirmation that "Jewish is beautiful." It thus had the same kind of appeal that Black nationalism had for African-Americans or feminism had for women—it insisted that an oppressed group did not deserve its oppression.

WERE THE ZIONISTS AN EXTENSION OF WESTERN COLONIALISM?

Because the Zionists were overwhelmingly Europeans who settled a distant land based on nationalist claims and brought with them an aura of Western superiority, Zionism has sometimes been understood as an extension of Western colonialism.

Wikimedia Commons

Some Jewish immigrants walked to Palestine. Often poor and destitute, they sought a homeland with the security they could not find in Europe.

Palestinian Arabs, with the Crusades fresh in their historical memory, not surprisingly regarded the waves of Jewish immigration as a colonial phenomenon. This may seem strange to Americans with their lack of historical memory, but not at all to Jews and Muslims, whose lives are filled with rituals that keep the past fresh.

Yet the claim that Jews were coming to Palestine to colonize it on behalf of Western colonial powers—though occasionally made by Herzl and a few other Western Zionist leaders in their attempt to get the colonial powers to support the Zionist effort, and then used by anti-Zionists as a way to demean the entire Zionist enterprise—makes little sense once one understands the history of the Jews. The Jews were not an integrated and accepted element in colonial Europe, nor did they share with the colonial powers a desire to extend colonial rule around the world. What brought most

Jews to Zionism was not a desire to extend European power and culture but the promise that Zionism could protect Jews against the oppression they faced in Europe. Whatever one can say about the ways Western powers used the Jewish migration to Palestine to further their own interests, the migrants' *intentions* were not Western colonialist.

The vast majority of Jews who actually came to Palestine in the early waves of immigration (*aliyot*) came from Eastern Europe. They fled oppression, having lost hope of ever changing the deeply ingrained anti-Semitism of the Christian world. While the overwhelming majority of those who fled Eastern Europe sought refuge in the West (many in the United States), those who went to Palestine were the most idealistic, the most hopeful about the possibility of establishing a just and even socialist society, and the most committed to a world of justice and peace. Their motivation was to escape centuries of oppression, not to overpower or exploit some other group on behalf of European political or economic powers.

Here it is important to distinguish between the motivations of the masses of Jews who eventually came to Palestine in the first half of the twentieth century and the statements of Western European Zionists who raised money and sought Western political support for the Zionist movement. The latter, sometimes materially quite comfortable themselves, were watching the growth of anti-Semitism in Europe that revealed its depth during and after the trial of Alfred Dreyfus, a Jew falsely accused by the French military of being a traitor. Their own attempts at assimilation seemed less certain to succeed as hatred of Jews became more visible in the last decade of the nineteenth and the first decades of the twentieth century. For the masses of Jews in Eastern Europe, already living in extremes of poverty and facing government-supported pogroms, the need for refuge was more immediate.

The claim that Zionism was, from the beginning, a movement of white people against people of color is similarly groundless. The impetus to return to Zion was part of the cultural heritage of Jews from the Middle East and North Africa. The vast majority of Jews who eventually came to Palestine—Sephardi and Mizrachi Jews—were ethnically similar to the Palestinian people.

When people on the Left use the term "white" they often don't mean the actual color of skin, but rather they mean by "white" those who are the primary beneficiaries of the West. Conversely, peoples of color are those who have been victimized by Western powers. Given this way of understanding "whiteness," Jews have not historically been "white." For most of the past two thousand years, Jews have been the victims of Western colonialism—first as it took form in Hellenistic and then Roman imperialism, later as it manifested in the church and in regimes influenced by the church, and finally by the great nationalist forces of Europe, the overwhelming majority of which were explicitly anti-Semitic. If Jews have been able to make good advantage of the openings given to them by capitalist society, they nevertheless retained their status as a demeaned Other for many of the societies in which they were "making it" in material terms.

A small proportion of Jews, freed from the ghettos of Western Europe in 1848 and 1871, quickly entered into the economic mainstream, and some succeeded in obtaining positions of power or wealth. However, for the majority of Jews it was only in the second half of the twentieth century, after Europeans had managed to murder millions of Jews, that Western hateful attitudes toward Jews were put on hold. All Jews were finally allowed to succeed economically in Western society and reach positions of real power in the corporate and political world—thus becoming "white" in Western societies that had previously treated them as a different and lesser species. But this is a very recent phenomenon that has little to do with the historical circumstances that led

Jews, many of them at the edge of economic destitution, to seek refuge in their ancient homeland. When Zionists first began their struggle for a national homeland in Palestine, the Jewish people were an oppressed minority living in a largely hostile European environment.

On the other hand, if one asks, "Did colonial powers succeed in using Zionism to advance colonial goals?" then the answer is: "Yes, they did."

The larger, oppressive, imperial order always seeks to co-opt liberation movements as much as possible, with varying and partial degrees of success in each case. American capitalism seized on the emancipation of formerly enslaved blacks first as an opportunity to employ them as strike breakers; they relegated most of them to an underclass working at cheaper wages than labor unions demanded. Similarly, the American capitalist order later used women's entrance into the work force to lower the relative economic power of men. This forced both adults in traditional families to work in order to supply an income comparable in purchasing power to what men alone had been able to provide in an earlier age.

In a similar but not identical way, Zionism has also been used to serve imperial interests. Yet in the liberation struggles of Jews, blacks, and women, the vast majority of the participants had no interest in serving the powerful—neither was that their intention nor did most of them even suspect that they were doing so. In my estimation it would be more appropriate to say no to the question of whether these were colonialist or imperialist movements in their essence.

Like other national liberation movements, the Zionist movement included people who thought that they could find allies by selling Zionism to European colonial powers as serving their interests, just as some in the Palestinian movement sought to do the same with England and later with Nazi Germany. Just as

Martin Luther King Jr. and Gloria Steinem took time to court the political powers of the United States at the height of American imperialist power, hoping thereby to win greater understanding and support for their movements, so too leaders of the Zionist movement appealed to the "powers that be" in their quest for support of a Jewish alternative to European oppression. And just as the struggle for the rights of women and African Americans sometimes involved quotas and approaches to affirmative action that sometimes unfairly disadvantaged white working-class men, Zionism in the first decades of the twentieth century sought to repair the damage done to the Jewish people through centuries of oppression in Christian and Muslim countries in ways that sometimes unfairly disadvantaged Palestinians.

To understand Palestinian anger at the Jewish immigrants fleeing Europe, we must recognize that some European Jews did, in fact, have contemptuous attitudes toward non-Jews (a contempt rooted in the morally abhorrent way that non-Jews had treated them). These attitudes found expression in the way some of these Jews perceived Palestinians.

Some European Zionist leaders even sought to exploit the anti-Arab racism of the European nations to gain support for the Zionist cause. The tragic reality of racism is that often victims of racism will join members of the dominant culture in bashing other victims of racism in order to advance their own status. This happens regularly in America. Minority groups will sometimes seek to get a leg up over other minority groups by identifying with the elites who run the corporate economy, rather than with their potential allies in other oppressed groups. In the course of the twentieth century, both Jews and Arabs at times jockeyed for position by playing up to the English colonialists and other European colonial forces.

Some European Jews explicitly supported the Western imperial worldview, sharing with Western Christians an arrogant

attitude toward Arabs and Muslims (and later, a similar attitude toward the Sephardi and Mizrachi Jews who immigrated to
Israel from Arab and Muslim lands). This was best exemplified
by the early Zionist claim that Eretz Yisrael, the Land of Israel,
was "a land without a people for a people without a land." To
Western minds, the native inhabitants were literally invisible, or,
if their physical presence could not be ignored, their cohesion
and identity as a people could.

There were counter tendencies. The much beloved Jewish
writer Ahad Ha'am, who was later known as a "cultural Zionist,"
may have shocked many Zionists when he wrote in 1891, after
a visit to Palestine: "We abroad are used to believing that Eretz
Yisrael is now almost totally desolate, a desert that is not sowed....
But in truth that is not the case. Throughout the country it is
difficult to find fields that are not sowed. Only sand dunes and
stony mountains ... are not cultivated."

Some Zionist leaders like Yitzhak Elezari Volkani, the founder
of Zionist agronomy, were able to acknowledge that in many ways
"traditional" Palestinian agricultural techniques were superior to
"modern Zionist techniques." But many European and American
Zionist enthusiasts were unable to see the strengths of this indigenous people. They instead continued to describe the land as
empty of inhabitants and refused to acknowledge the people who
lived there.

According to Israeli historian Benny Morris, "the Arabs were
generally seen by the *olim* (Jewish immigrants to Israel) as
primitive, dishonest, fatalistic, lazy, savage—much as European
colonists viewed the natives elsewhere in Asia or Africa." Many
agreed with the Zionist activist Moshe Smilansky, who by 1914
saw Palestinians "as a semi-savage people, who have extremely
primitive concepts." Smilanksy continues: "And this is his nature: If he senses in you power—he will submit and will hide
his hatred for you. And if he senses weakness—he will dominate

you.... [They have the tendency] to lie, to cheat, to harbor grave suspicions and to tell tales ... and a hidden hatred for the Jews" (quoted in Benjamin Morris's *Righteous Victims*).

These are xenophobic perceptions of the Other that are near universal. You can read the same accounts, with only slight variations, by Europeans describing the lives of Jews in *shtetls* (small villages of Eastern Europe) and the West European ghettos, by American colonists describing the Africans they enslaved and Native Americans they murdered, by Germans describing Poles, by Spanish conquistadors describing the civilizations they snuffed out in Central and South America, by Christians describing the people they forcibly converted to Christianity, or by Muslims describing some of the populations they conquered. The humanity of the Other remains invisible to those who imagine themselves on a higher or more civilized plane of existence, and this very perception is often used to legitimate barbarous acts of oppression by the colonizers.

To complicate the picture further, even in difficult circumstances, there have always been some Jews who, through their own cunning and ability, have escaped the degradation and extreme poverty suffered by the vast majority of Jews by serving the interests of Christian or Muslim ruling elites. These Jews' contemptuous attitudes toward non-Jews were based on the fear that their good fortune might be quickly changed by sudden eruptions of Jew-hating. The largest community of Spanish Jews experienced this sudden shift: their prosperity turned to poverty when hundreds of thousands of them (all who refused to convert to Christianity) were expelled from Spain in 1492 and a few years later from Portugal as well. A similar catastrophe occurred in Poland in 1648 when hordes of Khemelnitzky's populist rebels raped and murdered tens of thousands of Jews throughout much of Eastern Europe.

Being the victim of arrogance in one context does not prevent a group from being the perpetrator of arrogance in another context—in fact, sometimes it makes it more likely. Eastern European Jews who had been treated with little respect were often dismissive and arrogant toward Arabs and the Arab culture they encountered in the Holy Land, though fearful of Arab power. That attitude would soon extend to Jews who came from Arab lands, who were perceived as culturally backward by Eastern European Jewish settlers. So it appeared to Ahad Ha'am, who wrote that the Zionist colonists "behave toward the Arabs with hostility and cruelty, trespass without justification, beat them shamefully without sufficient cause, and then boast about it."

Given this circumstance, it is not surprising that many Palestinian Arabs developed an early antagonism toward these newcomers who did not speak Arabic, showed little interest in getting to know Arab culture, had little respect for local religious institutions (most of the early Jewish immigrants were socialists and atheists), and were ignorant of local customs (e.g., allowing local shepherds access to common pastureland). Nor is it hard to understand why Palestinians might perceive these attitudes as reflecting a kind of arrogance very similar to the arrogance of non-Jewish colonialists, despite the difference in origin.

Yet it's important to note that the Muslim religion as it had been refracted through the eyes of Arab landlords was replete with negative images of Jews and a long history in which Jews were expected to play a subservient and sometimes obsequious role in Arab-dominated societies. For Christian Palestinian Arabs, there was Christianity's long tradition of representing Jews as "Christ killers." For Muslim Palestinian Arabs, there were portions of the Koran that seemed to indicate that Jews had betrayed and become enemies to the Prophet Muhammed. These prejudices also influenced how Palestinian Arabs understood and dealt with the Jewish refugees from Europe.

Dealing with the Colonial Powers

European colonialists in Africa and Asia encouraged European Jews' identification with European culture by giving Jews and Christians in African and Asian colonies some advantages over native groups, thereby creating antagonism between what otherwise would have been equally non-colonialist minorities. The British, who would soon become the imperial masters of Israel/ Palestine, were particularly skilled in using this "divide and conquer" technique.

Some Zionist leaders from Western European countries had strategic reasons for associating themselves with colonialism. Theodore Herzl and Chaim Weizmann used Western imperialist justifications to convince the major colonial powers that a Jewish state was in their interests, just as some leaders of the growing Palestinian nationalist movement sought to convince those same powers that they could be good allies of the colonial powers. For example, Herzl, the ultimate Zionist pragmatist who at one point was willing to consider making the Jewish homeland in Britain's Uganda colony, contended that a Jewish state would be "an outpost of civilization against the barbarism of the desert," and at one point went so far as to advocate the transfer of Palestine's indigenous inhabitants out of the country. We know that Herzl did not identify as closely with Western imperialism as quotations like this would indicate because he was simultaneously pleading his cause to the Ottoman Empire, using language drawn from Ottoman ideology.

Once the Zionists felt their goal was legitimate, they were not averse to trying to play power politics with whoever had power. In this sense they were political realists.

Nor was the attempt to make deals with colonial powers something unique to the Zionist movement. Every other national liberation movement has at one point or another formed alliances with one set of colonial powers to defeat another set. George Washington, Ho Chi Minh, Mahatma Gandhi, Nelson Mandela, Fidel Castro, the influential Palestinian Husseini family, and many others have been willing to play to the interests of forces whose long-term agenda was antithetical to their own goals, but who in the short run might help them advance their national interests.

A national liberation movement does not automatically become an imperialist or colonialist venture just because it seeks support from imperial or colonial forces, not even if it does in fact advance the interests of that larger power. The African National Congress (ANC) worked with and sought the aid of the communist party and of the Soviet Union, but the ANC was far more than a tool of the communists. Similarly, it may have aided the Zionists to align with various colonial forces, including at times the British and more recently the United States, but the Zionist movement was far more than a tool of those from whom it sought aid.

The basic reality of the Zionist movement is that it grew out of Jewish despair over European Jews' inability to normalize their existence in Europe and overcome Jew-hatred among the masses of Europeans. Zionism began as a national liberation movement by a people who desperately wanted to move from a condition of homelessness and statelessness to a condition of being like other peoples, with a state of their own in their national homeland.

Millions of Jews in the late nineteenth and early twentieth centuries were living in conditions of insecurity and threat, and these millions were all candidates to make aliyah to the land of Israel. The more those threats became overt—first in Western and Central Europe, then in Arab lands (from which hundreds of thousands of Jews fled from 1948 to 1967), and finally in Ethiopia and the Soviet Union—the more the Zionists saw a need for land to resettle Jewish refugees.

No wonder, then, that the Zionists were always reluctant to define the borders of the state they desired—they knew that their borders would have to expand continually to meet the increased need for refuge.

This is a very different kind of dynamic from a colonialism that expands in order to increase the wealth of a colonial mother country. Indeed, it was precisely because they acted out of a feeling of despair, fear, and weakness, rather than out of a belief in their strength, that Zionists rarely understood how they could be perceived as colonialists by the native population of Palestine. Jewish settlers from 1880 to 1925 could not see how their attempts to make deals with colonial powers could be taken as anything more than an oppressed group's stratagems for survival.

Perhaps if the Zionists had been lousy deal makers, Palestinians would not have been so worried. But the Zionists were great deal makers, largely because their efforts played into the global strategies of the colonial powers. The Zionists' greatest success in this kind of deal making came toward the end of World War I, when they were able to gain the support of British Prime Minister David Lloyd George.

Dedicated to overthrowing the Ottoman Empire and securing British control over the Suez Canal, the British planned to become the dominant player in the Middle East after the war, thereby securing control over the vast oil reserves of that region, which were becoming increasingly indispensable for the industrializing and fossil-fuel-dependent West. Lloyd George believed that a Jewish colony in Palestine would be helpful in advancing British imperial interests in the area. A small part of this calculation included the belief among some in the British government that Jews in the United States (which had not yet entered the fray) were ambivalent about the war but might become more supportive if they believed it would help the Zionist cause.

On November 2, 1917, the British Foreign Secretary Lord

Balfour sent the following statement to Lord Lionel Walter Rothschild, the head of the Zionist movement in England:

> His Majesty's Government views with favor
> the establishment in Palestine of a national
> home for the Jewish people and will use their
> best endeavors to facilitate the achievement
> of this object, it being clearly understood that
> nothing shall be done which may prejudice the
> civil and religious rights of existing non-Jewish
> communities in Palestine or the rights and
> political status enjoyed by Jews in any other
> country.

The Balfour Declaration gave important international legitimacy to the Zionist movement. Its use of the words "national home" was understood by both the British and the Zionists to suggest that the Jews would have their own state in their ancient homeland. Because of its clear and strong language in favor of a Jewish national home, the Balfour Declaration is often cited as the legal basis for the State of Israel.

From the standpoint of the Arabs, however, the Balfour Declaration was just one of many pronouncements by an invading colonial power; it had no legitimacy beyond the practical fact that Britain had managed to conquer the land of Palestine by defeating the Ottoman Empire.

What concerned the Palestinians was that the Balfour Declaration provided the first mainstream support for a new political reality in the Arab world: a Jewish state carved out of what Arabs perceived to be their land. Under the sponsorship of this major Western imperial power, the little group of Zionists moved from being seen as a nuisance to being seen as a real threat. In that context, Palestinian Arabs began to feel hostility not only toward the newly arriving Jews, but also toward the religious Jews with whom they had previously lived in peace. These religious Jews were now welcoming other Jews into the land.

Palestinian concern about growing Jewish power was not pure paranoia. During the 1880–1920 period, as millions of Jews fled the waves of anti-Semitism that were engulfing Europe and Russia, some Zionist leaders argued that the only real safety for their persecuted people would come through political control of the land of Palestine. Thus, for example, Meir Dizengoff, the first mayor of Tel Aviv, imagined creating a "state within a state" in the neighboring Arab town of Jaffa before the Jewish town was established, while Zionist leader Arthur Ruppin wrote in his diaries that the goal of Tel Aviv was to "conquer Jaffa economically." This economic conquest of the land had at least as much significance as the political conquest to come.

Clash Over the Land

Though officially Zionists talked about "a land without a people for a people without a land," in fact Palestine was densely populated and intensively cultivated, except for some swampy areas, so the Zionists found that they would have to purchase land. In the first half of the twentieth century, the Jewish National Fund (JNF or Keren Kayemet LeYisrael) and Keren Hayesod purchased land in the name of the entire Jewish people—land that was then restricted for exclusive Jewish use. This exclusionist policy was not one democratically endorsed by the Jewish people, but rather pursued by those who supported this particular project and donated money on its behalf. Yet by the middle of the twentieth century, trees were being planted on this purchased land by contributions from Jewish children around the world who brought money to their Hebrew schools to donate to the JNF.

Much of this land was purchased from absentee landlords who lived in Beirut, Cairo, Damascus, and Baghdad, although some of it was purchased from landlords living in Palestine. A smaller percentage was purchased from Palestinian peasants. Land purchased by the JNF often included Palestinian villages or "commons," lands that had been used for generations by Palestinian families. The land was withdrawn from Palestinian use. The people who lived on it were often forced to move and look for work in an urban economy in which Jewish-only economic institutions were making it hard for Palestinians to find employment.

Imagine yourself living in a village whose agricultural lands have been worked for generations by your family and the families of your small community. Then one day someone arrives to tell you he has a piece of paper proving that he has bought all the land of your village, so you must move. To where? How will you and your family make a living? The land has been bought by "the Jewish people" and it has been bought from some absentee landlord whom you've never seen and maybe never even heard about. And you hear that this is happening to others around your country. The Jewish people are throwing you off your land and putting your family and the families of many, many others into crisis. How would you feel?

And what would you think if not too long afterward a group of Jews who speak no Arabic arrive on your land, telling you that they are "socialists" who are building a new world? They are building collective farms—kibbutzim—and in these kibbutzim they are going to experiment with shared ownership, raising children collectively, women's equality, sex outside of marriage, and developing a new consciousness for Jews who had previously never been allowed in European societies to own or work the land. But you can't join because you are an Arab. These socialists have no interest in your plight or your well-being. And when you

Wikimedia Commons

This photo of the Muslim quarter of Safed, a city in northern Israel, was taken in 1908. At the time, the city was home to a mix of Jews and Arab Muslims.

express rage at what is happening to you, they respond by calling your feelings "anti-Semitism," which they've experienced for hundreds of years from all non-Jews, so they're not surprised that you are feeling it too.

Your anger is discounted and dismissed as nothing more than an irrational holdover of prejudices, and these "progressive" Jews' main response to it is the formation of local defense militia (called "the Haganah") to defend the kibbutzim. If some of your friends start getting involved in acts of terror against those who are taking your land, might you "understand" their outrage? Might you even wish that you could participate in some action to stop these people from coming and displacing your fellow Palestinian Arabs? Might you even give credibility to anti-Semitic stories being told in Europe about Jews as being insensitive, selfish, and out for themselves?

Yet viewed from a larger historical perspective, what was happening in Palestine had been happening all over the world from the sixteenth through the twentieth centuries. The process of peasant displacement from the land was not initiated by Jewish immigration or Jewish purchase of the land, but was a universal phenomenon of the emerging world capitalist system. In fact, these dynamics, which had shaped the British industrial revolution back in the eighteenth century, had reached Palestine by the mid-nineteenth century, before the Zionist movement began, and they increased in the twentieth century. But JNF land purchases greatly accelerated the process.

Arab landlords and their political agents were not slow to redirect peasants' growing anger at the unfair class structure of the emerging capitalist economy toward property-buying Jews. Nor was this anger totally without foundation, because the property was being bought by Jews acting in the name of the Jewish people and not simply as individual capitalists. These Jews were carrying out a significant part of the expropriation of the Palestinian peasantry in the twentieth century. Yet from their standpoint they were merely doing what everyone else on the planet was doing—buying land at market prices.

So when Palestinians reacted with anger and eventually with violence, Jews were stunned and outraged. Anti-Jewish violence and racism are understandable but tragic and immoral responses to the economic exclusion and the feelings of threat that some Arabs were experiencing as the Jewish presence in Palestine grew. (Remember that we are talking about a time when the Jews were the minority and had no political power over Arab society.) Nor is it moral to demean a whole people for the actions of a few, even if those actions are done "in the name of" that people. The act of blaming an entire group for the offensive behaviors of some individual members leads people to blame all African Americans for the crimes of a few, or to blame all Muslims for Al-Qaeda's acts of violence, or to blame all Arabs or all Palestinians for acts of violence committed by Hamas. People can reasonably be held accountable for others' acts only to the extent that they know about the acts in question and have plausible (democratic or other nonviolent) mechanisms to stop them.

Palestinians would have been far more successful, and closer to a moral course, had they collectively sought a path of peace and mutual cooperation with the Zionists. This is something that might in fact have been possible for the first forty years of Jewish settlement, up until 1920 and maybe even up until 1929. But most Palestinians were illiterate and got their information from leadership elites who had their own goals of retaining power and rebuffing the ideas coming from the West carried by these new Jewish immigrants. So the stories told to most Palestinians in their mosques, in Palestinian newspapers sent to local villages where they were read aloud to the villagers, and through the words of their own feudal elites tended to inflame emotions rather than promote paths of cooperation with the Jewish settlers. Moreover, Palestinian society was very fragmented, and there was no mechanism for democratic participation or selection of legitimate leadership or spokespeople. So it would have been very difficult for small groups of Palestinians who might have had a desire to find a path of cooperation to get their ideas circulated, much less implemented by the entire Palestinian people.

Who Has a Right to the Land?

Jewish land acquisition was perceived by Palestinians as a threat. Shouldn't Jews have been more sensitive to this and known that they were taking over the land that "by right" belonged to Palestinians?

Not so fast.

Jewish land purchase was based on the same market assumptions that were being used by nearly everyone in the expanding global capitalist world since at least the seventeenth century. This expansion was increasingly taking hold in China and India, Europe, Africa, and the Americas. The core of this capitalist thinking went: "If I buy the land, I have a right to it, and I do not have a responsibility to worry about the well-being of those who previously worked the land. They did not, as tenants, own a piece of paper that gave them 'the right' to block the sale of that land or to continue to work it once sold." Historically, some have argued, this was an advance over the previous system in which land ownership was based primarily on military conquest.

Imagine saving up money for many years and then buying some land and the property on it—perhaps a house and a barn. Then imagine some people who previously rented your property declaring that they do not recognize the validity of your purchase. The government recognizes your purchase and the person you bought it from recognizes it, but the previous tenants don't. Well, if you have no other place to live, after a while you might think about forcing those people off the land so that you can live there and work the land yourself.

Now suppose that the people you force off begin to steal things from the land you purchased, or kill your livestock, or even kill some of the people in your community who are working the land. Might you not be inclined to call in the local police? And if the police don't step in—perhaps because they don't care much about your needs because you are Jewish and they don't like Jews, or perhaps because they are corrupt and taking bribes—might you not be inclined to create your own defense forces to protect yourself? That is what the Jewish settlers did when they created the Haganah.

The focus on whether Jews legitimately purchased their land in Palestine is becoming less relevant with time, as there is considerable evidence that the amount of land actually purchased by Zionists before 1948 has been vastly overestimated in an apparent effort to give the impression that the Zionists simply bought their way into a Jewish state. This whole argument may be moot if we consider that by 1947, Jews owned only 6.6 percent of pre-1948 Palestine. So the violence with which they were met cannot be explained away as a response to another people being wholly dispossessed—because that had not yet happened to most Palestinians. And yet by 1948 there had already been more than twenty years of violence against the Jewish settlers.

"Well," you might argue, "the Palestinians could foresee what would happen if the Jews were allowed to come without restraint. They knew that the Palestinian people would lose their land."

But it could equally be argued that this was a self-fulfilling prophecy and that a more open and generous reception to Jewish immigrants, coupled with plans to include them in a new binational state and take seriously their need to help their families find a safe place to live, might have produced a very different outcome. That was the proposal coming from Martin Buber, Judah Magnes, and a small group of Jewish visionaries from the 1920s to the middle of the 1940s, but they were unable to find a group of Arab intellectuals or community leaders willing to espouse a binational alternative.

My point, of course, is to show that each side had a story to tell that seemed perfectly understandable and reasonable within the context of its own assumptions, and that neither had to be evil or racist or colonialist in order to think that what they were doing and how they were responding to the Other made perfect sense.

But this is clear only once we understand the whole context of capitalist society and its assumptions as it increasingly managed to turn every aspect of life into commodities. In the context of a globalized capitalist society, market assumptions become dominant, and they enter into the consciousness of everyone.

This was already happening in Arab society before the Jews arrived. Some Arabs were already using their capital to buy land and throw villagers off that land before the Jews became a significant factor. But this was a minor phenomenon because the absentee owners needed people to farm the land in order to make any money. It was only when Jews offered inflated prices for the land that it became profitable for the landlords to sell the land to the Jews and thereby empower them to evict the Arab farmers.

So, if you want to argue within the context of an international capitalist society, then the Jews who bought land were acting reasonably and those who used violence against them were not.

The Palestinians who were working the land when the Zionists arrived had access to it because someone had conquered the land from people living there previously and had devised a system of ownership that favored them. Ottoman and, previously, other Muslim ownership of the land of Palestine was based on military conquest from those who owned it previously, and those previous owners' claims were derived from Roman and, previously, Greek conquest of the land from the Jews. And ancient Israelite ownership derived from conquest from someone else, and so on, into the unknowable past. Jews were one of the indigenous groups whose previous working of the land gave them historic claims to it that were just as legitimate as every other group that had used force and violence to take it from some previous group. And that, by the way, is where all ownership is really rooted: in acts of force and violence that are forgotten in subsequent generations. Afterward, ancient Israelites could set up a system of redistribution of land as commanded in the Torah's Jubilee. Or later Muslims could create a notion of collective ownership sanctified by Islamic law. Or still later Americans could set up a legal system that regulated the sale of land by contract. Yet all of these systems would be built upon original acts of violent conquest.

Once we recognize that "ethically legitimate" ownership of land is itself a questionable concept and that it is largely based on conquest and domination of one group over another, where do we go?

Some people avoid discussing these issues at all on the grounds that we can't critique anyone's ownership of anything, because the moral foundations of ownership are so weak that all we can rely upon is the legitimacy of current arrangements. If we don't want to revert to a "war of all against all," they argue, then we have to accept the current distribution of land as legitimate and operate within the context of the actually existing power arrangements of the modern world.

Within that context and using those standards, Jews who bought land in Palestine were operating by the same laws as everyone else and could not be faulted for acting immorally, and Palestinians who resisted the Jews' purchase-based claim had no right to do so.

I've argued in my book *Jewish Renewal* and in *Tikkun* (www.tikkun.org), that spiritual progressives should question the very legitimacy of the notion of ownership. In the Torah, for example, God warns the people not to get excessively connected to what they have acquired through the marketplace. So every fifty years, the Torah tells us, society should revert to its original (roughly equal) distribution of land, wiping out all previous market transactions. It's called the Jubilee.

To underscore why the land must revert to this equal distribution, the Torah challenges any notion of private property and attributes to God the statement, "The whole earth is Mine." Given that view, land can be held privately, but only if it is used to strengthen the larger system of love, justice, peace, and community that God has created human beings to establish on earth. Human beings have a "right" to land only to the extent that we use it in ways consistent with our moral and ecological obligation to guard and protect it, to produce food made available to all, and to use it as the foundation of a just social order created in accord with the Torah's mandate to "pursue justice" and to "love the stranger."

On these criteria, the original Zionist enterprise could be faulted. It was an attempt to acquire the land without regard for the well-being of those already there, and it stands in sharp contrast with the Torah injunction to "love the stranger." But this criticism is relevant only for those who always and consistently use this criterion. It has no place in the discourse of those who regularly use market criteria rather than moral criteria to judge financial transactions and uses of the land on our planet.

It's simply racist to use a higher standard for judging some Zionists' behavior than one uses in judging one's own behavior or that of other national groups. So, if a person is willing to critique his/her own behavior in the capitalist marketplace and to judge one's right to one's own house and other property by the criterion established in Torah, then this person has the right to fault the Jewish people as well for not having lived up to those spiritual standards.

The reality is that neither Zionist nor Palestinian societies thought about their practical daily economic lives in primarily spiritual terms—they both accepted market categories (as in "this is mine because I own a piece of paper that says so"), and they both accepted notions of ownership based on the flawed social system in which they lived. Nor have Christian, Jewish, or Islamic fundamentalists been particularly consistent when it came to enforcing the elimination of debts every seven years and the redistribution of land every fifty years.

So if we want to make a pragmatic argument, then we do so within the context of the current power relations and what they have established. But if we want to make an argument from the standpoint of a world that we really believe in, then we are not going to accept as convincing the notion that somebody has property rights on a particular piece of land. Instead, as spiritual progressives we are going to ask about all land on the planet: how do we share it most effectively so that everyone can have enough and still be ecologically sustainable and responsible? And that is a very different kind of question than the question of how we reestablish previously existing rights to land that were unfairly taken away. The latter question is difficult in part because so many different people have mixed their labor with the same land over the course of history and hence have conflicting claims to it.

Could a middle path have been found, based more on pragmatic empathy than on capitalist, Marxist, or spiritual progressive ideology? Could the Jews have been able to see the Palestinians as equal children of God worthy of full respect and to mitigate the harshness of the capitalist marketplace by offering security and cooperation to sitting tenants, so that they became partners in the land rather than dominators? Or could the Palestinians have been able to feel compassion for these refugees from Western oppression, even when the refugees were arrogant or, like some Palestinian leaders, eager to cooperate with colonial powers? Under these circumstances, perhaps an entirely different history might have unfolded. But how many of us have been able to rise to the occasion in this empathic and generous fashion when our community's lives and livelihoods are at stake? How many of us have made dialogue and mediation with political, religious, or ethnic opponents so central to our communities in easier times that we would be collectively equipped to work out pragmatic, caring solutions with opponents in such hard times as were faced by the Jews and Palestinians in their decades-long encounters? Even now, small minorities on each side are working with this kind of practice but are not visible enough to swing the majorities.

THE ECONOMIC CLASH

Jewish immigrants who arrived in the second wave of immigration after World War I brought with them a thick socialist ideology, but it was their Jewish nationalism that eventually shaped their choices about how to relate to the Palestinian Arabs.

Just as nationalism undermined the internationalist aspirations of the European working-class parties that ultimately lined up to support their nations' involvement in World War I, so too nationalism overwhelmed the internationalist emphasis that had been part of the official ideology of many early Zionist socialists.

The Zionists argued that Jewish life in the Diaspora was abnormal and distorted in part because Jews had become separated from the means of production—from land and factory work. Historically Jews had been either economically marginalized or allowed only into professions like money-lending and intellectual life. Either way, they had no intrinsic connection to the creation of wealth. So, the Zionists reasoned, the first priority for creating a healthy Jewish society would be to create Jewish farmers and Jewish laborers.

Yet that was not so easy, because Jewish capitalists who began to invest in Palestine (starting toward the end of the nineteenth century and through the first decades of the twentieth century) often put their class interests above their nationalist interests. These capitalists hired Arab laborers who would work for low wages. If the Jews were going to build a working class, Zionists argued, these Jewish capitalists would have to make it possible for Jews to work. The solution: make it a central demand of the Zionist movement that only Jews be employed in factories or agricultural enterprises that were to do business with the Jewish immigrants and their supporters abroad.

In this way, a new kind of socialist workers' movement emerged—one that supported Jewish labor and excluded from membership Arabs who wished to work together with Jews. Political parties were formed, including Poalei Zion (Workers of Zion), led by David Ben Gurion. The party's distinguishing ideology was its strong commitment to creating an exclusively Jewish economy.

As the Jewish labor movement became ever stronger, it formed a powerful organization, part union and part welfare operation, known as the *Histadrut*, and started establishing factories and other economic institutions meant exclusively for Jews. The Histadrut was a very unusual trade union organization because it not only represented workers but also owned some of the institutions in which workers worked. Moreover, it created one of the most advanced and humanitarian networks of social services ever. It established a health insurance program or sick fund (*Kupat Holim*), pension programs, and training and educational programs. Through its outreach to workers, the Histadrut became the backbone of a powerful labor movement whose Labor Party became the major force in building the Israeli state. Yet all these benefits were restricted: Jews only.

Take, for example, the health program. Working with an international women's Zionist organization called *Hadassah*, Kupat Holim was able to create a health service that provided hospitals, nurses' training schools, school playgrounds, and public health programs that reduced trachoma and malaria among Jews. "As a consequence of these," argues Samih K. Farsoun, "the death rate among Jews was less than half that among the majority of

Palestinians." It was only after the introduction of public health programs by the British that the entire population began to see the benefits of modern medicine and that population increase became possible among Palestinians.

Closely connected to economic strength were residents' levels of education. Jewish culture had long given primacy to education, so Jews were well positioned to take advantage of opportunities whenever they became available. When European and American institutions allowed Jews to enter and advance on equal footing with their Christian neighbors, Jews excelled.

But such opportunities were not abundant in the first half of the twentieth century. Many elite institutions in the United States and other Western countries had heavy formal or informal quotas on the number of Jewish students and faculty they would take. And Jew-hating was prevalent among many university students throughout Europe in the first four decades of the twentieth century. No wonder that some of the most talented thinkers and intellectuals were attracted to the Zionist movement with its promise that Jews could become "a people like all other people" and not face special disadvantages that came with their peculiar social location in diaspora societies.

These intellectuals embarked on what many saw as an amazing feat—the revival of ancient Hebrew into a spoken contemporary language. In so doing, the Zionists were consciously breaking with the Yiddish language, which had become the spoken tongue of the Jewish masses of Eastern Europe. Many Zionists believed that Yiddish reflected the "pathology" of ghetto Jews' passivity and powerlessness. The revival of Hebrew also constituted a sharp break with religious Jewry's perspective that Hebrew was *lashon hakodesh*, the holy language that should not be spoken in profane daily use.

With British consent, the Zionists were able to create a segregated Jewish school system that went from kindergarten through university (the Hebrew University in Jerusalem and the Technion in Haifa). But the British denied similar autonomy to the Palestinian Arabs, who were forced to attend British government schools or private schools and had to leave the country if they wished to attend university. As Samih Farsoun puts it, the educational systems were "separate and unequal in terms of quality, financing, levels, and delivery, especially in the rural areas." Farsoun quotes the director of education in the British Mandate government to illustrate the extent to which the British contributed to a growing separation between the peoples: "The natural result of the disparity between the educational facilities offered to Arabs and Jews is to widen the cultural gap between the two races, to prevent social intermixture on equal terms, and to tend to reduce the Arabs to a position of permanent inferiority."

Now imagine you are a Palestinian Arab watching as this new group of people arrive in your society and begin to build economic institutions with the help of outside financial backers—institutions that explicitly exclude you. Might you begin to feel that your own well-being, and certainly the well-being of your children and grandchildren, is being threatened by this group of immigrants? Imagine you are already inclined to see these immigrants as agents of European colonialism. Then you hear them publicly articulate a desire to establish a Jewish homeland in your neighborhood. And next you hear the British declare in the "Balfour Declaration" of 1917 that they intend to support this Zionist movement. Your conclusion? You might well see these institutions as prefiguring a political state that would deny you your rights.

Now, turn around and imagine you are an early Zionist. You live in a world where Jews are an oppressed group. You feel that for some period of time it is necessary for your people to have some institutions of your own so that you can overcome the internalization of demeaning self-conceptions that have limited your ability to function.

As a whole, liberal and progressive people have tended to support this kind of development as a necessary step toward the empowerment of groups that have endured demeaning treatment and abuse. Few progressives today oppose forms of affirmative action that include privileging various oppressed groups in one way or another. While most would oppose a government founded on such exclusivist principles, many of us have been very supportive of voluntary organizations being formed to allow previously oppressed groups to organize institutions that are exclusive.

Well, this is precisely the reasoning that was at the heart of the Zionist insistence on a Jewish-only economy in the midst of what was at the time a majority non-Jewish society. Creating Jewish-only institutions in an area that was majority Arab and in a country run by British colonialists could easily be understood as an act of national self-determination and resistance to oppression. That is certainly how the Jewish Fund organized itself as a Jewish-only socialist organization in Eastern Europe.

One might object that whether or not Jews intended to be agents of British colonialism, they came to Palestine with the active support of the British after 1920 and were often helped by the British in settling in to their new homeland. It's undeniably true that this dynamic created a situation very different from that of other minority groups in advanced industrial societies.

The relationships here are complex, however, and call for a sophisticated understanding of the situation. Historical research has revealed that the British were far more ambivalent about Zionism than their official pronouncements often suggest and wavered between moments of support for aliyah and moments of hostility. The hostility was real and led to an actual armed struggle between the *Yishuv* (the Jewish settlement in Israel) and the British army. In particular, the Zionist embrace of socialism scared British capitalists. If the Holocaust had not led to the prevalence of a nationalist-protective discourse in

the Jewish people, Israel might have become a socialist country aligned with anti-capitalist forces. Just because the British
at times showed hostility toward the Yishuv, some Zionists have
gone in the other direction and argued that Britain was actually
against the Zionists. That was not the case either because, as Tom
Segev has demonstrated in his book *One Palestine, Complete*, the
Zionists cooperated with the British far more than traditional
Zionist histories acknowledge.

The government in England veered sometimes toward the interests of the Yishuv but more frequently toward the interests of
the Arabs. Doing so was necessary to preserve British access to
Arab oil and Arab support for the United Kingdom's continued
rule over India. However, the Brits who actually lived in Palestine
were often more supportive of the Yishuv.

Since the British and the leadership of the Zionist movement
employed a shared discourse of "development," the Brits generally saw the Zionist movement as an agent of "modernization,"
even when political circumstances set them in opposition to each
other. The Brits' deeply ingrained racism led them to see the
Arabs as backwards.

To complicate the picture further, there were many Brits in
Palestine who harbored a deep anti-Semitic revulsion against
Jews. This revulsion played out in British attempts to curtail immigration and send illegal Jewish immigrants to detention camps
in Cyprus.

Did Palestinians Have a Right to Keep Jews Out of Their Country?

There are people in the United States who oppose immigration
from South and Central America. Currently just 16 percent of the
U.S. population identifies as Hispanic on the U.S. Census, but

Latinos have accounted for more than half the nation's growth in the past decade. Some analysts are predicting that by the year 2125 there will be more Latinos than non-Hispanic whites in the United States and that Latinos will make up 36 percent of the nation's total population.

Some whites argue that it was their families who built this nation into the powerful and rich country that it has been for many generations. They believe that Latinos will take their jobs and cause high levels of unemployment or that they will bring a Spanish-speaking culture and unfamiliar worldview into their Anglo-Saxon-dominated schools and culture. Their American ancestors made similar arguments against Jews, Irish, Italians, Poles, and German immigrants.

Blacks moving north to Boston from the 1960s to the 1990s were confronted by Irish communities who feared that these newcomers would destroy the communities that they and their parents and grandparents and great-grandparents had built. They used violence and coercion to try to stop these "outsiders" from "taking over" what they perceived to be their schools, their jobs, and their heretofore safely homogeneous communities. The blacks, aided by the huge power of the federal government of the United States and the capitalist media, were able to overcome the resistance of the Irish residents. Many Irish men did in fact lose jobs, and many faced higher rates of crime than had been present when these communities were primarily Irish.

If you side with the white nativists and then support Palestinians' claim that Jews had "no right" to come to Palestine, at least your position is consistent. But if you believe that countries should not restrict immigration on ethnic, religious, or racial criteria, then you may begin to question the moral righteousness of Palestinians who sought to bar Jewish refugees who were fleeing oppression.

Latino immigration to the United States is supported in part by the interests of powerful agricultural and industrial corporations that believe they can benefit by exploiting immigrants for cheaper labor. Jewish immigration to Palestine was supported in part by imperial European powers. I'm not saying these separate cases are truly parallel. But in neither case does the partial and unreliable support of an oppressive force (whether capitalist or imperialist) justify callousness or xenophobia toward individual immigrants and refugees in an urgent and vulnerable situation.

There is something suspicious, perhaps even immoral, about those on the Left who demean white nativists who fear that their culture will be undermined by immigrants, yet see as legitimate the Palestinian fears that shaped Palestinian resistance to Jews seeking refuge in Palestine.

The egalitarian rhetoric (and even sometimes behavior) of the many socialist Zionists who were part of the second aliyah (1904-1914) was not welcomed by Arab landlords. Egalitarian ideas were not then considered a legitimate part of the Palestinian cultural world except by a very small group of Palestinian intellectuals whose writing and teachings were not accessible to most Palestinians.

The point here, as throughout this discussion, is not to justify the choices of the Zionist settlers or the Palestinian farmers and the Arab elites, but to see how those on each side could have had reasonable foundations for doing what they did. Those on each side had some reasonable grounds for feeling that the other side was acting in ways that were insensitive, provocative, and hurtful.

Chapter Three

THE EMERGENCE OF A JEWISH STATE

W HEN THE LEAGUE OF NATIONS INCORPORATED the Balfour Declaration into its "Mandate for Palestine," it essentially gave international approval to British rule and to the British elevation of Jewish interests over the interests of the Palestinians. As a result, Jewish immigration dramatically increased and many Palestinian Arabs were outraged at the imposition of these outside forces' visions on an Arab society.

By 1920, Palestinians had begun to riot against Jewish immigration, causing many deaths on both sides. Attacks against Jewish settlements increased. Though the official leaders of the Palestinian movement—usually the scions of wealthy landowners and feudal families who traced their lineage back to the early conquest or to the struggle against Crusaders—were organizing in the large cities, it was the peasants who were most radicalized by the growing economic power of the Jewish community and its land purchases. It was largely the peasants, rather than the official Palestinian leadership, who demanded of the British Mandate authorities that taxes be reduced, schools and roads be built, and agricultural cooperation be fostered. At this point there was barely any Arab working class, much less a significant Arab communist or socialist party.

Wikimedia Commons

Students at Hebron's yeshiva pose for a picture in the 1920s. All but one were killed in the 1929 massacre.

Violence broke out again in 1929: 133 Jews and 116 Palestinians were murdered by angry mobs before the British authorities could restore order. Though the violence was precipitated by specific struggles over conflicting claims to Jewish and Islamic holy sites in Hebron and Jerusalem, a British investigatory commission concluded that the basic cause of the riots was the "disappointment of [Palestinians'] political and national aspirations and fear for their economic future." Yet listening to the actual language used by those involved, it's clear that anti-Semitic themes on the Arab side and anti-Arab prejudices on the

Jewish side made everyone involved more willing to believe inflammatory rumors. At times, a false rumor about the other side having massacred people provided rioters with a justification for more violence.

Please note the outrageous slaughter of innocent Jews in Hebron. For centuries a small group of religious Jews had prayed and lived near the Machpelah in Hebron, a cave that has traditionally been seen as the burial site for Abraham and Sarah (and, in some religious Jewish accounts, of Adam and Eve). On this site sacred to Jews, Muslims chose to erect a mosque. So for many subsequent centuries it was a shared site of holiness, just like the area of the Dome of the Rock Mosque, which was built on the site of what Jews believed to be the ancient Temple of Solomon, to which the Israelites brought sacrifices in Jerusalem. The Arab mobs who murdered dozens of religious Jews in Hebron in 1929 left a scar on the memory of some Jews that would resurface in the late twentieth century in the establishment of a Jewish settlement there. The fundamentalists who created the settlement often recall this earlier massacre to justify their contemporary hatred of Palestinians and their violent attacks on Palestinian civilians (children included).

As the first few decades of the twentieth century wore on, underlying tensions in Palestine continued to fester and radicalize both sides. Gradually, an increasing number of Jews came to agree with Chaim Arlosoroff, the director of the Jewish Agency's political department from 1931 until 1933, that force was necessary to achieve Zionist aims. Meanwhile politically sophisticated Palestinians became increasingly convinced that an armed conflict with the British was necessary to preserve Palestinian society. When economic conditions worsened in 1936, therefore, many Palestinians were ready to join a general strike in protest of continued Jewish immigration. Jewish immigration to the region had escalated dramatically in the few years since Hitler had come to power in Germany: only 4,075 Jews immigrated in 1931, but by 1933 the number was 30,327, and by 1935 it was 61,854.

In 1936, Palestinian nationalists called not only for an end to immigration, but also for an end to the British Mandate and for the creation of a parliamentary Palestinian Arab government. Guerilla bands known as Ikhwan Al-Qassam or Brothers of Al-Qassam (named after a guerrilla leader who was killed by British troops) attacked Jewish immigrants and British officials. Older and more established Arab voices tried to calm or restrain the shabab for fear of an open conflict with the British Mandate authorities.

The Arab Revolt of 1936 to 1939 began with a six-month general strike and an armed insurrection that lasted longer. The British declared the strike illegal, censored or closed down newspapers, imposed tough curfews, imposed collective punishments, and jailed or deported key leaders. They set up a new investigation, the Peel Commission, which came to the same conclusion that earlier studies had: that the central cause of the revolt was local Arabs' desire for national independence and their fear of a Jewish national homeland in Palestine.

Many Jews were shocked. While Ben Gurion, a leader of the Jewish community in Palestine, understood that Arabs feared losing their homeland and hence had resorted to a violent struggle, other Zionist leaders saw the revolt as little more than an extension of centuries of hatred of Jews. For many Jews it was easier to liken Palestinians to Jew-hating Cossacks and street gangsters than to see them as representatives of an Arab nationalist movement with claims to legitimacy equal to those of the Zionist movement.

To the extent that most Zionists were willing to acknowledge the Arab Revolt as a nationalist movement, they characterized it as an immoral terrorist movement. Yitzhak Tabankin, one of the ideologues of the kibbutz movement, went so far as to say: "The swastika, waved aloft in Hitler's Germany, and the green flag, the Arab 'national' flag now upraised by reactionary leadership of the Arabs of Palestine—they are the same flag, the flag of national hatred." This response of delegitimizing the Other was intensely prevalent on both sides.

The Peel Commission concluded that the struggle was "irrepressible" and the Mandate unworkable. Its proposed solution: to partition the territory. The Jews would receive one-fifth of it, including most of Galilee, Emek Yizre'el, and the coastal plain, while the Arabs would receive the Negev, the southern coastal plain, the Gaza Strip, and the Judean hills and central plains—all of which would be united with Transjordan into one large Arab state.

Peel also recommended an exchange of populations—the transfer of some 225,000 Arabs from the Jewish state to the Arab state and the transfer of 1,250 Jews from the Arab state to the Jewish state. Picking up themes that had been part of Zionist thinking since Herzl, Jews welcomed the idea of transfer because they believed that a Jewish state would be impossible without a solid Jewish majority. Though few talked about this publicly, many believed that the Palestinian Arabs should be resettled in the lands of their brothers and sisters across the Jordan. They saw no problem with this plan if the transfer was well compensated, was done in a humane manner, and was not forced.

While Jews publicly welcomed the partition plan and privately celebrated the legitimization of transferring Arabs from the proposed Jewish state, few Zionist leaders believed that the Jewish state would be able to live within the narrow boundaries proposed by the Peel Commission. Yet by 1937 there was a perceived urgency to have some place to settle the Jews of Europe unrestricted by the kind of ethnic-based immigration quotas that kept Jews from being accepted in the United States or in Palestine. For that reason, the possibility of transferring Arab populations to neighboring states made the Peel Commission proposal seem reasonable to many Zionists.

The Peel Commission proposal did not seem at all reasonable to most Palestinian Arabs, who were outraged at the idea that their homeland should be divided. The Palestinian Arabs of Galilee led the opposition, unwilling to consider either transfer or living under Jewish rule. Thirty years before, there had been few Jews. Now, Palestinian Arabs asked themselves in astonishment: are the Jews going to transfer us from our homes or make us live as a minority in a Jewish state? The Arab Revolt continued and intensified.

Until 1937 the organization of Jewish settlements and settlers (called the Yishuv) had followed what they called a "policy of restraint," but an increase in acts of Palestinian Arab terror in October 1937 provided the "grounds" for a Jewish terrorist group, the Irgun, to plant bombs in Arab civilian crowds and Arab buses. As Benny Morris reports in *Righteous Victims*:

> Massive bombs were placed in crowded Arab centers, and dozens of people were indiscriminately murdered and maimed—for the first time more or less matching the numbers of Jews murdered in the Arab pogroms and rioting of 1929 and 1936. This 'innovation' soon found Arab imitators, and became something of a 'tradition'; during the coming decades. Palestine's (and, later, Israel's) marketplaces, bus stations, movie theaters, and other public buildings became routine targets, lending a particularly brutal flavor to the conflict.

The Arab Revolt was put down forcibly by the British as the approach of World War II reinforced fears about Great Britain's ability to maintain control of the routes to Arab oil and to India. That same concern for oil led the British to back away from the Peel Commission's notion of partition and to focus instead on winning Arab support for the coming conflict with Germany, Italy, and Japan.

Given Nazi anti-Semitism, the Jews had no choice but to side with the British in a struggle against Germany, but anti-colonial feelings in the Middle East gave Arabs their reason to find a Hitler victory potentially appealing. This caused additional worry to the British, who needed to secure their access to Arab oil. So on May 17, 1939, the British issued a new statement of policy designed to appease the Arabs, called the White Paper of 1939, which proposed a ceiling of 75,000 on Jewish immigration during the next five years, set severe limitations on Jewish land purchasing, and promised an independent Palestinian state within ten years.

The British hoped that the White Paper would appease the Palestinians and buy Arab support for the war in Europe. Because the proposal did not immediately establish Palestinian independence, it was rejected by Palestinian Arab leaders. And because it restricted immigration, it was rejected by the Zionists. So the British were forced to implement their policy unilaterally.

Jews had already sought to break the British immigration quotas through illegal entry by sea. Between 1934 and 1938, about 40,000 Jews arrived illegally. But after 1939, with the British more determined to keep Arab support, the number of illegal entries decreased, with less than 16,000 making it into Palestine between 1940 and 1945. Seeking to appease Arab anti-Zionist sentiment, the British captured boats filled with Jewish refugees seeking escape from Nazi Germany and sent them to special island camps in Mauritius and later in Cyprus.

These policies did little to convince Palestinians that the British were really on their side. The British had consistently prevented Palestinians from developing their own democratic institutions, still refused to give Palestinians their independence, and were not challenging Zionist aspirations. Many Arabs cheered when the Nazis began to defeat the Allies militarily in the early war years. They hoped that the weakening of England's and France's militaries would eventually lead to a loosening of the two countries' colonial power throughout the Arab world. (France played a major colonial role in Syria and Iraq.)

Given the absence of a strong democratic tradition inside the Arab world, the dictatorial approach of the Axis countries did not cause huge tensions. However, the racist ideologies of the Axis (Hitler had once called the Arabs "half-apes") would certainly have come into conflict with Arab aspirations had the Nazis succeeded in dominating the world. But for many Arabs the immediate need to break free from British or French colonialism made an Axis victory seem preferable.

In 1941 the Iraqi military revolted in favor of the Nazi Axis. There were mass riots in Baghdad and in other Arab cities against the Jewish populations there, and hundreds of Jews were killed. These anti-Jewish attacks set the stage for the subsequent mass exodus of Sephardi and Mizrahi Jews to Israel as soon as that became possible after the creation of a Jewish state. The exiled ex-mufti of Jerusalem, Amin Al-Husseini, a leader of the Arab Revolt, tried to organize support for the Axis among Arabs and eventually fled to Berlin, where he was greeted as "a great champion of Arab liberation and the most distinguished antagonist of England and Jewry." He later befriended Hitler and helped organize Arab volunteers to fight on the side of Germany. He also tried to interfere with the emigration of Jewish children to Palestine.

This history of Arabs tilting toward the Axis, though motivated largely by anti-colonial feeling rather than by allegiance to
Nazism, made it easier for the Allies, whom the Jews were unequivocally supporting, to more fully support the Zionist cause.
Similarly, the tilt of Zionism toward the Allies was not based on
an inherent affinity between the Zionists and British and French
colonialists, but by a reading of what would be best for allowing
Jews to establish a safe haven for Jews who were at the time beings massacred in Europe.

The legacy of Arab willingness to close the doors of Palestine
when Jews were seeking refuge from mass extermination at
the hands of the Nazis would set the stage for similar moral insensitivity years later, when Jews shut their ears to the cries of
Palestinian refugees.

THE HOLOCAUST

The destruction of European Jewry by the Nazis was a decisive
factor in convincing Jews that they needed a state of their own
to protect them from what many saw as the inevitable and periodic resurfacing of the world's basic anti-Semitic tendencies. Adherents to this worldview saw the situation of the German Jewish
community as proof that assimilation into other states could never
ensure Jews' safety.

No Jewish community in history had ever been better integrated into the life of its host country than the German Jews. Jews
had reached positions of command and respect in academic and
cultural life, in the media, in a wide array of professions, and in
some corners of the business world. Yet none of this was enough
to protect Jews from the recurring curse of anti-Semitism.

Even those whose families had converted to Christianity were
not safe. The Nazi doctrine of racial origins led Nazis to trace birth

National Archives, Washington

Piles of Jewish bodies were found at Buchenwald concentration camp when the camp was discovered by Allied forces.

records back several generations, unearth hidden "Jewish blood" in families that had no previous knowledge of their Jewishness, and send them to the death camps along with other Jews.

There is little question that the Nazis were the indispensable element in organizing the mass murder of the Jews. But, on an experiential level, Jews were equally shocked at how quickly their non-Jewish neighbors abandoned them. Many refused to take risks to stand up on their behalf and too often even actively betrayed Jews to the Nazis. In some places in Eastern Europe, large numbers of Poles, Latvians, Estonians, Lithuanians,

Ukrainians, Croats, and Russians enthusiastically helped hunt down Jews who were in hiding or seeking to escape, and then murdered the Jews in large numbers and with disturbing brutality.

Even in the Austrian, Czech, French, and Dutch populations, which Western European discourse portrayed as "more cultured," there were all too many people eager to cooperate with the Nazis and turn in the Jews. Neighbors, coworkers, employers, employees—no matter where Jews turned, they were amazed to find so little support. Nor did this hatred come out of nowhere. The centuries of Christian anti-Semitism had created among the European masses a predilection to hate and distrust Jews. This was then built upon by fascist and openly anti-Semitic political parties that flourished in the 1930s in many European countries. Though it was hard to find anyone in France after 1945 who wanted to boast about their affiliation with fascist parties, a significant section of the French population had manifested intense anti-Semitism in the 1930s, welcomed the creation of the anti-Semitic Vichy regime, and cooperated with the rounding up of Jews who were packed into trains and sent to Auschwitz and other Nazi death camps.

There were, of course, righteous non-Jews who did risk, and in some cases actually lost, their lives defending, hiding, or protecting Jews. A room in the Yad Vashem Holocaust memorial in Jerusalem commemorates these courageous people. But by and large the experience of the Holocaust tended to renew the historically-based memories of non-Jews as essentially hateful toward Jews or at best indifferent to their fate.

There was nothing secret about Hitler's plans. The Left had plenty of warning, yet it did little to counter the growing anti-Semitism in Europe's leftwing parties.

Jews on the Left were often reluctant to raise this issue, perhaps subconsciously aware that their non-Jewish comrades were unwilling to campaign seriously against anti-Semitism, or perhaps unwilling to seem parochial in a movement whose central theme was to overcome nationalism and become internationalist.

When the war came, too many of those non-Jews who had been affiliated with socialist or communist organizations were unwilling to protect their Jewish comrades and instead allowed racism to triumph. After the war, communists in Eastern Europe again used anti-Semitism to connect with the masses, show their nationalist credentials, and reestablish their credibility with a people whom Soviet troops had conquered in repelling the Nazis. Popular anti-Semitism was a reality that remained a significant force in Eastern Europe even after the Nazis had been defeated and their leaders had been brought to trial by the communists.

Meanwhile, the Allies also did little to save Jews. There was no concerted effort to destroy the death camps, interdict trains bringing Jews to their deaths, or support refugees who had managed to flee Europe by ship. The gates of the United States were closed—Jewish refugees were turned away from our shores—and Arab influence managed to ensure that the gates of the much closer Palestine were closed as well. British navy ships enforced the closure of Palestine to refugee ships.

Meanwhile in most of Europe Jews were rounded up and herded into ghettos, where they died by the tens of thousands by being slowly starved to death. Others were shipped to concentration camps, where they were worked to death or simply sent to the gas chambers and crematoria. Tens of thousands of Jews being murdered turned into hundreds of thousands, and then millions. Yet the world paid little attention as the death machine worked with remarkable efficiency toward the stated aim of exterminating every last Jew on the planet, despite feverish appeals from Jews around the world.

It should be stressed that the goal of destroying the Jews was quite unique in that it did not flow from some other economic or

Wikimedia Commons

These Jewish women were forced to disrobe and pose for a picture before being murdered themselves. They were among 2,749 Jews murdered by Nazis on the beach near the city of Liepaha, Latvia, from December 15 to 17, 1941.

political goal. Even when destroying Jews required a diversion of resources and energy away from the front lines of military struggle, the Nazis gave the gas chambers first priority. They were willing to sacrifice other goals, even the goal of winning the political war, to accomplish this evil end. At a time in the twenty-first century when people throw around the term "genocide" loosely, it is important to remember what genocide means: intentional killing of everyone in a particular racial, ethnic, or national grouping whom the perpetrators can manage to kill. The mass murder of Tutsis by Hutus was genocidal in this sense, as was the mass murder of Armenians by Turks, the murder of Native Americans by white settlers in the United States, the murder of aboriginals in Australia, and the murder of the kulaks by Stalin in the Soviet Union.

The impact of the genocide perpetrated by the Nazis remains a major factor in Jewish consciousness in the twenty-first century. The humiliation of being treated like vermin who ought to be exterminated; the murder of one out of every three Jews alive at the time; the fear facing all Jews on the planet as they contemplated their fate should Hitler win, coupled with the subsequent lies by people who had collaborated; the denial of what had happened; the failure of the world to allow Jews to find refuge from Nazism; and the failure of the world to come to grips with what had produced this tragedy and what could be done to prevent future recurrences—all these combined to create an ongoing trauma for the Jewish people. This trauma has never healed; it must be central to any attempt at understanding the current realities of the Middle East.

The political impact of the Holocaust on Jewish consciousness went in two opposite political directions. For some, the horror of racism and genocide led to a deep commitment to never again allow anyone else in the world to face this kind of horrible reality. Though Jews had already played a leading role in labor, socialist, and communist movements and various other progressives struggles, the overwhelming nature of the Holocaust gave a deeper immediacy to Jews' drive to fight racism and other forms of oppression. No wonder, then, that many young Jews growing up in advanced industrial societies in the 1960s, who were born immediately after the Holocaust yet had their childhoods dominated by its stories, became leaders of movements against racism and imperialism. They became advocates for the civil rights of African Americans, women, gays and lesbians, the disabled, and other victims of neglect and abuse.

Wikimedia Commons

A Jewish woman in Ivangorod, Ukraine, attempts to protect a child with her own body as they are shot dead at close range in 1942.

Many—perhaps most—other Jews, however, drew a quite opposite set of conclusions. They thought: "We Jews cared about everyone else, but no one cared about us, no one protected us, and no one ever will. When we sought refuge, the countries of the world closed their borders to us and few did anything to assist us in escaping the Nazi genocide. We are alone in the world and we can't count on anyone but ourselves, so we need to focus all our energies on protecting ourselves to ensure that it will never happen to us again."

Judah L. Magnus Museum

Jewish refugees escaping death camps in Europe arrive in the Holy Land.

Jews who responded to the Holocaust in this way tended to focus more on building the Jewish state and became impassioned advocates for Zionism. Indeed, they became increasingly intolerant toward anyone who criticized the State of Israel. From their perspective, history had proven that the Jews could count only on themselves and that therefore the need for a Jewish state was paramount in importance.

Moreover, in the aftermath of the war there were hundreds of thousands of Jews in displaced persons camps around Europe— homeless, hopeless, and in need of urgent care. To the Zionists it

Wikimedia Commons

The SS Exodus left France on July 11, 1947, seeking to take its 4,515 passengers—most of them Holocaust survivors—to Palestine. Following wide media coverage, the British Royal Navy seized the ship and deported all its passengers back to Europe.

was obvious that the place for them was the ancient homeland of the Jewish people, though many of those refugees had never been connected to Zionist aspirations before the war.

As soon as it appeared clear that the Allies were going to defeat the Axis powers, the fight for Palestine resumed. But this time the Zionists managed to bring in another important ally: the United States. The strong Jewish population of the United States played an important role in the Democratic Party. Growing

Jewish influence in the Democratic Party at times was sufficient to balance the strong pressure on U.S. leaders to accommodate the needs of American global oil interests by tilting toward the artificially created Arab states. This ensured U.S. access to the oil in exchange for U.S. military support against the Arab leaders' own populations and U.S. political support when the Arab leaders felt it necessary.

The historical gains of democratic movements in the American past made it possible for ordinary citizens to have an impact on global politics, even when their perspectives conflicted with those of ruling elites. So Zionists in the United States were able to effectively use their growing power in the Democratic Party and the popular revulsion at what had happened to the Jews in the Holocaust to mobilize support for Israel even when doing so seemed to conflict with the interests of the powerful oil and auto lobbies.

Of course, this was not the only way Jews might have chosen to use the democratic arena. Some argued for the elimination of all immigration quotas for Jews and for the mass acceptance of hundreds of thousands of Jewish refugees into the United States. But this choice was unthinkable to many Jews under the influence of Zionism; for them, the revelations of the Holocaust seemed to show that this was the moment to claim national sovereignty and not just national safety.

Demanding the immigration of hundreds of thousands of Jewish refugees was a choice unthinkable to many of the most assimilated leaders of American Jewry, who still felt wary about testing American tolerance, given the strong anti-Semitic themes in Christian theology and the enduring quotas against Jews in major American universities. All the better, most agreed, to send these refugees to Palestine. Some leading anti-Semitic figures in the U.S. Senate concurred, hoping that perhaps American Jews would also depart for the Holy Land.

As the United States started to lean on Britain to provide a more satisfactory arrangement for Jewish immigrants, the Yishuv also stepped up their struggle for statehood. The Yishuv now included thousands of men who had participated in the Allied armies of World War II, and many had stolen or illegally purchased arms that could be used in the coming struggle. With the post-war British seeming more tentative about the Zionist enterprise, two Jewish terrorist organizations—the Lehi and Irgun Zvai Leumi (IZL, led by Menachem Begin)—initiated an armed struggle for Zionist independence in February 1944. The press dismissed them as "misguided terrorists" and "young fanatics crazed by the sufferings of their people into believing that destruction will bring healing." But even before the war fully ended, the more mainstream Haganah (Jewish defense forces) joined in attacks on the British.

For the next three years, from 1945 to 1948, a guerrilla war was fought between the British and the forces of Jewish national liberation. The most notorious act of this guerrilla war took place on July 22, 1946, when the IZL placed bombs in the King David Hotel, killing ninety-one people (Britons, Arabs, and Jews). The Haganah condemned this terrorist attack.

Yet the British were far less repressive toward the Jewish Revolt than they had been toward the Arab Revolt of 1936 to 1939. For example, during the Arab Revolt, British forces killed thousands of Palestinians and arrested, detained, or deported the entire leadership of the Palestinian movement. During the Jewish Revolt of 1945 to 1947, the British killed thirty-seven Jews fighting for their own independence. The standard Zionist claim that the British systematically tilted in favor of the Arabs throughout the Mandate period ignores the relatively less repressive methods used by the British fighting against the Yishuv.

Without U.S. support for the Mandate, the British were in an untenable position and began to make plans to leave. They

Wikimedia Commons

The Irgun, a Jewish terrorist organization, bombed the King David Hotel on July 22, 1946. Ninety-one people—most of them civilians of diverse nationalities—were killed.

proposed a British-run international "trusteeship" with local autonomy for Jews and Arabs over municipal affairs, agriculture, and education, leading eventually to a binational state. Neither side agreed. The Palestinians wanted majority rule in an independent Palestinian state (they were still the majority in Palestine in 1946), whereas the Zionists insisted upon partition and a separate Jewish state.

Instead of solving the problem themselves, the British, limping from the Second World War, resolved to leave. They turned the issue over to the United Nations, where both the United States and the Soviet Union announced support for partition. Using its considerable political power, the United States pressured some of its client states into voting with it, and partition received the two-thirds vote necessary for passage in November 1947.

The partition agreement gave the Jews, who were 37 percent of the population in 1947, about 55 percent of the land. The Arabs believed they were being asked to pay the price for the pain Jews suffered during the Holocaust. Why, they wondered, shouldn't the Jews be given a portion of Germany or some other country that had actually persecuted them? And if Jews didn't want to be a minority in a Palestinian state, why should Palestinians have to be a minority within a Jewish state? Outraged, Arab states walked out of the United Nations and declared that partition, if implemented, would lead to war.

As with India and Pakistan, which was partitioned into two states in this same time period, the partition of Palestine was a decision against a pluralist, multinational state with aspirations for tolerance and cooperation between rival groups. In other places, notably Yugoslavia, previously feuding communities were forcibly bound together into one country by a powerful communist party, with consequences that turned genocidal fifty years later.

There were a few Jewish voices in Palestine who called for compromise with the Palestinians and for a binational state before the outbreak of the 1948 War. The Jewish philosopher Martin Buber (author of *I and Thou* and a proponent of the wisdom of East European Hasidism), Judah Magnes (president of the Hebrew University), and a handful of others argued that a Jewish state created under these circumstances would be in perpetual conflict with Palestinians and with its Arab neighbors.

Jews, they believed, should do more to seek accommodation with the Palestinian people before declaring independence.

Most Jews, however, felt that these idealists were out of touch with reality. With hundreds of thousands of Jews incarcerated in displaced persons' camps, and with Palestinians involved in guerrilla actions against the Yishuv, there was, most Zionists believed, no time to waste. After 1,800 years of statelessness, and three years after the conclusion of the Holocaust, the Jewish people, Zionists insisted, were no longer willing to wait for the fulfillment of messianic dreams. They wished to take control of their own history by creating their own state.

In grabbing the opportunity that history had presented them, the Zionists embodied the ethos of activism and self-affirmation that had been so long absent in Jewish history. A people who had faced 1,800 years of cultural demeaning, oppression, and genocide and had developed a culture of passivity and otherworldliness had been transformed into a people who could act decisively in their own self-interest and shape their own future. From the standpoint of social-psychological development, this was a powerful indication that an oppressed people could revive and rejuvenate.

Jews rejoiced to see that "dead bones" (in the words of the Prophet Ezekiel) could still live. "Am Yisrael Chai"—"the people of Israel live"—was not simply a nationalist chant; it was an affirmation of life that many Jews felt was a miracle just a few years after the Holocaust. Unfortunately, while this moment helped overcome the nationwide post-Holocaust emotional depression that might have reasonably afflicted Jews for a few decades, it also repressed the ability to fully mourn the loss that the Jewish people had experienced. As a result, those feelings would continue to play an unconscious but powerful role in shaping the ways Jews perceived their own reality.

There is little record of Palestinian voices calling for acceptance of the 1947 partition plan or a binational state that gave equal or close to equal power to both sides. As Israel's first prime minister, Ben Gurion, put it, many Palestinians were convinced from the public statements of Zionist leaders in the 1920s and 1930s that once the Jews had established an independent state in Palestine, they would push for more and more land. This would continue the expansionism that had been a central dynamic of the Zionist movement. It's not hard to see why Palestinians, who had constituted the vast majority of people in their own land a mere thirty years before, should imagine that millions more Jews might soon arrive and continue the dynamics that had already resulted in the loss of Palestinian land and livelihood. In fact, that same fantasy was shared by some Zionists.

And yet there is little doubt in retrospect that the failure of the Palestinian leadership to accept partition and attempt to negotiate a peaceful transition to statehood for both Jews and Palestinians had disastrous consequences for the Palestinian people. For all their bluster, the Arab states were in no position to win a war with the Yishuv. Accepting partition would have allowed for the establishment of a Palestinian state in 1948 and would have made it much more difficult for Israel to receive support for future expansion.

Much has been made of the claim that "the Palestinian people rejected partition." Uri Avnery, who fought as part of the Israeli army in 1948, was later elected to the Knesset, and is now the leader of the Israeli peace movement Gush Shalom, sought to clarify this history in an article he wrote in 2011:

> It is indeed a fact that the Zionist leadership accepted the partition plan—formally. Many Zionist leaders objected, but were persuaded by David Ben Gurion to agree to the official acceptance. However, in several secret meetings

Wikimedia Commons

Palestinian Arab volunteers fought against Jews in Palestine in 1947.

Ben Gurion made it clear that the partition
borders were unacceptable and must be rectified
at the first opportunity. The minutes of these
meetings are there for all to read.... No one asked
the Arab Palestinians whether to accept or reject
anything. If they had been asked, they would
probably have rejected partition, since—in their
view—it gave a large part of their historical
homeland to foreigners. The more so, since the
Jews, who at the time constituted a third of

the population, were allotted 55 percent of the territory—and even there the Arabs constituted 40 percent of the population.

The Yishuv had used the years of the Mandate to build the infrastructure of a state, complete with mechanisms for taxation, a school system, settlement agencies, a well-functioning labor movement, and a governmental apparatus (the Jewish Agency). Meanwhile, the Palestinian infrastructure and leadership had been severely crippled by the British occupation, particularly during the Arab Revolt. Further, while Jews were developing the institutions of a parallel government underground in preparation for potential statehood, the Palestinians continued to work through the British Mandate authority and to rely on its institutions. They had built no independent infrastructure to create a state or run it. Nor could the Palestinians really rely on their fellow Arabs. Surrounding Arab states had huge populations but tiny armies that had fewer military supplies available to them than did the new Jewish State. Militarily, some Israeli historians have argued, the Zionist movement bested the Palestinian Arabs in command and control, weapons production, trained manpower, and political unity.

Nevertheless, the Yishuv faced serious challenges from Palestinian guerrilla forces who began a civil war in November 1947 and continued to be a major factor in the conflict until Arab armies invaded in May of 1948, the day after Israel declared its independence. These guerrilla forces were not strong enough to conduct a frontal war. Instead, they focused on cutting off the roads between settlements, isolating them and in some cases seriously threatening their survival.

The Jewish population of Jerusalem (100,000 Jews) was cut off from the rest of the Yishuv and was under intense siege in the early months of 1948. Convoys of Jews bringing supplies to nearby Gush Etziyon and to Jerusalem were massacred. Jews in Jerusalem faced a desperate food situation in March of 1948, and the attack on convoys bringing relief made many in Jerusalem feel cut off and scared. Meanwhile, as the civil war raged, the IZL killed or wounded hundreds of Arab civilians. There were moments when the Haganah joined with IZL in reprisal attacks on Palestinians, but mostly the terror against Palestinian civilians was perpetrated by IZL and Lehi.

As in all such situations, the cycle of violence and counter-violence makes it difficult to say who started first. Jewish terror attacks in response to Palestinian guerrilla actions were met by vicious attacks on Jewish civilians by Palestinians. The attacks by Palestinians, in turn, led to more Jewish terror attacks. Throughout most of Palestine, both Jews and Palestinians felt that they were deeply threatened by the other side, and both used violence against civilians as part of their strategy to demoralize and terrorize the other side.

The campaign to secure the road to Jerusalem was particularly intense. Jerusalem had not been part of the area given to Israel in the UN partition plan—it was to be an international city. Yet the attack on its Jewish residents by Arab guerillas and the cutting off of its food supplies convinced the Yishuv that its Jews were in immediate danger and that Jerusalem must become part of the new Israeli state. So several convoys were sent to Jerusalem and a set of battles took place in Palestinian villages along the road. The most prominent Palestinian military leader was killed in those battles.

One of the battle sites was Deir Yassin, a village that had gone out of its way to establish good relations with the nearby Jewish neighborhoods of Western Jerusalem and had refused to host Palestinian units or to let them use the village as a base for attacks against Jerusalem. In coordination with the Haganah, the

IZL and Lehi planned to expel the inhabitants of this village to further secure the road to Jerusalem. Haganah machine gunners provided cover for the attack.

The Deir Yassin residents resisted the attack, and five members of the IZL and Lehi were killed in the battle; thirty were wounded. But Deir Yassin stands out in the memory of the Palestinians because of the atrocities committed there against Palestinian civilians. Men, women, and children were massacred by the IZL and Lehi troops.

Benny Morris quotes an Israeli commander who made this report on April 12: "The conquest of the village was carried out with great cruelty. Whole families—women, old people, children—were killed, and there were piles of dead." In a report the next day, this same Haganah commander reported: "Lehi members tell of the barbaric behavior of the IZL toward the prisoners and the dead. They also relate that the IZL men raped a number of Arab girls and murdered them afterward." The number of dead has been estimated at about 250, with some pro-Zionists insisting that the count was much lower (around 120 dead) and some Palestinian partisans claiming numbers closer to 350.

The Jewish Agency immediately condemned the massacre. (Many Palestinians took that condemnation with the same kind of skepticism that decades later Israelis would use to greet Yasir Arafat's condemnation of acts of terror against Israelis.) Just as Israelis later came to believe that Arafat secretly supported terrorism but publicly condemned it for the sake of public relations, so many Palestinians saw the actions of IZL and Lehi as just another dimension of the Zionist tactics to rid the land of Palestinians.

Some historians believe that this and other acts of terror in the pre-1948 period played an important role in pushing surrounding Arab states to move beyond empty rhetoric and actually enter the war against the Yishuv. But the main effect of the massacre at Deir Yassin was to demoralize and terrify many Palestinians, leading them to flee from their homes. Deir Yassin, after all, was a village that had sought to have good relations with the Israelis. Deir Yassin Palestinians had resisted attempts to recruit them into the civil war and had expected that they could live in peace with the emerging Jewish state. If even these people were brutalized and massacred, many Palestinians reasoned, what could they personally expect from Israeli forces?

It made little impact on the Palestinians that many unarmed Jews had also been killed in the course of the previous years or that a few days later Arab militiamen from Jerusalem attacked a convoy of mostly unarmed doctors, nurses, and others on their way to the Hadassah Hospital and Hebrew University camps on Mount Scopus. More than seventy Jews were murdered in this single attack.

Just as present day acts of Palestinian terror are not put into the context of the larger cycle of violence generated by both sides, the terrible massacre at Deir Yassin was not similarly contextualized in 1948. Palestinians did not see their own acts of violence as anything more than defensive acts against Jewish terrorists. So when the news of Deir Yassin became known, it spread panic among Palestinian civilians who drew the conclusion that unless they left their homes quickly, they too would be targets for massacre.

Nor was this panic without foundation. Future Israeli Prime Ministers Menachem Begin and Yitzhak Shamir were leaders of the terrorist groups that were proud of their accomplishments at Deir Yassin. They openly advocated that Palestinians should be terrorized into flight.

In the next weeks in April 1948 and the beginning of May, the struggle accelerated. From the standpoint of the Jews, the struggle was to save Jewish populations in cities and kibbutzim whose supplies of food were being cut by Palestinian forces controlling access. From the standpoint of Palestinians, the struggle was to save Arab villages that would soon be wiped out just as villagers at Deir Yassin had been.

The Jewish forces prevailed in most of these battles. After rebuffing an attack on Kibbutz Mishmar Ha'emek, Jewish forces counterattacked and wiped out ten surrounding Palestinian villages. Teverya, Haifa, and the Arab Katamon section of Jerusalem were conquered. In the case of Haifa, the Jewish mayor urged Palestinians not to flee, though Palestinian leaders were asked to make an unconditional surrender to the Jewish forces; instead, fearful of what might happen, most Palestinians fled.

The pattern spread: Jewish forces conquering Palestinian neighborhoods or villages, and Palestinian civilians fleeing for their lives. The same happened in Jaffa, Eastern Galilee, and Western Galilee. In fact, by May 15, many of the population centers of Palestine had been conquered by the Jews, and much of the Palestinian flight had already taken place. It was only in the Etzion bloc of settlements that the pattern was reversed and the Jewish settlements were crushed by a Palestinian offensive. There, angry Palestinian villagers yelling "Deir Yassin" massacred more than 160 Jewish civilians.

Jewish noncombatants in the Yishuv did not flee. For them, there was no place to flee to—they were surrounded by hostile Arab states, many of them were refugees from Europe where their families had been murdered, and they faced a world that continued to discriminate against them with restrictive immigration laws. They saw the Land of Israel as their only potential home. Most had no other place of even temporary refuge.

The situation for Palestinian refugees was horrendous. Though they could enter the West Bank or neighboring countries, they did not have a place to stay, and many ended up in temporary tent cities that evolved over the course of the next sixty years into "refugee camps" that had few of the amenities or comforts of their previous lives in Palestine. Often they remained in makeshift tent cities or shantytowns into which large families were squeezed, often without running water, sewage, or electricity. Some of these camps have improved slightly over time, but many remain sites of deplorable living conditions. As a result the Palestinian refugees felt homeless and in deep despair.

From the standpoint of Palestinian Arabs, the rapid conquest of many Palestinian population centers and the resulting flight of Palestinian civilians reconfirmed their worst fantasies about what would happen under Jewish rule. Surrounding Arab states showed little real interest in the fate of Palestinians, but after they had postured about caring for their fellow Arabs, the developments of April and early May 1948 forced the hands of Arab feudal regimes and required that they show at least token support.

Once it became clear that the Zionists were intent on declaring their own independence and that the creation of a Jewish state would begin with the departure of the British on May 15, 1948, the Arab states began to talk about exterminating the Jews and eliminating the Jewish State. There was fervent talk about sweeping the Jews into the sea. A few hours after the Yishuv leadership declared independence and created the State of Israel, Arab countries invaded with the intent of wiping out that state. Yet the Arab elites had done little to educate or mobilize their own masses for this struggle.

The Arab forces were much smaller than the Zionists had calculated, and only part of their strength was ever used in Palestine. Things might have been different for the Palestinians had the huge Arab world responded to their plight with hundreds of thousands of volunteers to fight against Zionism. In fact, not more than 5,000 volunteers from the Arab world joined the Palestinian cause—far fewer than the number of Jews and non-Jews who came to volunteer for the Yishuv.

Most Arabs were not invested enough in this struggle to want to get directly involved. They may have felt some sense of solidarity with their fellow Arabs in Palestine. However, this sense of solidarity was not sufficient to overturn the rhythms and customs of what were in fact largely peaceful village societies and submit to the hateful diatribes of their unelected feudal leadership and reactionary, anti-Semitic clergy. In contrast to the belief in the Jewish world that the Arab masses just couldn't wait to be involved in wiping out the Jews, most Arabs chose to stay out of the struggle.

There is little reason to doubt that the Arab armies sent to invade would have wiped out the Jewish State if they had prevailed, but historical revelations from that period now make it possible for us to know that the Arab leaders doubted that they could achieve such a result. Their military experts cautioned them that they would not be able to win an all-out war with the Zionist state. Most entered the conflict with the goal of grabbing as much land as possible while avoiding blame for the loss of Palestine— an outcome they suspected was inevitable.

Yet the fact is that their clearly stated intentions were to destroy the Yishuv, and that could not have been accomplished without the killing of tens of thousands of Jews in Palestine, if not more. It was this recognition that made the Yishuv leaders ever more determined to mobilize every possible resource to resist this invasion, made it easier for the Zionists to generate international support (including arms from Czechoslovakia), and united nearly all Jews and most Westerners in support of the newly emerging Jewish state. This was seen by many as a fulfillment of the prophecy that "the dead bones will yet live." Israel's subsequent military victory proved easier than anyone had expected.

The constant intrigue among the Arab states about how to divide Palestine made it impossible for them to develop a serious coordinated effort. Instead, there were several separate Arab armies with little in the way of shared planning or cooperation. The one plan developed by the Arab League Political Committee was ignored by Jordan; its Legion (the only force with previous battle experience) was directed instead to capture the West Bank for Jordan.

There was also no attempt by the Arab armies to incorporate the Palestinians into planning or participating in the struggle, partly because Arab leaders were not willing to take seriously the needs of the Palestinian people. The Arab countries' own disregard of the Palestinians made it easier for the Zionists to discount the Palestinians after 1948.

The war was bloody and horrific on both sides. More than 1 percent of the Jewish population of Palestine at that time was killed. (In contemporary terms, that might be the equivalent in the United States to a war that killed approximately three million Americans.) Arab forces massacred Jewish settlers. Jewish forces massacred Palestinian civilians and prisoners of war at Eilaboun, Saliha, Safsaf, Jish, Hule, Major, Al-Kurum and elsewhere.

Israel won a powerful military victory and secured its existence, while the Arab states were shown to be militarily powerless. Palestine was de facto divided, with Israelis retaining control over a significantly larger part of pre-1948 Palestine than had been envisioned by the United Nations in 1947. And the enmity between Israelis and Palestinians had dramatically intensified.

Chapter Four

PALESTINIAN REFUGEES . . . AND THE CONFLICT CONTINUES

ONE OF THE TERRIBLE AND LASTING CONSEQUENCES of the war was the creation of a large population of Arab refugees. Israel claimed that there were 520,000 Palestinian refugees, while Palestinians estimate somewhere between 900,000 and one million.

Benny Morris's classic study *The Birth of the Palestinian Refugee Problem 1947–1949* shows that neither the official Israeli account—that Palestinians left voluntarily or in response to an appeal by Arab leaders—nor the Palestinian account—that all refugees were systematically and with premeditation expelled—turns out to be true.

Morris cites private statements by David Ben Gurion and other Zionist leaders in the 1930s and 1940s; these statements show they had a penchant for using "transfer" of Arabs to reduce the Palestinian presence in what they hoped would emerge as a Jewish state, while simultaneously acknowledging that they could not talk about this publicly without endangering their own cause. It was this proclivity to see transfer as an appropriate way to deal with "the Palestinian problem" that set the background for many specific military actions during the 1947–1949 struggle, in which there were outright acts of expulsion either by Lehi and IZL or by the Haganah.

Morris maintains in *Righteous Victims* that almost every instance of Palestinian mass flight from April through June of 1948 "was the direct and immediate result of an attack on and conquest of these neighborhoods and towns. In no case did a population abandon its homes before an attack; in almost all cases it did so on the very day of the attack and in the days immediately following." But Morris is equally insistent that during the first stage of the war "there was no Zionist policy to expel the Arabs or intimidate them into flight, though many Jews, including Ben Gurion, were happy to see the backs of as many Arabs as possible. And without doubt, Jewish—both Haganah and IZL—retaliatory policies and the IZL/LHI terror bombings were precipitants."

On June 16, 1948, the Israeli cabinet resolved to prevent the return of Palestinian refugees and to greet them with live fire should they attempt to return. Morris writes: "Abandoned villages were razed or mined or, later, filled with new Jewish immigrants, as were abandoned urban neighborhoods; fields were set alight, and landowners still in place were urged to sell out and leave; and new settlements were established and began to cultivate the abandoned fields."

In the next phase of the war, in July 1948 and then again in October and November of 1948, another 300,000 Arabs were made refugees.

Morris's gripping account of one battle (originally published in *Tikkun* as part of "The New Historiography: Israel Confronts its Past" in November 1988 and then reprinted in *Best Contemporary Jewish Writing* in 2001) illustrates how Palestinian civilians became refugees:

> On July 12 and 13, the Yiftah and Kiryati brigades carried out their orders, expelling the fifty to sixty thousand inhabitants of the two towns, which lie about ten miles southeast of Tel Aviv. Throughout

the war, the two towns had interdicted Jewish
traffic on the main Tel Aviv-Jerusalem road,
and the Yishuv's leaders regarded Lydda and
Ramlah as a perpetual threat to Tel Aviv itself.
About noon on July 13, Operation Dani HQ
informed IF General Statt/Operations: "Lydda
police fort has been captured. The troops, led
by Lt. Col. Yitzhak Rabin [later to become
Israeli Prime Minister] are busy expelling the
inhabitants." Lydda's inhabitants were forced
to walk eastward to the Arab legion lines, and
many of Ramla's inhabitants were ferried in
trucks or buses. Clogging the roads (and the
Legion's possible route of advance westward),
the tens of thousands of refugees marched,
gradually shedding possessions along the way.
Arab chroniclers, such as Sheikh Muhammed
Nimr Al-Khatib, claimed that hundreds of
children died in the march, from dehydration
and disease.... Many of the refugees came to rest
near Ramallah and set up tent encampments,
which later became the refugee camps supported
by the United Nations Relief and Works
Agency [UNRWA] and the hotbeds of today's
Palestinian rebellion.

Yet Morris, who carefully investigated the Israeli archives, insists that there is no evidence of a systematic expulsion policy at
the level of the Cabinet or IDF staff. Individual commanders in
the field made their own decisions, some expelling villagers, others leaving them in place.

In *Righteous Victims* Morris concludes that the attacks by the
IDF were the major precipitants to flight, but "the exodus was,

overall, the result of a cumulative process," rather than a pre-meditated plan. In the countryside, he writes, many factors were involved:

> ... isolation among a cluster of Jewish settlements, a feeling of being cut off from Arab centers, a lack of direction by national leaders and feeling of abandonment by the Arab world, fear of Jewish assault, reports and rumors about massacres by the Jews, and actual attacks and massacres.

Morris's conclusions have been subsequently challenged by Arab and Israeli post-Zionist Jewish historians who believe that the evidence is far more ambiguous and who point to the ways that many Zionist leaders privately (and a few, publicly) endorsed the notion of "transfer" of Arabs from their homes as early as the 1930s in order to achieve a Jewish majority in some part of the land of Israel. The problem had long predated the actual war: if Zionists were to have a state that went beyond the narrow areas around Tel Aviv, they would have to find some way to move the Arab majority, and that is exactly what happened. On this account, though, the transfer may have never been consciously planned; it was the inevitable consequence of the logic of creating a Jewish state in a society with a majority of non-Jews.

Yet many Israeli historians emphasize that at the time there was far more chaos than organized plans and that many more Palestinians left their homes than Israelis had imagined would. The Palestinian flight went far beyond anyone's expectations.

Historian Avi Shlaim says that although there were many reasons for the Palestinian exodus, including the early departure of the upper classes and Palestinian leadership when the going got tough, the most important reason was Jewish military pressure.

Wikimedia Commons

Palestinian refugees flee their homes during the 1948 War. Palestinians call this war "Al-Nakba," or "the Catastrophe."

The infamous Plan Dalet called for the Haganah to capture Arab cities and destroy Arab villages. The objective of the plan was to clear the interior of the country of hostile and potentially hostile "Arab elements." Though that plan was defined in narrow military and territorial objectives, Shlaim argues that "by ordering the capturing of Arab cities and the destruction of cities, it both permitted and justified the forcible expulsion of Arab civilians" by the Israeli army (the Haganah), and that is exactly what happened even before the official outbreak of hostilities on May 15, 1948 (Avi Shlaim, *The Iron Wall*).

Once the flight began, there were explicit orders not to allow refugees to return. One such, from General Moshe Carmel on October 31, 1948, told troops to "do all in your power to clear quickly and immediately from the areas conquered all hostile elements in accordance with the orders issued. The inhabitants should be assisted to leave the conquered areas." This was understood by the IDF commanders as orders to expel.

In the course of subsequent expulsions, the IDF perpetrated massacres at Majd Al-Kurum, Al-Bi'na, Dayr Al-Assad, Nahf, Safsaf, Jish, Sasa, Saliha, Ilabun, and Hula. Historian Benny Morris argues that the

> uniform or at least similar nature of the
> massacres points to a belief among the
> perpetrators of central direction and
> authorization.... Almost all the massacres
> followed a similar course: a unit [of the IDF]
> entered a village, rounded up the men folk in
> the village square, selected four or ten or fifty of
> the army-age males ... lined them up against a
> wall and shot them. Some of the massacres were
> carried out immediately after the conquest of
> the village by the assaulting troops, though most
> occurred in the following days.

In July 1949, Israel offered the Arab states an overall peace settlement in which 100,000 refugees would be let back if the rest were resettled in Arab lands; or, if Egypt would give up the Gaza strip, Israel would take its 200,000 refugees and let them stay there. But the Arab states insisted that Israel allow all the refugees to return to their homes. In subsequent years, Israel insisted that the Arab states resettle the refugees, but the refugees insisted on remaining in camps, hoping someday to return home.

Wikimedia Commons

A Palestinian man overlooks his crowded refugee camp in 1948.

Who could blame the refugees for being outraged at not be-ing allowed to return to their homes once the hostilities had stopped? Many of them had been forcibly evicted. Others had fled from a war zone, imagining that they would be able to return home once the war was over. No wonder the creation of the State of Israel was for them *Al-Nakba* (the disaster)—it meant the loss of their homes and a life of some stability and regularity, and the start of economically desperate life in refugee camps.

The decision not to allow refugees to return was the single most significant decision ever made by the Israeli government. It guaranteed incalculable human suffering for the Palestinian people—and a time bomb for Israel that would explode in the coming decades.

Yet from the standpoint of many Zionists, the expulsion of

Palestinians was a necessity. Even though most Palestinians had not joined the armed struggle against the Yishuv, many had. And how could one be sure that those who had not yet joined would not soon join?

There were few Palestinian voices calling for coexistence and peace in 1948. The Yishuv perceived itself as faced with a huge threat both externally from Arab states and internally from a hostile Palestinian population. Moreover, these Palestinians had seemed united in their opposition to allowing Jewish refugees to enter the country just a few years earlier. Perhaps, reasoned some Jews, the Palestinians would get a taste of what they had done to the Jews whom they had prevented from entering the Land of Israel during the Holocaust.

Ben Gurion frequently told Westerners, "Israel did not expel a single Arab." The official story, now historically discredited, became that Palestinian Arabs who subsequently became refugees had all left voluntarily, in response to an appeal from Arab leaders who wanted a clear path to massacre all of the Jewish inhabitants of the land. In so doing they proved that they were an element who sought the destruction of the Jewish State, a goal that they would be empowered to advance should Israel allow them to return. If allowed to return, the Palestinian refugees would, in the minds of most Zionists, destabilize and perhaps destroy the Jewish State from within.

This fear was not without foundation. The new Israeli state was surrounded by hostile Arab states. Even after the mass flight of Palestinians, there were at least 150,000 Palestinians who remained within Israel's total population of 850,000. To bring back the refugees could easily have caused turmoil and possible internal dissolution of the Jewish State. This is how even the most humanitarian Israelis explained to themselves a decision that would lead to Israeli instability for the next many decades.

Instead, Israel turned its attention to resettling Jews who

had been living in camps in Europe and elsewhere after the war and to opening its gates to the hundreds of thousands of Jews who had previously lived in the Muslim world; these Jews now sought refuge from the anti-Semitic backlash that the Zionist movement had produced in Islamic countries.

The Zionist movement argued that what had in effect happened was a population transfer similar to what had happened in India/Pakistan after India had achieved independence; millions of Muslims had fled to Pakistan while millions of Hindus had fled to India. Yes, a large number of Palestinians had lost their homes. But hadn't that happened to millions of people after World War II as well as during the breakup of the post–World War II colonial world? What was important to note, these voices said, was that other refugees had been resettled. From the standpoint of the world's refugee problem, Israel had been a net gain—resettling more refugees than it had dislodged. The reason the refugee problem continued to fester for the next many decades, Zionists argued, was that the Arab states refused to resettle the Palestinian refugees in decent conditions. Instead, they kept them in refugee camps in horrific conditions, using them as a political football to demonstrate why Israel had no right to exist as a country. Israelis refused to do the same with Jewish refugees from Arab states and made a good-faith effort to resettle them in the new Jewish state.

The Palestinian people, of course, did not see things quite that way. They were not looking at the situation from the standpoint of the world refugee problem, but from the standpoint of their own lives. In that context, what had happened was an outrageous wrong that Israel refused to acknowledge and refuses to acknowledge until this very day. Israel had resettled Jewish refugees in Arab homes and villages and had given some of the Arab agricultural land to kibbutzim and moshavim. More than 350 Palestinian villages had been destroyed. These actions would make the return of Palestinians to their homes virtually impossible.

It is hard to fully grasp the impact of the Palestinian Nakba. In an essay entitled "The Palestinians and 1948: The Underlying Causes of Failure" in *The War for Palestine,* historian Rashid Khalidi points out that, at the beginning of 1948, Arabs

> constituted over two thirds of the population of the country and were a majority in fifteen of the country's sixteen sub-districts. Beyond this, Arabs owned nearly 90 percent of Palestine's privately owned land. In a few months of heavy fighting in the early spring of 1948, the military forces of a well-organized Jewish population of just over 600,000 people routed those of an Arab majority more than twice its size.... More than half of the nearly 1.4 million Palestinian Arabs were driven from or fled their homes. Those Palestinians who did not flee the conquered areas were reduced to a small minority within the new State of Israel (which now controlled about 77 percent of Mandatory Palestine). At the end of the fighting Jordan took over the areas of Palestine controlled by its army west of the Jordan River, while the Egyptian army administered the strip it retained around Gaza, adjacent to its borders.... The Palestinians found themselves living under a variety of alien regimes, were dispossessed of the vast bulk of their property, and had lost control over most aspects of their lives.

I am telling this story in a way that attempts to show that this outcome was a product not of evil intentions, but of the way each side perceived and defined its reality and the way each side ignored the needs and legitimate concerns of the other.

There is no question that had the Palestinian people responded to Jewish refugees' need for a haven they would have been in a stronger position to have argued for one democratic country and against partition. And had they embraced partition and accepted the need for a Jewish state, they might have ended up with far more land and security than a war yielded for them.

Conversely, had the Zionists been able to understand Palestinians' legitimate concern about losing their right to national self-determination, and had they extended a hand of cooperation and friendship rather than perceiving the Palestinians as an extension of all the hurtful forces that had historically confronted the Jewish people, they might have been able to work out agreements and arrangements that could have prevented Israelis from continuing to fight the same battle for legitimacy for the next sixty-three years (and counting) of Israel's existence.

It makes little sense to demonize either side. Each was incapable of seeing the pain of the other. It certainly would have been better for the long-term well-being of the Jewish people if they could have found a way in the early years of 1948 to 1952 to start a process of bringing back Palestinian refugees. If, for example, they had allowed back 50,000 per year, with the clear understanding that the process of bringing them back would stop if violence from these returnees became a significant reality, that humane gesture could have influenced Palestinian consciousness. If, in addition, Israel had sought to reach out to the refugees in a spirit of reconciliation and recognized them as victims rather than as a monolithic group of enemies, a very different relationship might have been established.

But now imagine the Jewish people in 1948, three years after the Holocaust, just barely even beginning to acknowledge to itself the level of pain and trauma it had suffered, and then fighting for what it perceived to be its survival in Palestine. Imagine the experience as fear turned to jubilation: many Jews felt that a modern

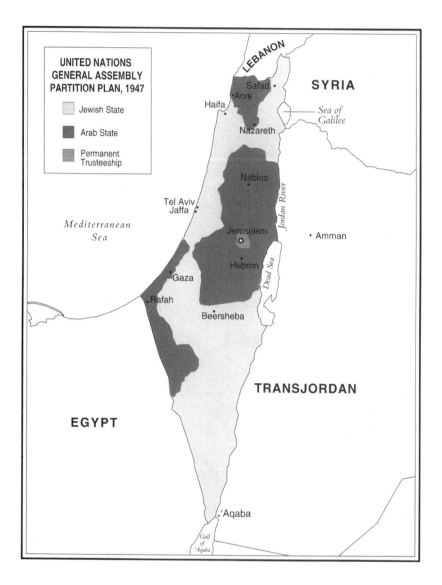

UNITED NATIONS
GENERAL ASSEMBLY
PARTITION PLAN, 1947

Jewish State

Arab State

Permanent
Trusteeship

miracle had taken place. The people who had been treated as vermin to be exterminated just a few years before had finally refused
to be pushed around any more. At such a moment, talk of compassion for a group that refused to allow Jewish refugees to escape the

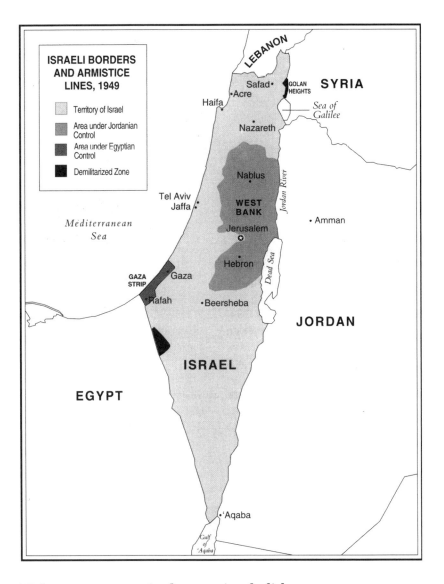

Holocaust was perceived as utopian foolishness.

Now think your way into the consciousness of the Palestinian people by the end of 1948. Imagine that only a few months have passed since you were thrown out of your home or since you fled for the complex reasons described above, expecting you would return as soon as the war was over. Imagine the rage you would feel at having your worst fantasies confirmed: that the Zionist enterprise was in fact causing you to lose your homeland. You would hardly believe your ears and eyes upon learning that the Zionists kept your house or apartment, forbad you to return to your village (if, indeed, it even existed anymore), and rejected a resolution calling for the return of refugees (Resolution 194) from the same United Nations whose vote had been used to legitimate the State of Israel in the first place. At such a moment, talk of acknowledging past errors, repudiating Palestinian leadership, or pleading for another chance with the State of Israel would also have been perceived as utopian foolishness or downright traitor talk.

And yet, it was precisely this kind of prophetic thinking that was necessary on both sides. Indeed, sometimes the only truly "realistic" position is precisely to be prophetic and utopian. But that kind of thinking was dismissed by the mainstream in both the Palestinian and Zionist communities. And so both cocreated the struggle that has plagued both sides for the past sixty-four years (and more by the time you read this).

So what did happen? In the early years of the State of Israel, some Palestinians sought to return to their land, sneaking over the borders, attempting to work their own farmland and occasionally grabbing back property that had been theirs. Eventually these incursions led some to steal food or property from the kibbutzim or others who occupied the land that had previously been theirs.

At first, they came to steal crops, to graze their flocks, to engage in smuggling, or to cross from Israel into the Jordanian-occupied West Bank. They were mostly unarmed, but the IDF began to use violent repression; it gave orders to shoot at any Arab "infiltrator," armed or unarmed, who attempted to cross the lines; several thousand Palestinians were killed in this way. More and more Palestinians began to carry arms, and some committed acts of revenge for what they had lost. They perceived Israel as an immoral robber that had stolen Palestinian lands, and they felt justified in striking back.

After 1954 they were joined by Egyptian *fedayeen* (self-sacri-ficers) who struck against Israelis. From 1948 to 1956, approxi-mately 200 Israeli civilians and scores of soldiers were killed by the combination of Palestinian infiltrators and fedayeen.

Some Israeli leaders understood the motivation of the Palestinians seeking to cross back into Israel. In *Righteous Victims*, Benny Morris cites the following quote from General Moshe Dayan, responding to criticism after a particularly hor-rendous anti-infiltration move by the army at the end of May 1950; a whole group of "suspected infiltrators" were pushed across the Jordanian frontier in the desert land of Arava, and thirty of them died of dehydration and exhaustion:

> Are [we justified] in opening fire on the Arabs
> who cross [the border] to reap the crops they
> planted in our territory; they, their women
> and their children? Will this stand up to moral
> scrutiny...? We shoot at those from among the
> 200,000 hungry Arabs who cross the line [to
> graze their flocks]—will this stand up to moral
> review? Arabs cross to collect the grain that they
> left in the abandoned villages and we set mines
> for them and they go back without an arm or a
> leg.... [It may be that this] cannot pass review,
> but I know no other method of guarding the
> borders. If the Arab shepherds and harvesters
> are allowed to cross the borders, then tomorrow
> the State of Israel will have no borders.

Had the Israelis exhibited this type of sensibility, they might have found a better way to deal with the infiltrators. But increasingly these infiltrators were defined not as hungry Arabs looking for some means of physical survival, but as terrorists seeking to destroy Israel. From 1951 to 1953, the IDF struck against villages on both sides of the border that were suspected of harboring these infiltrators/terrorists.

A special IDF commando group, Unit 101, was created in August of 1953 to execute these retaliatory actions. It was commanded by Ariel Sharon. In response to a grenade attack that killed an Israeli woman and two children in the settlement of Yehud, Unit 101 and a paratroop company struck at the Palestinian border village of Qibya, killing sixty inhabitants. In this case, the IDF acted according to orders from above, because it had been told to execute "destruction and maximum killing."

Chief among the hardliners was David Ben Gurion himself, who at the time publicly denied the IDF's involvement in the Qibya massacre. But privately he and others made clear to Foreign Minister Moshe Sharrett (the voice in the ruling party, Mapai, which was most critical of these policies) their belief that Arabs understood only the language of force. They believed that Israel would be destroyed unless Israel demonstrated a clear willingness to use force in a devastating and highly effective manner.

In construing their situation this way, the Israelis refused to take seriously the desperate plight of the Palestinian people. Instead, they focused only on the activities of the surrounding Arab regimes, believing that all reference to the Palestinian refugees was nothing more than ideological window dressing. After all, if the Arabs really cared about the Palestinians, Israelis reasoned, they would resettle them in decent economic conditions. Instead, these dictatorial governments used Palestinians as a political football for the sake of rallying the masses behind their anti-Israel policies.

The anger of the Palestinian people was thus dismissed by

Israelis as little more than a replay of the anti-Semitism that Israelis had experienced through the ages. Unable to recognize or acknowledge their own role in the creation of that anger, many Israelis brought to this most pressing problem the ghetto mentality—"everyone is against us and always will be"—that Zionism had originally thought to transcend.

Struggle with the Arab States, 1949–2011

Israelis' belief that the Arabs would understand nothing except force, their inability to imagine that any Arabs really cared about the Palestinian people, and their dismissal of the needs and demands of the Palestinian people having any real legitimacy set the basic frame for Israeli/Arab relations over the next sixty-plus years of Israel's existence.

What I've found is that the struggle between Israel and the Arab states, like every other part of the story, can be told persuasively from each side's perspective. I have listened to Arabs tell the story of growing anti-Semitism in Arab states as a logical outgrowth of the anger that people felt at the terrible treatment inflicted on their fellow Arabs by a group of people they perceived as Westerners. And, to the extent that they had historical memory, they saw these Westerners as part of yet another wave of Crusaders seeking to establish and maintain a Western presence in a Muslim society.

Though these sentiments were, to be sure, manipulated by the ruling elites of Arab countries in various destructive ways, the core of these sentiments was a genuine and legitimate outrage at what was happening to fellow human beings.

Some Arabs have used the analogy of American politics after September 11 to explain these dynamics. George W. Bush, Dick

Cheney, and other opportunistic politicians manipulated the legitimate outrage Americans felt at the attack on the World Trade Center and channeled it into militaristic justifications for imperial ambitions in Iraq that long predated that attack. Yet the core feeling of outrage and pain at the unjustifiable suffering of our fellow citizens was not a product of media manipulation alone. It was in part a genuine feeling of deep empathy and also a (somewhat exaggerated) feeling of vulnerability that the rest of us might soon be murdered. It is this same kind of dynamic, some Arabs have told me, that helps explain why Arab states could manipulate legitimate anger at Israel in ways that were fundamentally illegitimate and more intent on propping up support for Arab elites than on relieving the suffering of the Palestinian people.

Yet in my research I've come to believe that anti-Semitism also played a role. Arab countries allowed the widespread dissemination of classic anti-Semitic literature including *The Protocols of the Elders of Zion*. (As recently as 2002 Egyptian television state-owned channels cited this classic forgery to demean the Jewish people.) Arab governments integrated former Nazi scientists and operatives into their defense and intelligence systems. They refused to allow Jews from anywhere in the world to visit their countries, including American Jews who were in the diplomatic or military service. And they did little to distance themselves when Arab terrorists in countries around the world struck at Jewish targets that had nothing to do with the State of Israel (Jewish community centers, for example). It was not hard to make the case that a deeper dynamic than identification with the suffering of the Palestinians was being played out in these behaviors.

Indeed, after overthrowing the old feudal order, Arab nationalists who emerged in the 1950s used the struggle against Israel as a rallying point to divert attention from the fact that, for all their courageous anti-imperialist rhetoric, their nationalist regimes had little interest in seriously empowering ordinary people or re-distributing the wealth that could be amassed through Arab oil.

These regimes eventually yielded leaders like Gamal Abdel Nasser, Anwar Sadat, Hosni Mubarak, Hafiz Al-Assad, and Saddam Hussein. Each of these leaders presented themselves at first as progressive nationalists who sought to counter the old feudal regimes and to create a secular society free from the domination of Muslim fundamentalists. However, they each used the threat of Israeli expansionism as their explanation for why democratic processes could not be introduced, why a free press was impossible, and why more wealth could not be redistributed since it had to be spent on arms procurements (which in fact were used to strengthen the power of new capitalist elites that these dictators supported). It remains to be seen whether some variant of this manipulation of legitimate grievances into anti-Semitic sentiments will recur now that democratic revolutions in Egypt, Tunisia, and elsewhere in the Arab world have over-thrown the past set of demagogues.

The tensions between Jews and Arab nationalists spilled over into outrageous campaigns of anti-Semitism (and occasionally anti-Semitic violence) in some Arab countries in the 1940s. These campaigns were particularly pronounced in Iraq, but also took root in Egypt, Syria, Algeria, and Morocco.

By the time of the creation of the State of Israel, large sections of Jews in Arab countries felt imperiled, and many responded to vigorous recruiting by Zionist agents. These agents fanned the flames of fear and discontent and urged Jews to leave. What followed was a mass exodus of Jews from Arab countries. Many of them left what had been relatively secure lives to join a mass flight to the newly established State of Israel. The hundreds of thousands of Jews who left these Arab countries were not forced from their homes by threatening armies like those that forced many Arabs to leave their homes in Palestine. Historians today continue to debate how unsafe Jews really were in the 1940s and 1950s in Arab lands. Some have even argued that Jews would have been safer had they remained in Arab lands, that they were stampeded by Zionist propaganda and paranoia into a mass exodus. But very few of these refugees agree with that perspective.

Given the experience of having fled from Arab lands, it was not a difficult step for these new immigrants to focus their resentment of Arab societies in ways that proved their patriotism and allegiance to their new homeland. Faced with an Israeli culture dominated by European (Ashkenazi) Jews, the Jews from North Africa and Asia encountered severe discrimination and contempt in Israeli society in the first few decades after they arrived. Rather than engage in a struggle against the Israeli society to which they had fled, these new immigrants sought to demonstrate their solidarity with their new homeland by outdoing the *Sabras* (Israelis born there) in patriotic anti-Arab fervor. They did so by hating Arabs in general and Palestinians in particular. Yet it must also be noted that many of these Mizrachim retained fond memories of personal relationships that they had with individual Arabs and had a better understanding of Arab culture than did the dominant Ashkenazi population of Israel. Some have argued that these Mizrachim remain culturally more attuned to Arab consciousness and more likely to be able to shape an Israel that could become a Middle Eastern state living in peace with its neighbors than would a state run by the descendents of European immigrants.

All this contributed to the ease with which Israel came to portray itself as a lone island in a sea of hostility from surrounding Arab states. Israel developed a "Left" that was progressive on social and economic issues but highly hawkish on issues relating to Arabs in general and Palestinians in particular. It was this socialist Left, embedded in the Labor Party, that created an ethos of hostility to Arabs that persisted long after the creation of the State of Israel.

PALESTINIANS WHO REMAINED IN ISRAEL

Few Israelis today remember the fact that immediately after the 1948 War, the Palestinians who remained in their homes were put under martial law and thus imprisoned in their own country for the next eighteen years. Instead of seeing these Palestinians as people who had proved their loyalty by remaining in Israel, many Israelis saw them as a potential fifth column, just as, according to *Exodus*, the Pharaoh saw the Israelites who moved there some 3,600 years ago.

While David Ben Gurion and other Israeli leaders at the time flirted with the idea of expelling local Palestinians or convincing them to leave and join their refugee brothers and sisters, the more progressive Zionists prevailed and Palestinians in Israel were offered citizenship and the right to vote. This was a considerable achievement for a Jewish state filled with refugees from around the world. But even the Palestinians who had not left during the war were often expelled from their homes and barred from returning. Many found that the agents of the office of the "Custodian of Absentee Property" had expropriated their property, even though they insisted that they were not absent at all. Many Palestinians were forcibly evicted from their homes and resettled in the poorest parts of Haifa, Jaffa, Ramla, and Lydda.

Military rule included checkpoints at the entrances to villages and the kind of harassment that has become a fact of life for Palestinians in the West Bank. Israeli military personnel started controlling entrance to or egress from Palestinian villages, leaving residents subject to the whims of soldiers.

Living under martial law prevented many Palestinians from traveling beyond their village or region. It made travel to educational facilities precarious, blocked the development of small businesses and commerce, and prevented Palestinians from taking jobs in the Israeli economic infrastructure that was rapidly growing. This growth was thanks to aid from Western countries and contributions from Jews around the world.

To its credit, the *Histadrut* (Israel's largest labor union federation) did begin to accept Arabs as members in 1953. The major Labor Zionist party, Mapai, also sought to draw Palestinian votes, particularly after the mass immigration of Jews from Arab lands added to the electorate a significant number of Sephardim/Mizrachim attracted to Mapai's rival, Herut. This more virulently anti-Arab party was led by former terrorist leaders Menachem Begin and Yitzhak Shamir.

When the Arab Israelis were finally freed from military rule by Prime Minister Levi Eshkol in 1966, they found themselves still suspect and facing discrimination in housing and employment. Though Israel did not impose legal apartheid or segregation, and Israeli Palestinians were able to organize political parties that together regularly accounted for about 10 percent of the vote in national elections, there was another method of discrimination that persisted. Many employers and landlords only hired or sought tenants who had completed their service in the IDF, effectively excluding Arabs who did not serve in the army. This pattern of discrimination continues even at the time of this writing.

Moreover, in the budget allocations to support education and local government services, Arab cities and towns have consistently been given dramatically less financial support than their Jewish counterparts. As a result, it has been harder for Palestinian Israelis to get high-quality education in their villages and cities. Those who excel, however, are accepted into Israeli universities with little discrimination. (This is something that deserves more recognition than it normally gets from those who dismiss Israel as "an apartheid society.") After graduating from excellent undergraduate, graduate, or professional schools, Palestinian Israelis often have to accept jobs significantly below their level of education and training, if they can find employment at all in

Kareem Jubran, B'Tselem

The home of the Damiri family in Beit Hanina was destroyed on July 4, 2005, on the grounds that it was built without a permit.

the Jewish-dominated economy. What we have here, in effect, is not segregation or apartheid, but more akin to an acute and less hidden form of the racist discrimination against minorities that persists in the U.S. and in many Western European countries.

Yet it's also important to note that few Palestinians living in Israel today would wish to live in the surrounding Arab societies. While life in Israel involves daily discrimination and hardships, the material standard of living there is perceived by most Palestinian Israelis to be considerably higher than in neighboring states; many prefer the relative security, freedom of the press, and freedom of public assembly that are protected in Israel but have been dramatically absent in much of the Arab world for decades. The Arab uprisings of 2011 may eventually change that reality. However, for the past decades Palestinian Israelis have not yearned for the right to become citizens of other Arab states, but rather have sought equal social and economic rights with Jewish Israelis.

Many Palestinian Israelis wish to see Israel transformed into a secular state in which Judaism and Jews no longer receive special benefits for being part of a "Jewish state" whose national anthem (*HaTikvah*) and flag reflect the history of the Jews. If Israel were no longer a religious state, its national holidays would need to include Islamic and Christian holidays as well as Jewish holidays, it would need to stop discriminating against Palestinians in the leasing of land, and much more.

Significant discrimination continues to this moment. An editorial in Israel's prestigious newspaper *Ha'aretz* on April 14, 2011, attempted to remind Jewish Israelis that Palestinians Israelis (also referred to as "Arab Israelis" or the "Arab minority") should be seen as partners, not enemies, even though this is not the way they are viewed by the Israeli majority:

> Forty-five years after the military regime within the Green Line was revoked, public officials and state authorities continue to treat the Arab minority in Israel as a suspicious group of second-class citizens.... Apart from ongoing discrimination in resource allocation and access to senior public positions, the Arab minority's "daily life" consists of insensitivity to its identity problem in a state that defines itself as Jewish. Legislative initiatives that reek of racism are further excluding the country's non-Jewish minority groups and alienating them from their Israeli identity, and driving many young people to nationalist and religious extremism.

It is this situation—largely invisible to the majority of Jewish Israelis, who often have too little contact with Palestinian Israelis—that gives some credence to those who describe Israel as a racist society. When, for example, Israeli politicians talk about moving Palestinian Israelis into a Palestinian state—despite the fact that few Palestinians want that—or when they refuse to consider as "legitimate" a government that relies on Palestinian votes in Knesset or that would put Palestinian parties into a ruling coalition, the subtext of racism is there.

Some argue that Israel is not racist. Rather, they see it as "an affirmative action state" for a Jewish people battered by the violence and indifference of most of the world. In their view, the special treatment of Jews in such a state appears no different from, say, the privileging of Christians when choosing entrants to a Christian university or of blacks when choosing entrants to a historically black college or university. Yet human rights advocates point out one major significant difference: one can choose whether or not to go to such a university or join such an organization, but a government that rules over everyone in a given physical location is necessarily compelling people to be part of the state. As such, it has an obligation to treat all its citizens equally or at least not to discriminate on the basis of ethnic, national, or religious affiliations. However, when we consider most of the countries of the world, we are hard-pressed to find many who live by this high standard in their actual practice. True separation of religion and state remains a great but not yet fully realized democratic ideal. Just ask any Christian-majority country how quickly they are willing to give up the special status of Christmas in their country's calendar, and you'll quickly see what I mean.

ARAB STATES AND THE 1967 WAR

Many of the Arab elites saw Israel as the tool of Western expansionism—a perception based in part on the fact that the United States gave so much economic aid and political support to Israel. For most Israelis, the notion that the new Jewish State was an extension of Western colonialism seemed absurd. They perceived themselves as the victims of Western anti-Semitism, and they had made common cause with the British and the French in 1956 when Egypt tried to nationalize the Suez Canal. When the United States abandoned them by demanding withdrawal from Sinai in 1956, Israelis perceived themselves as isolated.

That isolation reached a peak in 1967 when Egyptian dictator Gamal Abdul Nasser generated a new crisis by calling for the UN force (set up to protect Israel and Egypt from each other) to withdraw from Sinai, by closing the straights of Tiran to Israeli shipping, and by inflaming dormant anti-Israel feelings in Egyptian and Syrian societies. Egyptian radio repeatedly broadcast messages talking about "pushing the Jews into the sea" and calling upon Arabs to join in this struggle. Recent diplomatic and military papers in the Israeli archives give some evidence that the top military leadership of Israeli society had reason to believe that Nasser had no serious intention of invading Israel; like the Arab states of 1948, he may have been merely posturing.

It's hard to know whether Israeli military leaders believed that evidence or whether their own perceptions of powerlessness led them to feel more endangered than their information would have warranted. But for the vast majority of Israelis, and for Jews around the world, the rhetoric of "pushing Jews into the sea" re-stimulated the anger and fears lingering from the Holocaust—feelings that had largely been suppressed during the intervening years when the Jewish State had to focus its attentions on survival and resettling immigrants. For many of us who lived through the spring of 1967, the possibility of the destruction of the State of Israel and a new Holocaust seemed very real. Once again, as had happened so many times before in Jewish history, the nations of the world sat silent as Jews faced the threat of destruction.

Today, many Israelis dismiss world opinion criticizing Israel's treatment of Palestinians as irrelevant and unimportant. These Israelis often hearken back to this experience in which UN forces positioned supposedly to protect Israel from Egypt and vice versa were removed on Egypt's request. The Israeli people (and Jews around the world) were then traumatized by explicit statements made by Egyptian leaders suggesting that they sought the elimination of Israel altogether in 1967. Yet this time, the Zionists proclaimed, unlike the passive Jews watching the rise of fascism in Europe, Jews would not respond to this potentially genocidal threat by averting their eyes and praying for the best possible outcome.

No wonder then that so many Jews around the world experienced almost religious ecstasy when Israel's leaders used this moment to launch a preemptive military strike against Egypt and Syria. The Six Day War was so short, many Arabs pointed out, because there was no serious plan on the part of Egypt and Syria to attack and hence no serious mobilization of those societies in preparation for war. Yet the perception of that threat by Israelis was caused by the demagoguery of Nasser's Egypt. The memory of that moment lives in the minds of many Israelis and diaspora Jews when they think about the current situation in the Middle East. They are often unable to fully grasp how militarily and economically powerful Israel has subsequently become.

In the days leading up to its sneak attack on Egypt and Syria, Israel made overtures to King Hussein of Jordan, seeking to keep him out of the war. Instead, he joined, and attacked Israel a few days after Israel's attack on Syria and Egypt. Israel's counterattack conquered the Arab sections of Jerusalem and from there proceeded to conquer the West Bank. There was little resistance to Israeli forces moving into the West Bank for two main reasons: First, the Palestinian people had been living under Jordanian rule since 1948 and did not feel particularly attached to that occupying power. Second, the Palestinian people had nothing to do with starting or engaging in the 1967 War. They would be amazed to later be told, "You lost the war in 1967, so now you have to bear the consequences." Most Palestinians had not been involved except as passive witnesses to a swift battle fought by foreign armies.

Israeli forces occupied the West Bank, and very soon thereafter many sane voices in Israel—including Moshe Dayan and David Ben Gurion, who had both quit the Labor Party they had previously led—called upon the Israeli government to withdraw and create an independent Palestinian state in this territory.

There was a debate from the outset between those who thought that strategic depth (adding miles between Israel and its neighboring states and their potential hostile assaults) most ensured Israel's security. Others, however, thought peace was the best guarantor and that the lands should be used as a bargaining chip in negotitations with Arab states that were still technically and politically at war with Israel. In September 1967, the Arab states issued in Khartoum what came to be known as The Three No's: no peace with Israel, no recognition of Israel, no negotiations with it. The three Khartoum "no's" did much to undermine those advocating for peace negotiations and confirmed widespread Israeli and Western perceptions that there were no Arab partners for peace. Blinded by their glorious military victory, those who were now leading Israel could see no point in making an accommodation with the Palestinian people. In fact, many of them denied there was such a thing as a Palestinian people. They insisted instead that there was only an Arab people and that the only problem regarding Palestinian refugees was that they were not being resettled in Arab lands.

Israeli political scientist Neve Gordon estimates that between 200,000 and 250,000 residents of the West Bank—more than 30 percent of the West Bank's inhabitants—fled to Jordan in the aftermath of the conquest of the West Bank. Only approximately 17,000 were eventually allowed to return to their homes. Israel faced an immediate problem: If these Palestinians were to be treated like the Palestinians who had remained in Israel after the 1948 War and given full citizenship rights, including voting, the Palestinians might outnumber Israelis in a few generations. They might then use their democratic rights to transform Israel into a secular democracy rather than a Jewish state. This concern seems racist to those outside the Jewish experience, but quite reasonable to those whose historical experience of living as a minority entailed oppression, rape, property theft, expulsion, and mass murder. Given their determination to live as a majority in their own land, even otherwise moderate or ethically sensitive Israelis thought that the goal of self-protection, as they understood it, would justify stealing other people's lands.

For most Israelis the desire to maintain the Jewish majority in Israel and keep Israel safe from potential enemies in Jordan, Iraq, Syria, Lebanon, and Egypt played an important role in the decision not to allow these new refugees to return. It also played an important role in the decision to deny citizenship rights to the one million Palestinians whom they now governed as a result of the 1967 War.

What proved decisive in keeping Israel on the path of expansion and retention of the West Bank was the emergence of religious Zionists (*Dati Leumi*). Inspired by their reading of the philosophy of the former Chief Rabbi of the Yishuv, Rav Kook, these religious Zionists believed that Zionism was not an accident or tragedy brought upon Jewry by a secular movement (as many of the ultra-orthodox Haredi believed), but the realization of God's will. So Kook's followers in 1967 and thereafter, led by his son Rabbi Tzvi Kook, preached that it was forbidden for Jews to return land to the Arabs. They believed that the land had been given to the Jewish people by God in Torah, and it was now being given back to us again by God's will.

These religious Zionists argued that the outcome of the wars by the Israeli army were actually a product of divine intervention, and that God's will had thereby been made known. So, while the Israeli government argued that it needed to hold on to the West Bank and Gaza for strategic and military reasons, a growing number of religious Zionists began to see a different reason: God's manifest destiny for the Jewish people. It was these religious Zionists who created settlements in the West Bank and have been at the center of pushing the agenda of Israeli expansionism. Over the course of the next forty-plus years, they encouraged some 300,000 Israelis to settle in the West Bank and Gaza. These settlers sometimes bought land but often occupied and expropriated land from Palestinian farmers and landholders, sometimes with overt or covert government and military support.

Emergence of Nationalist Fundamentalists in Israel After 1967

A common misunderstanding is to describe these Jews as "fundamentalists" and then fail to distinguish between them and the religious fundamentalism of the Haredi Jewish world, which includes many Hasidic sects as well as other ultra-Orthodox groups. In fact, many of the settlers are fundamentalist only in their nationalist/ Zionist reading of Jewish history—not in their dress, observance, or understanding of Jewish texts. Many of them have more in common with the "modern orthodoxy" that emerged in the United States. This notion is not surprising given the fact that a significant number of Orthodox Jews actually moved from the United States to the West Bank. They moved not to escape persecution but to escape the alienation and meaninglessness of life in the midst of competitive capitalism with its selfishness and materialism. The ultra-Orthodox, who dress in clothing styles from sixteenth-century Poland, are a different group; few of them are involved in the settlements of the West Bank.

Through much of the past decades ultra-Orthodox Haredi fundamentalists have been more interested in supporting their yeshivot (religious schools) and in shaping Israeli society than in holding on to the West Bank. They earn the enmity of the secular Israeli Jewish majority because they have been able to obtain from both left- and right-wing governments the right to shape issues of "personal status." This includes determining "who is a Jew" and establishing standards and requirements for conversion, marriage, divorce, and burials. Because the proportional representation system of Israeli elections allows the 10 to 20 percent of Israeli Orthodox Jews to play a central role in forming a governing coalition, given that no secular Israeli party has ever been able to win a majority of voters on its own, they are able to use their representation in the Knesset to become part of right-wing or left-wing government coalitions in exchange for obtaining money for their yeshivot and exemptions from serving in the IDF for their students.

Secular Israelis are hostile to ultra-Orthodox fundamentalists; they see them as narrowly self-interested and not willing to share the burden of "defense" of the Land of Israel. The secularists are particularly outraged when the ultra-Orthodox begin to take over neighborhoods in major Israeli cities and try to force secularists to not ride on the Sabbath. (Some ultra-Orthodox even throw rocks at cars driving through the religious neighborhoods.) The ultra-Orthodox also push secularists to close businesses on the Sabbath, including movies and night clubs, and make it difficult to obtain non-kosher food that some secularists want. And since the Orthodox establishment has banned secular marriage and divorce in Israel, many Israelis, rather than participate in a ceremony that has no meaning to them, fly to other countries in order to obtain secular marriages or divorces. (Quite shockingly, Jewish Israelis who wish to marry non-Jews are forced by Israeli law to marry abroad.) The level of contempt for "the religious" in Israel is so pervasive among secularists that they are likely to blame many of Israel's problems on this minority part of the population. So secular Israelis often mistakenly blame them for the Occupation itself, though that Occupation was originally a secular Labor Party project.

It is true though that in the past decades more of the ultra-Orthodox have come around to supporting the Occupation. Chabad (the Lubavitcher Hasidim who were followers of "the Rebbe" Schneerson) and others of these Haredi groups committed to *Ahavat Yisrael* (the Jewish obligation to love one's fellow Jews) and have invested time and resources in supporting the policies of the Israeli government. They have also opposed withdrawal from the West Bank, claiming that doing so would put Jews in danger. Some others in the Haredi world have joined peace-oriented governments that were willing to concede land for peace.

The Israeli government, instead of seeking a way to reconcile with the Palestinian people in the West Bank and Gaza, began a path of Occupation that would shape the destiny of Israel for many decades to come. The government of Israel began to call the West Bank "Judea and Samaria" in accord with the religious Zionist position that these lands were part of what God had given to the ancient Israelites. The Israeli government has changed its map labels and educational curricula to erase the "Green Line" (the border established after the 1949 armistice with surrounding Arab states), just as maps in many Arab countries have consistently depicted all of Mandatory Palestine as Palestine with no "Israel" in the picture.

The Israeli government offered low-cost, suburban-type housing in the settlements to Israeli families who could not afford comparable housing inside the Green Line. They also built roads to the settlements through the West Bank that made it convenient for Israelis who had no particular ideological commitment to "Eretz Yisrael HaShleymah" (the ancient full land of Israel) and who simply wanted easy access to their jobs in Tel Aviv or Jerusalem. This gave the Israeli Army the primary task of providing security for these settlers. It was a time bomb that has subsequently gone off many times and is likely to go off many more in the future.

THE 1973 WAR AND ITS AFTERMATH

The return engagement of the 1967 War occurred in 1973 when the Egyptians launched a retaliatory strike to win back what they had lost in 1967. They faced an Israel newly armed by the United States, which had become convinced that Israel could be a useful ally in the global struggle against communism.

The 1973 War produced a stalemate, and much suffering among Israelis, so it was with great joy that Israelis welcomed Egyptian president Anwar Sadat to Jerusalem in 1977 and then proceeded to sign an agreement with him. The agreement returned the Sinai desert to Egypt in return for a peace treaty that has kept the border mostly quiet and has allowed Israelis and Egyptians to visit each other's countries in recent decades.

Yet even after a peace treaty with Egypt and—after the Oslo Accords—an additional peace treaty with Jordan, the Arab states continued to exhibit deep hostility toward the State of Israel. In the 1970s they used their considerable power to get the United Nations Assembly to pass a resolution condemning Zionism as racism. Yet this move itself was a racist singling-out of the

Jewish people and its particular sins. It was as though somehow their transgressions were qualitatively worse than the oppression of Tibet by China, the suppression of millions of people in the then Soviet Union and Eastern European states occupied by the Soviet army, the pervasive denial of human rights in Arab countries, and the systematic denial of rights to minorities in many countries at the time. Yet other countries went along with this double standard, in part out of genuine and legitimate sympathy for the ongoing plight of the Palestinian people and in part to build good relations with the oil-producing Arab states.

In singling out Israel, a world that had previously abandoned the Jewish people during the Holocaust was once again showing a particular willingness to ignore the suffering of the Jews and focus only on our sins. This kind of behavior, in turn, strengthened the hands of Jews who would say: "The world is filled with so much anti-Semitism that there is no point in paying attention to what non-Jews think. Our only hope is to develop our military strength in Israel to protect ourselves against the inevitable resurgences of anti-Semitism, of which this UN resolution is an example."

Right-wing forces in American politics were similarly able to use this unfair resolution as an important weapon in their campaign to discredit the United Nations more generally. Thus, the distorted attack on the Jews, an attack motivated at least in part by genuine and legitimate outrage at the fate of the Palestinian people, took a form that was so unfair that it gave strength to the forces most willing to ignore the well-being of the Palestinian people. This is an important lesson: sometimes the tactics of support for a cause can do more to harm the cause than to aid it.

In the aftermath of the September 11 attacks on the World Trade Center and the subsequent U.S. decision to wage war in Afghanistan and Iraq, many Arab states, believing U.S. policy to be inordinately shaped by the Israel Lobby, sought to end the

Israeli-Palestinian struggle by offering Israelis what they had always claimed they wanted: a permanent peace agreement. Under the leadership of the king of Saudi Arabia, more than twenty Arab countries signed a manifesto offering peace and security to Israel in exchange for Israel's return to the pre-1967 borders and a just settlement of the needs of Palestinian refugees.

Unfortunately, Israel has not responded to that offer by the Arab states. To some Arab leaders it appeared as if their own turnaround, their willingness to accept and live in peace with Israel, was no longer consequential to the Israeli government or its people. Indeed, many in the Israeli peace movement have pointed out that the Arab states' offer in 2002 would have been welcomed as almost messianic if it had been offered in 1952, 1962, or even 1972. However, Israel has subsequently grown so attached to the Palestinian territories that this offer no longer seems important to the Israeli leadership in the early twenty-first century.

1977 and Beyond: The Triumph of the Israeli Right

Sephardi Jews' growing resentment of the Ashkenazi elite for the way they tended to demean Sephardim and to discriminate in the way the State's resources were allocated, combined with general disillusionment with the Labor government and its purported military smarts in the aftermath of the 1973 War, produced a radical change of government in 1977. The ultra-right Likud party came to power and former Jewish terrorists Menachem Begin and Yitzhak Shamir became the leaders of a new Israeli government. It was they who concluded peace with Egypt and they who, having pacified the Arab country with the largest population, sought to consolidate their power over the larger Land of Israel that had been acquired in the conquest of 1967.

The U.S. government never accepted the legitimacy of Israel's conquest of the West Bank. Neither did it accept Israel's conquest of the Golan Heights, which Israel won from Syria in the 1967 War, or Israel's incorporation of the Golan and Eastern Jerusalem, which were populated exclusively by Arabs in 1967. The U.S. State Department embraced the overwhelming consensus of the international community articulated through the United Nations: that in the aftermath of World War II it was no longer legal for countries to expand through conquest. Land occupied during a war must later be returned to its inhabitants rather than incorporated into the territory of the military conqueror.

This position has continued to be the official policy of the U.S. State Department. The U.S. Congress, however, plus a significant section of the military-industrial complex that shapes the policies of the United States, has done much to undermine this policy. They have given Israel a relatively free hand to do whatever it wishes to do in regard to the Palestinian territories and the Palestinian people.

Meanwhile, in the aftermath of the 1967 War, the Palestinian people—themselves largely apolitical and still traumatized into quiescence by the shock of Al-Nakba (the 1948 "disaster") and the daily problems of surviving in horrendous refugee camps with minimal rations from the United Nations—began to awaken to the challenge of the Occupation. Palestinian activists began to develop a national liberation struggle calling for the elimination of Israel and the return to a single democratic Arab-dominated state. They called on their neighbors to support the Palestinian Liberation Organization (PLO), which was led by Yassir Arafat and formed before the 1967 War.

The extremism of calling for the end to the State of Israel in the PLO charter was matched by extremism espoused by Israeli leaders like Israeli Prime Minister Golda Meir, who denied the very existence of a Palestinian people. It was also matched by right-wing Jews who to this day insist that the Palestinians have no national rights and should be transferred to Jordan to rejoin the Arab nations that surround Israel.

As Arafat became more successful in mobilizing and radicalizing exiled Palestinians, it became increasingly obvious to PLO activists that the first goal would have to be the replacement of repressive Arab regimes that had used the Palestinian cause for their own purposes but not provided serious support for a struggle against Israel. Needless to say, this kind of analysis was not welcomed by conservative Arab elites, so it was no surprise when the PLO and its supporters were physically driven out of Jordan by King Hussein's forces and later attacked by Syrian and Lebanese forces in Lebanon. But as the Lebanese were not able to fully defend themselves against an increasingly militant PLO, which had, by the late 1970s, moved its main presence to Lebanon, the PLO became a major factor in shaping the lives of people in southern Lebanon.

It was on the flimsiest of pretexts that former terrorist Menachem Begin, who became prime minister of Israel in 1977, sent the Israeli Army into Lebanon under General Ariel Sharon to wipe out the PLO in 1982, breaking a de facto truce that had been fully operative for the past year. The ensuing struggle left tens of thousands of Lebanese and hundreds of Israelis dead over the course of the next eighteen years. Israel's Christian Phalangist allies slaughtered men, women, and children in two Palestinian refugee camps called Sabra and Shatila, bringing the Lebanese war worldwide attention. The Sabra and Shatila massacre precipitated protest demonstrations by more than 300,000 Israelis coordinated by the newly formed Peace Now group; these activists were led by Israeli army members who felt distraught that Israel had lost its ethical way. The massacre led to considerable questioning of Israeli policies among American Jewish liberals and eventually led to a public commission of inquiry that forced

Paul Walsh

Egyptian President Anwar Sadat, U.S. President Jimmy Carter, and Israeli Prime Minister Menachem Begin clasp hands at the White House after signing the Egypt-Israel peace treaty in March of 1979.

Israeli Defense Minister Ariel Sharon to leave the government. The greatest destruction of life and property, however, resulted not from the massacre but from the shelling and bombing of Lebanese cities by the IDF.

Israel's behavior in Lebanon contributed to the continuing hostility of Arab states toward Israel. President Sadat of Egypt had made a peace visit to Israel in 1977, after having worked with President Jimmy Carter to reach a peace agreement with Israel involving the withdrawal of Israeli troops from the Sinai and the creation of nonpermeable borders with Egypt. Even after the 1977 peace treaty, however, Egypt felt the need to transform the peace it had contracted with Israel into a "cold peace"—one in which there was little real friendliness and only minimal cooperation.

Though Israel was anxious to develop deeper ties, it paid scant attention to Egyptian sensitivities about the role Israel was playing in the Occupation of the West Bank or in the invasion of Lebanon. In turn, the Egyptians, while scrupulously living up to the terms of their treaty, continued to teach hatred of Jews and hostility to Israel itself. And later, under the leadership of President Hosni Mubarak, who became Egypt's dictator after President Sadat was assassinated by Islamic extremists hoping to end the peace with Israel, Egypt participated in the anti-Israel rhetoric that pervaded the Arab world.

Though Israel did succeed in routing Arafat's forces in Lebanon (who withdrew to Tunisia), the war produced a peace movement in Israel, thereby breaking what had until the early 1980s been the virtual uniformity of Jewish Israeli support for aggressive action against Arabs.

The construction of West Bank settlements accelerated during the 1980s and 1990s. On one hand, the Israeli government was offering attractive housing at rates far below market prices within the Green Line. On the other hand, more and more religious Jews were supporting the enterprise and seeing it as a fulfillment of the Torah command to settle the Land of Israel (Eretz Yisrael).

In response to the continuing Occupation and the growth of settlements, Palestinians in the West Bank and Gaza began to demand self-determination, and many claimed that their real representative was the exiled PLO. When Israel ignored the repeated appeals for democratic self-determination, the Palestinian people began a spontaneous uprising in 1988 called the First Intifada—a war of stones against the bullets of the occupying armies and the Jewish settlers.

Stones can be scary. I remember in 1989 driving through an Arab section of Jerusalem between the Old City and the Hebrew University, when my front window panel was shattered by stones thrown at my car by a group of teenage boys. I barely managed to drive the car out of that section of Jerusalem, and I had grounds to fear for my safety. But of course I knew that bullets sometimes used against demonstrators by the IDF are not exactly benign either.

In response to the Intifada, IDF general and then Israeli defense chief Yitzhak Rabin ordered his forces to "break the bones" of the teenagers throwing rocks. We in the Israeli peace movement protested to no avail. Ariel Sharon used his new position as housing minister in the coalition government to provide massive assistance to Israelis who agreed to buy apartments in West Bank settlements. As a result, the settlements mushroomed in size and in suburban accoutrements.

But Israel was unable to end the Intifada, which sputtered out only after the United States convened a new set of peace negotiations in Madrid following George H.W. Bush's war against Iraq in 1991. The goal of the negotiations was to develop a comprehensive Middle East settlement.

To Israelis, the idea that the Arab states could demand a resolution to the conflict seemed ludicrous, both because the Arab states had been proven militarily ineffective and because the Arab states had shown so little concern about the fate of the Palestinian people.

It was not only Zionists who saw Arab states using the Palestinians as a political football. One of the Palestinians' most respected advocates, Columbia University Professor Edward Said, wrote in 2001 about the Arab countries' "scandalously poor treatment of the refugees themselves." He continued:

> It is still the case, for example, that the 40,000–
> 50,000 Palestinian refugees residing in Egypt
> must report to a local police station every month;
> vocational, educational, and social opportunities

for them are curtailed and the general sense
of not belonging adheres to them despite their
Arab nationality and language. In Lebanon
the situation is direr still. Almost 400,000
Palestinian refugees have had to endure not only
the massacres of Sabra, Shatila, Tell Al-Zaater,
Dbaye and elsewhere, but they have remained
confined in hideous quarantine for almost
two generations. They have no legal right to
work in at least sixty occupations, they are not
adequately covered by medical insurance, they
cannot travel and return, and they are objects of
suspicion and dislike.

It remains to be seen how the democratic revolutions and mass uprisings in the Arab world in 2011 may rectify some of these injustices.

In most Arab countries—with the important exception of Jordan—the fate of Palestinian refugees became a pretext for anti-Israel mobilization but not for actual concrete measures to protect and care for the refugees themselves. And it was this continuing cynicism of Arab states that gave credence to the supposition of some Israelis that they were surrounded by people who were implacably opposed to them and that the particulars of Arab grievances were only a cover for underlying irrational anger at the Jewish people.

From the standpoint of the Palestinian people, Arab states' attempts to keep the Palestinian refugee issue alive were a blessing in a world that would just as easily have forgotten their fate. No matter how cynical the intent of the interventions of the Arab states, their own perceived need to keep the refugee issue alive may have served the interests of the refugees. Or maybe not— maybe the refugees could have been resettled in Arab land and taken the same stance toward return to their homes that Jews took after the Roman defeat—they maintained the dream but built new lives for themselves in the lands of their diaspora.

The Palestinian refugees themselves had a very clear message: we want to return to our homes and villages. But unfortunately most of those homes and villages no longer existed, having long been replaced by Israeli villages, towns, and apartment complexes in which new generations of Israelis had been born. As one Israeli put it to me: "How do you think Americans would react if the urban poor, who had been forced to leave their homes in the wake of thirty years of "urban renewal," demanded the "right of return" to the places where new high-rise apartment buildings now stand? How much serious attention do you imagine Americans would give to such a demand, even if they agreed that the urban renewal programs had been racist and classist and had treated the poor in an unethical manner?" While the analogy is inexact, this unempathetic political analysis is reflected in the way that Americans have been largely indifferent to the fate of Native Americans or the urban poor.

Facing the growing upsurge of support for the PLO and its secular nationalist vision of Palestinian independence, Israel decided in the 1980s to support the newly emerging Islamic fundamentalist movement in Gaza called Hamas. While Hamas is best known in the West for its acts of horrific terror against Israeli civilians, its large base was built by providing the social services to the Palestinian population that international law requires of all occupying forces but that Israel was unwilling to provide (e.g., health care and education).

Imagining that Hamas would be a counterweight to the PLO, Israeli agents worked with and provided material support for the development of the Hamas infrastructure—even though Hamas was 100 percent clear in its total opposition to the existence of a Jewish state in any part of Palestine at any time. In supporting the development of Hamas, Israel followed a path that had also been followed by the United States when it funded Osama Bin Laden to organize Afghan "freedom fighters" in the struggle against the Soviet occupation of Afghanistan.

It was to please the Arab states, which had allowed George Bush, Sr. to station troops in Saudi Arabia to fight against Saddam Hussein during the Gulf War of 1991, that the United States pressured Israel to participate in the international negotiation in Madrid over a multilateral peace agreement. But while Israel agreed to participate, its Likud government felt no incentive to concede anything. Israel's then Prime Minister Yitzhak Shamir later revealed that his strategy was to sit in negotiations for the next ten years. He reasoned that as long as Israel continued to occupy the West Bank and to expand settlements, there was no problem in having representatives sit through a meaningless process preordained to produce nothing.

Bush, however, was determined to reward Arab states in some way for their support. So when Prime Minister Shamir requested that the United States back ten billion dollars in "loan guarantees" to provide housing and support for Russian immigrants suddenly able to move to Israel after the collapse of the communist regime, he threatened to refuse unless Israel agreed to a complete freeze on new settlements in the West Bank. Shamir refused, and Bush stuck to his guns.

Some Bush supporters later argued that this move cost him his reelection because it alienated American Jewish conservatives so much that they were unable to mobilize Republican votes in the 1992 election. The event was also seen by many as a central cause of Shamir's loss in the election of 1992 to Yitzhak Rabin of Labor. Many right-leaning Russian immigrants felt that Shamir had shown he could not deliver the material help that they imagined would be coming their way if the loan guarantees from the United States enabled new construction in Israel.

Although the public negotiations continued to go nowhere, a private channel was opened in which Yossi Beilin and others representing a new generation of Israeli leaders met with the new generation of Palestinian leaders. By the spring of 1993, they publicly announced a breakthrough that became known as the Oslo Accords. It was clear to both parties that for a moment the two sides had taken the time to get to know each other and each other's needs. It was in that context that they could recognize each other's humanity and begin to work out a plan not about one side winning but about both sides winning. This human connection allowed a thawing of previously militant commitments to a "power over the Other" view. Getting to "yes" from both sides was not a matter of having some clever new political idea—the actual terms of the Oslo Accords were made possible because first there was a development of trust and willingness to understand the experience of the Other. It was only when that had been established that both sides were able to think their way into political arrangements that would work for each other.

Unfortunately, this new attitude, the spirit of Oslo, did not survive the 1990s. Even the participants in the process of Oslo failed to fully understand the significance of creating on a mass scale the kind of trust-building that they themselves had engaged in as the prerequisite for their own breakthroughs into a new consciousness. So instead of providing leadership in how to engage in that process, they instead focused on the content of their ideas. They thought that they could win over their own populations just because their solutions were so transparently rational. And that did not happen.

Chapter Five

THE OSLO ACCORDS
AND BEYOND

THE SIGNING OF THE OSLO ACCORDS in September 1993 at the White House ushered in a new period of hopefulness. Finally, it appeared that an end to the conflict had been negotiated. The core of the agreement was mutual recognition between the Palestinian Liberation Organization (PLO) and the State of Israel.

The agreement itself was far less wonderful than the hoopla around it. The PLO would return to the occupied territories and set up a government that would then be the official partner with Israel in implementing a peace agreement. The Oslo Accords called for a three-stage negotiation: 1) a short negotiation period, followed by an interim period of self-government for the Palestinian people in the West Bank and Gaza that would last no more than five years, 2) three stages of Israeli disengagement from the occupied territories, and 3) the negotiation of a permanent solution during the five-year period.

The best part was the preamble, which states: "It is time to put an end to decades of confrontation and conflict, recognize mutual legitimate and political rights, and strive to live in peaceful coexistence and mutual dignity and security and achieve a just, lasting and comprehensive peace settlement and historic reconciliation."

Privately, Israeli officials involved in the negotiations told the Palestinians flat out that the interim "self-government authority" (SGA) was a fancy yet indirect way to say that the Palestinians would have a state of their own in five years and that Israel would be out of the territories. The first few years would involve gradual transfer of authority to the Palestinians. During this time the Palestinians would build a strong police force to guarantee public order and internal security, while Israel would have the right to defend the security of Israelis in the territories.

From the standpoint of Israeli negotiators, the gradual process of transfer of power would be critical, because it would allow for the building of confidence among Israelis who had, over the course of decades, developed deep anger and antipathy toward the Palestinian people. With little understanding of the oppression Palestinians were experiencing during the Occupation, and with righteous indignation at the acts of terror that the PLO had sponsored during the preceding two decades, Israelis felt they could not trust Palestinians to live up to agreements with a state they had sworn to destroy. If the Palestinians could demonstrate to Israelis during this period that they were using their new power in responsible ways, that would make it easier for the government to build the political support it would need to implement the final settlement.

For this same reason, the Israelis left many issues undefined. They hoped that as support built for the peace process in Israel they could make greater concessions in the future without endangering the political support that the Yitzhak Rabin government would need to survive inevitable criticism from the Zionist Right.

The great fear shaping the strategy of Israeli negotiators was that somehow they would provoke the Israeli Right into resistance, and that resistance could lead to civil war. The Rabin strategy was to gradually show the Right that there was nothing to fear from Palestinian control of the West Bank. (This was something that the military experts agreed upon and that had become obvious to a large section of the Israeli public during the Gulf War, when missiles from Iraq sailed over Jordan and the West Bank and hit targets in Tel Aviv. These attacks proved that holding these extra few miles of territory did not necessarily enhance Israeli security in an age of advanced weapons technology.) The Rabin government reasoned that if Israel could separate the "security hawks" (those who opposed peace arrangements with the Palestinians because they genuinely feared for Israel's safety) from the religious messianists who wanted to hold the territories at all costs, it would be far easier to win majority support for the peace process. From that standpoint, the step-by-step process seemed plausible to negotiators like Yossi Beilin.

Of course, Rabin would have to ease close to 120,000 Israelis out of the territories. (Some had moved there for ideological reasons, others because of cheap housing and convenient commuting to Jerusalem or Tel Aviv.) So Rabin and others imagined that this interim period would allow him some wiggle room to establish trust and to win a larger and more solid majority in the Knesset, which would allow him to negotiate a more generous final settlement agreement.

Many Palestinians, on the other hand, saw the agreement as a massive sellout of Palestinian interests. It did not call for the uprooting of the settlements, which were often built on land seized from Palestinians. Moreover, the IDF would continue to exercise control over most of the West Bank and Gaza, and Israel would still control the borders with Egypt and Jordan. The future stage of final settlement had not been defined, so the final borders of the two states and the issue of what would happen to the Palestinian refugees were unresolved. In addition to all this, Israel was continuing much of the Occupation while seeking the use of the PLO as an anti-terrorism police force.

Some Palestinians felt that the real winner at Oslo was not the Palestinian people but the PLO, which claimed to be their "sole legitimate representative." The PLO was granted the right to bring in large contingents of police (12,000 in the West Bank and 18,000 in Gaza), as well as machine guns, rifles, and light armored vehicles. Yet the Palestinians had not freely chosen the PLO for this role.

It was Israel that had chosen the PLO. There had been no democratic election. Israel's focus was on its own security, which it believed the PLO could enforce, rather than on creating a democratic process for the Palestinian people. It is thus ironic that Israel later denounced the lack of democracy in Palestinian-held areas, when in fact it was Israel that imposed the PLO before conducting Palestinian elections.

Though local representatives of the PLO such as Faisal Husseini rejected the notion of local elections and insisted that only the PLO could speak for the entire Palestinian people (including the majority who were in exile), there were other organizations in the Palestinian world that would have participated in these elections. A representative voice could have been established for the Palestinians living in the West Bank and Gaza.

Some of those aligned with the Israeli peace movement protested this element of Oslo as a serious mistake, but the joy of having any kind of agreement overwhelmed these criticisms.

Israeli fears of such elections were also understandable. In the absence of a peace-oriented PLO policing the West Bank and Gaza, the elections might have been unduly influenced by the power of intifada militants and Hamas, the Islamic fundamentalist group that Israel helped build in the 1980s when it seemed a plausible alternative to the militancy of the PLO, but that by the mid-1990s had begun to orchestrate terror attacks on Israel. Even if the Israeli army could have ensured quiet and orderly elections, Israeli leaders feared that these militants would win the election and thus determine the shape of Palestinian politics. While professing a commitment to democracy, Israel did not have a similar commitment to Palestinians' national self-determination.

Despite this lack of an explicit commitment in the text of the Oslo Accords to the creation of a viable, independent Palestinian state and despite the introduction of guns by the PLO to run the West Bank, most Palestinians welcomed the Oslo Accords as an important first step toward the ultimate goal of a Palestinian state living at peace with Israel. Many had insisted on the PLO as "the sole legitimate voice of the Palestinian people" because the PLO represented not only the people who would be in a position to vote inside Gaza and the West Bank, but also those Palestinians scattered around the world (many in refugee camps) who had no other way to express their views except through the PLO.

Yet the PLO and the Palestinian Authority they set up eventually came to be perceived by many disillusioned Palestinians as an organization riddled with opportunists more focused on self-enrichment and power-aggrandizement than on the best interests of their own people. The irresponsibility of these opportunists helped discredit the larger Palestinian Authority leadership in the eyes of many Palestinians and eventually enabled Hamas to win a majority in the 2006 elections for leadership of the Palestinian Authority.

There was originally widespread approval in Israel for the Oslo Accords; polls indicated about the same percentage of Israelis and Palestinians supported the agreements (roughly two-thirds of the population). In the few weeks following the signing, jubilation spread through much of the Israeli population. That jubilation was equally intense when, a year later, Prime Minister Rabin and Jordanian Premier Abdul Al-Salam Al-Majali signed a Treaty of Peace.

Israel's ultra-democratic proportional representation gives a great deal of power to minor parties, including the religious and

Sephardi parties, which held the balance of power in the Knesset. The religious parties did not share the popular enthusiasm for the Oslo Accords, nor did the right-wing secular party, Likud, nor did the more settler-oriented leaders of the Labor Party. (This included former IDF chief Ehud Barak, who was critical of the proposals when the Cabinet voted on them a few weeks before the signing in Washington.)

Because of this internal opposition, Yitzhak Rabin made a fatal choice in the aftermath of Oslo. He had the opportunity to challenge the anti-Palestinian discourse that had been taught in Israeli schools and that had dominated the media for decades. He had the opportunity to call for a move from enmity to friendship. Instead he played to Israelis' fears.

I was invited by Hillary Clinton to the signing of the Oslo Accords at the White House on September 13, 1993, and then to meet with Rabin at the Israeli embassy. (Mrs. Clinton had assured me in a previous meeting that she and her husband fully supported *Tikkun's* Middle East positions.) In a private conversation with Rabin that day in D.C., and in numerous conversations with his top advisers, I urged him to use that moment to define the highest patriotic duty of Israelis to be reconciliation with their former enemies. I asked him to tell Israelis it was their patriotic duty to make friends with at least one West Bank Palestinian family, to learn of their situation, and to find ways to help them as the process of ending the settlements proceeded. I asked him to urge Israelis to learn Arabic and to introduce an Arabic requirement for all students from kindergarten to twelfth grade and as an essential part of *bagrut* (the Israeli test for college entrance).

I talked with him about the importance of changing hearts, not just borders, and urged him to ask the Israeli people to open their hearts to the suffering of the Palestinian people.

I asked him to propose a massive fund to resettle West Bank and Gaza settlers inside the Green Line (the pre-1967 borders of

U.S. Government Press Office

U.S. President Bill Clinton applauds as Prime Minister Yitzhak Rabin and King Hussein shake hands at the Israel-Jordan peace treaty signing ceremony in October of 1994.

Israel). I asked him to start talking in explicit terms to the Israeli public about what the terms of a final settlement would be—to use this moment of enthusiasm to prepare people for the ending of the Occupation, the turning over of the settlements to the Palestinian people, and the sharing of Jerusalem as the joint capital of two states. The signing of the Oslo Accords was the moment to act decisively to change the dominant discourse in Israeli society, and Rabin had the opportunity to do so.

Rabin chose a very different path. Instead of building on the two-thirds of the population who supported him—something he could have done by dissolving the Knesset and calling for an election to give the Israeli people an opportunity to ratify Oslo— Rabin decided to play to the fears of people who did not support the agreement or who he felt might be influenced by right-wing criticisms. In many ways the Right and its ways of thinking were closer to Rabin's own personal militarist mentality than were talk of reconciliation and emotional bridge-building with Palestinians. So his focus went not to building the self-confidence of the peace forces and spreading a peace mentality, but rather to seeking approval from the Right. Here, as in the negotiations for Oslo, he acted foremost out of his fear of civil war. He placated the Right instead of mobilizing the political center.

So instead of trying to encourage a spirit of generosity, caring, and reconciliation, Rabin did the opposite when he returned to Israel. In a series of speeches to the Israeli public in 1993 and 1994, his main point was not how to build peace, but rather how little he had given away, how clever a negotiator he had been, how he still didn't really trust the Palestinians, how he would not move too quickly to implement various parts of the agreement, and how he and Israel would remain "tough."

In this way, Rabin reinforced narratives of distrust in Israeli public discourse at the very moment when Israel needed to build a climate of trust. And of course, the Palestinian leadership heard these speeches as indications that not much had changed in the consciousness of Israelis.

Many of his advisers, and even many of the leaders of the Israeli peace movement, opposed any attempt to push Rabin in a direction of explicitly embracing a message of peace and reconciliation, which would have led to an explicit confrontation with the Right.

In the next few years, I moved back and forth between my office in New York and the apartment I had rented in Jerusalem in order to help take care of my son on the weekends when he'd come home from his IDF service (the *Tzanchanim*—paratroopers). What I encountered from almost everyone in the pro-Rabin part of the Israeli electorate was the fear of civil war with the settlers. Faced with the choice of fighting settlers or remaining insensitive to the hope that Oslo had inspired in the Palestinian world, most chose the idea of Jewish unity as their number one priority.

Israeli peace movement leaders with whom I spoke in the next two years after Oslo, including Moshe Halbertal, Avishai Margalit, and Peace Now leader Janet Aviad, all were convinced that Rabin's path made sense and avoided the unpleasant possibility of civil war with the settlers. Their argument was this: by showing through confidence-building measures that land could safely be handed over to the Palestinians, Rabin would gain a larger vote of confidence in the next Knesset elections. Once reelected in 1996, Rabin could claim a mandate necessary to more forcefully and unequivocally bring peace. In the meantime, this logic went, Rabin had to show the Israeli "middle" that he was both tough and restrained, and that he would fight terror as though Israel still had the right to do whatever it wanted in the West Bank. I was assured that in order to get reelected in 1996, Rabin would have to appear unsympathetic to the Palestinian cause.

Even leaders of the peace movement agreed that reconciliation and openheartedness sounded too soft. They embraced the notion that one has to appear tough in order to win the confidence of the political middle or "the Israeli street." Yet by capitulating to that logic, they guaranteed that there would be no voice within Israeli public life challenging the mass psychology of suspicion and demeaning of the Other. This had been a major part of the Zionist ethos for decades and remained a stumbling block to any peace-oriented change of consciousness. Being perceived by their fellow Israelis as tough-minded seemed to most in the peace movement far more important than trying to convince Israelis to act in a generous way toward the Palestinians whose lands they occupied.

Rabin's confidence-building measures gave new credence to the right-wing critics of Oslo. The latent content of his message was this: We may have reached an agreement, but we still can't trust those Palestinians. We have to be careful that we don't give them too much.

And that's how Rabin acted.

When a series of terror attacks came, instead of responding narrowly to the specific terrorists who had attacked Israel, Rabin closed all borders with Palestine and imposed restrictions on access to the mosque on the Temple Mount. Checkpoints were established between various Palestinian towns, making transit more difficult for the Palestinian people. (This, as Israeli military authorities later conceded, did not even increase Israeli security—these towns were not on the borders with Israel, but inside the West Bank.) These checkpoints, which were later extended by Ariel Sharon's government, dramatically increased the daily suffering of Palestinians—yet they were instituted by Rabin as part of the "peace process" to reassure hard-line Israelis that he was not being too gentle with the Palestinians.

The underlying assumption was that Israel was still at war with the entire Palestinian people, who would be punished

Flickr/FREEPAL

Palestinian children often see tanks and army vehicles in their neighborhoods. This is their image of Israelis.

collectively for whatever action was taken by the minority who wished to thwart the will of the majority. Collective punishment of a civilian population had been banned by international law, yet that had little impact on Israeli military or civilian leaders.

Moreover, Rabin did little to confront the settlers with a new reality. On one hand, he talked in ways that settlers experienced as demeaning. On the other hand, he did not actually dismantle the settlements. As a result, settlers felt both under attack and free to mobilize counterattacks with impunity. Some acted on those feelings by taking aggressive actions against their Palestinian neighbors.

THE SETTLER RIGHT WINS THE HIDDEN CIVIL WAR IN ISRAEL

In the first phase of the implementation of Oslo, Israeli troops were withdrawn from major Palestinian cities. From Israel's standpoint, this, together with the creation of a Palestinian Authority democratically elected to run the new system, was a major benefit to the Palestinian people.

Palestinians, after all, could now run their own municipal services (education, taxation, municipal policing, garbage collection, etc.). Israeli police no longer shot Palestinian youth for waving a Palestinian flag, something that had happened frequently in previous years. Yet this was a long way from what Palestinians wanted: independence as a separate country with its own borders, its own representative in the United Nations, and its own ability to participate in international affairs. But quite apart from the dignity and self-respect that would come only with national independence, there was a much more concrete reality: daily life was becoming more, rather than less, oppressive.

Implementing Oslo involved the creation of different zones in the West Bank, and to go from one zone to another Palestinians found themselves standing in long lines, sometimes for hours, to get from one town to another. Try to imagine yourself in this situation every day.

The decision to respond to acts of terror by the then-still-marginal Hamas by punishing the entire Palestinian people proved to many Palestinians that they were still being treated as "the enemy," not as a friend who had just signed a peace treaty. The collective punishments involved closing the borders between Israel and Palestine. This effectively prevented many Palestinians from being able to work in Israel or to engage in trade with Israel. For much of the duration of the Occupation, Israel had prevented the Palestinians from developing their own economic infrastructure; this meant that hundreds of thousands of Palestinians were economically dependent on jobs based in Israel and on tourists who came through Israel to the West Bank and Gaza. When the Israeli government found that border closings were hurting the Israeli economy, they moved to a new tactic: bringing in foreign workers to take the jobs that Palestinians were no longer allowed to fill. In other words, massive unemployment and economic suffering became the hallmark of the peace treaty for many Palestinians.

With settlements expanding and new ones being created, roadblocks inflicting new levels of daily oppression, and economic dislocation worsening, it's no wonder that the Palestinian people became disillusioned with Oslo. Many Palestinians found it increasingly difficult to argue against the Hamas militants who were claiming that Arafat had sold out the entire Palestinian people. What the Israelis really want, Hamas contended, was for Arafat to be the jail keeper for the Palestinian people. He was enforcing the Occupation in exchange for pathetic gains of municipal self-governance.

Arafat could have countered Hamas by articulating a vision of national independence that would be achieved only if Palestinians chose nonviolent methods to continue their struggle. After elections were held and the PLO received a mandate, he could have used that moment to announce a relentless campaign against violence. Doing so would have played a major role in the confidence-building that was the primary requisite for the Oslo Accords to work. Arafat could have followed through by arresting, trying, and jailing Hamas leaders involved in organizing acts of violence. Moreover, he could have built a popular understanding of why it was important for Palestinians to engage in confidence-building measures to reassure Israelis that what they were "giving up" was not going to make them less secure, nor was it going to lay a foundation for future violent struggles against Israel.

Unfortunately, Arafat proved incapable of this, just as Rabin proved incapable of validating the aspirations of the Palestinian people to Israelis. He was a deeply flawed leader whose roots in terrorism and military struggle left him with neither the skill nor the imagination necessary to pursue a path of reconciliation. So instead of stopping terrorism in the period of 1994 to1996, Arafat mostly made empty pronouncements. Like Rabin, Arafat sought to placate the most extremist elements in his Fatah organization. Many of them had a hard time thinking of themselves as peacemakers rather than as militants engaged in armed struggle.

Without an end to terrorist attacks, the Israeli Right could easily argue that the Oslo Accords had not brought security but rather had ceded land to the Palestinians in exchange for zero peace.

Within this context of distrust, each side had a point. Even after Israel began to withdraw its troops from Gaza and small slivers of the West Bank, most Palestinians found their living conditions just as oppressive as ever. Israeli settlers continued to expand their settlements on Palestinian land and continued to

consume vastly disproportionate amounts of scarce water supplies. So when Israeli troops withdrew from inside some major
West Bank cities, relocating themselves on the periphery of those
cities, Palestinians experienced little improvement. The post-
Oslo prosperity Palestinians had expected never materialized.

Oslo's failure to improve Palestinians' lives was also connected
to the dominance that the Israelis had given the PLO. Many
Palestinians had come to believe that the PLO was rife with corruption. They suspected that buddies of Arafat and other top
leaders were embezzling funds meant for the Palestinian people
or directing those funds to projects useful to the PLO elite but
not to the masses of impoverished Palestinians. Without mechanisms of accountability, which Arafat refused to put in place, the
Palestinian Authority appeared to be an unreliable partner in al-
leviating the suffering of Palestinians. Under these conditions,
many Western governments that had previously promised aid
felt little inclination to sink monies into the PLO coffers.

While Israelis tended to see the emergence of the PLO in
Palestine as proof that Israel had been willing to give Palestinians
what they wanted, some Palestinians felt that the PLO was itself
part of the problem.

Had the Palestinian Authority been able to stop terrorist acts,
it would almost certainly have created the conditions under which
Rabin would have been able to start dismantling the settlements.
Though he still might have faced a civil war from armed settlers,
most Israelis in 1994 would have backed a dismantling of settlements had the settlers not been able to point to acts of Palestinian
violence as "proof" that it was not just they, but all Israelis, who
were in danger from the Palestinian people.

I can't make this observation without simultaneously acknowledging that the Palestinians faced many violent provocations
from the settlers in this period, including attacks on Palestinian
towns and the shooting of random Palestinian civilians by settlers

Sarah and Adam Cleaveland

Israeli soldiers stand guard near the Al-Ibrahimi Mosque in June 2005. A Jewish terrorist murdered twenty-nine Muslim worshippers at this mosque in 1994.

who were rarely restrained by the IDF. The best known was the slaying on February 25, 1994—five months after the signing of the Oslo Accords—of twenty-nine Muslim worshippers and the wounding of dozens more. This mass murder was committed inside the Tomb of the Patriarchs in Hebron by a Jewish settler doctor named Baruch Goldstein from the nearby settlement of Kiryat Arba.

In the riots that followed in Hebron, many more Palestinians were killed by the IDF, which was stationed there to protect the five hundred Jewish settlers who had provocatively set up a Jewish encampment in the heart of this Arab town. Goldstein became a hero for the Jewish Right, and to this day his grave is a pilgrimage destination for Jewish opponents of the peace process who travel there to honor his murderous deed. Just as those who seek to discredit any serious Palestinian intent toward peaceful coexistence point to the ways that suicide bombers from Palestine have been celebrated as martyrs, Palestinians point to the fact that the people of Kiryat Arba and many others treat Goldstein's grave as a holy place. Many wonder how Palestinians could be expected to build a nonviolent movement in this kind of a climate.

The attack on Palestinians at prayer in Hebron was only one of many moments when Israelis lost an opportunity to break the cycle of hatred. Rabin would have faced little serious opposition from the political mainstream had he used that moment to remove the settlers from Hebron and Kiryat Arba. This action would have demonstrated to the Palestinian people that they would no longer be at the mercy of violent settlers.

This is not to suggest that all or most settlers were or are filled with hatred or involved in random violence against Palestinians. Settler attacks on Palestinians were the actions of a fringe minority in Israel. When the Palestinians attribute these acts to "Israelis" as a whole, this is as misleading and racist as Israelis attributing Hamas or Islamic Jihad violence to "Palestinians." In fact, most settlers were not engaged in direct acts of physical violence against their Palestinian neighbors. It was the structural reality created by the institution of settlements itself that was oppressive even when individual settlers were gentle or sought ways to be sensitive to their Arab neighbors.

However, settlers were triggering the creation of new security checkpoints by building homes on hills around Palestinian towns and cities. Soon their settlements led to the construction of special settler-only roads that were prohibited to West Bank Palestinians. The settlements often appropriated water rights that had been previously available to those Palestinian towns and then recklessly squandered that water on fancy lawns and swimming pools. All this happened while the Palestinians below suffered with inadequate drinking water (and at some points in the hot summer absolutely no drinking water) and far less water for cleaning their bodies, clothes, and homes. Imagine how they felt trying to explain to their thirsty children why water had to be so carefully rationed when they could see the surrounding hills covered with swimming pools and well-watered lawns. Moreover, settlers often banded together and rarely reported acts of violence by fellow settlers against Palestinian civilians.

Sometimes partisans on each side of this struggle seek to show that a large percentage of people on "the other side" are covertly supporting the actions of the extremists. Very often the media contribute to this by putting before the viewing audience the most extreme (and therefore most visually interesting) scenes of support for some extremist act. "You see," say the partisans, "just look at those people—they prove that there is no real possibility of dealing with them."

This dynamic happened repeatedly on both sides. When missiles landed on Israel in 1991 during the Gulf War, a small number of Palestinians publicly celebrated. The world was made to believe that this was the universal response of the Palestinian people. And when two Israelis were brutally lynched in the fall of 2000, the footage of the crowd of Palestinian extremists celebrating and pulling their bodies through the streets was presented. Little public voice was given to the many Palestinians who were horrified by these acts.

Similarly, when Israel developed policies that caused widespread malnutrition among Palestinian children, such as the twenty-four-hour curfews that became a tactic of the IDF in 2002, the media gave little attention to the many Israelis who protested and attempted to deliver food to the besieged population.

Rabin eventually broke through this "blame the other side for everything wrong" dynamic. Two years after the Oslo Accords were signed, Rabin was deep into negotiations on the next step, called Oslo II, which was to involve the withdrawal of Israeli troops from the West Bank and Gaza. At this point, however, the Right began a political insurrection led in part by Benjamin Netanyahu, who said Rabin had "established the Palestinian terrorist state." The Right explicitly claimed that Rabin was turning over Israel to the terrorists and that his government was acting as the Nazis had acted to destroy the Jews. Right-wing forces sponsored daily acts of (sometimes violent) civil disobedience, blocking highway entrances to Jerusalem and attempting to wreak havoc in Israeli society.

Thus began the Israeli civil war that Rabin and others had feared so much.

It was under these circumstances that Rabin made a sharp turn in his public rhetoric in the last three months of his life. The path of compromise with the Right was not producing results, and Rabin was furious that his strategy to position himself as a center-right moderate was not succeeding. So Rabin unexpectedly adopted a more compassionate and accommodating attitude toward Arafat and the Palestinians. For the first time, he sounded as though he actually believed in peace.

The response of the Israeli Right was horrific: posters appeared throughout Israel talking about Rabin as an enemy of the Jewish State; some compared him to Hitler. In the religious world, a discourse of hate was aided by quotes from the Torah that authorize people to kill someone who is coming to kill them (a "chaser" or *rodeph*).

The argument that the entire Palestinian people were such chasers seeking the destruction of the Jewish people gave support to the notion, articulated in public discussions in some corners of the Orthodox world, that Rabin had either aided the rodephim or was himself a rodeph—and hence a legitimate target of murder. It was this kind of discourse that contributed to the climate in which a young Orthodox Jew named Yigal Amir, brought up in the Orthodox schools and yeshivas of Israel, assassinated Rabin at an Israeli peace rally on November 4, 1995.

The unthinkable had happened—a prime minister of Israel had been assassinated, and not by a Palestinian but by a fanatical, right-wing Jewish Israeli supporter of the settlers. The civil war had in fact already started and had claimed the democratically-elected leader of the Israeli people. The vast majority of Israelis were appalled and scared. They wondered where they had gone wrong as a society.

After Rabin

Shimon Peres, who succeeded Rabin as prime minister, was the wrong man for the moment. Peres had a career as an appeaser of the Right, and though he was known as a dove in comparison with the right-wing circles of the Labor party, he expressed contempt for Palestinians. Such contempt had been fostered among Israelis through decades of struggle, not only against the Palestinians but also against leftists in Peres's own party. So instead of defining the settlers and their ideology as the source of Israel's woes, Peres identified the possibility of civil war with the Israeli Right as the main enemy.

The Jewish world was told that the central post-assassination task for friends of Israel was to emphasize Jewish unity—including unity with the very forces that had created the circumstances of the assassination. Instead of confronting the settlers, Jews around the world were asked to embrace them, along with the messianic religious fanatics whose ideology had identified Rabin as an enemy of the Jewish people. Thus, the civil war that had manifested in this dramatic killing of a democratically-elected leader who was moving toward peace was hushed up. Denial became the order of the day.

This was a moment when it would have been possible to change the dynamics of Israeli society and accelerate the peace process. A decisive, peace-oriented leader could have called for an immediate referendum to authorize the government to evacuate the key settlements that had sponsored opposition to the peace process—Kiryat Arba, Ariel, Hebron, and dozens more—and to begin immediate resettlement of these ultranationalist zealots into the Negev, where new houses would be constructed for them. Simultaneously, such a leader could have immediately negotiated an end to the Occupation, which would involve Israel's return to its pre-1967 borders, with slight border adjustments to allow the continuation of Gush Etziyon and the sharing of Jerusalem. (Israel would retain the neighborhoods that in 1995 had a majority of Jewish inhabitants.)

An inspired leader could have won the support of the Israeli majority at this moment, when it was clear that the democratic process had been thwarted by violence from the Right. A forceful campaign to explain why the Occupation and settlements constituted a clear and present danger to the continuation of Israeli democracy could have produced democratic authorization for the IDF to move decisively.

And yes, this was also the moment of truth for the Israeli peace movement. Had its members rejected Peres's appeal and demanded serious moves to end the Occupation, they might have created a political crisis inside the Labor Party. Such a crisis, in turn, might have allowed for the ascendancy of dovish leaders such as Knesset members Yossi Beilin and Avrum Burg. But the Israeli peace movement had demobilized itself in the years since the Oslo Accords, accepting the strategy that everything would work out by allowing Yitzhak Rabin to be a moderate. Now suddenly faced with his assassination, the peace forces fell into line behind Shimon Peres, imagining that his accommodationist strategy, while unprincipled, would be smart politics and allow for Peres's reelection. After that, they told themselves, the Oslo process would continue.

So Rabin's assassination became a moment of quasi-religious introspection, calls for unity, the creation of a near-saintly status for Rabin (who was seen as the great symbol of peace rather than as a brand new recruit), and mourning rather than decisive action. The teaching that those who sought to work with the Palestinians and withdraw from the territories were rodephim whom it was appropriate to kill continued to be espoused in the settlements and in yeshivot throughout the State of Israel and in the United States as well.

Progress toward peace might still have gained ground had Peres made some genuine gestures in response to Palestinian needs. Instead, Peres used all the political credibility the assassination had given him to attempt to negotiate a deal with Syria. This deal failed because Peres was not prepared to return to the pre-1967 borders of Israel, as Rabin had indicated he was willing to do in secret messages sent to the Syrians through the United States.

Rather than make a new set of overtures to the Palestinians, Peres allowed the Israeli security apparatus to take vengeance on Palestinian terrorist leaders. Here was a way to show the Israeli public how tough he was. Rabin had approved the assassination of an Islamic Jihad leader in October, so in January Peres authorized Mossad operatives to kill Hamas member Yahya Ayash, known as "the engineer" for his bomb-making skills and allegedly responsible for major terrorist attacks inside Israel in 1994 and 1995. In short, Peres chose to use his window of opportunity to take vengeance on a suspected terrorist mastermind instead of closing down the most hate-filled settlements and preparing to have the rest of the settlers either move back to Israel within the following year or become citizens of a Palestinian state.

Peres's attempts to be perceived as strong after Rabin's death in some ways played into Hamas's hands. Hamas is an organization committed to the creation of an Islamic state in all of Palestine. Its strength has grown directly in proportion to the degree to which Palestinians have lost hope of establishing Palestinian rights through peaceful negotiation under the leadership of the secular Palestinian Authority. Hamas had no desire to see the peace process succeed, as this would have strengthened the Palestinian Authority.

Instead, the Islamic fundamentalist movement was committed to the full destruction of Israel and so had a stake in proving to the Palestinian people that every path to peace was a sham and a false start. For the same reason, Hamas has consistently sought to discredit the Palestinian Authority, seeing it as the enforcement arm of the Israeli Occupation.

By approving the murder of a Palestinian suspected but never charged with terror activity, Peres gave Hamas just the excuse it needed to break through the relative quiet that had followed in the months after the Rabin assassination. He also set a precedent that led to many more extrajudicial Israeli "targeted assassinations" of "suspected" Palestinian terrorists or, more broadly, "militants." As Palestinians absorbed the assassination of the one leader in Israel who had been willing to sign a peace treaty with them, and the willingness of Israelis to embrace rather than repudiate the settlers, the Hamas position seemed increasingly plausible to many.

In early February, Hamas began retaliating against the assassination of Yahya Ayash by killing Israeli civilians and soldiers. It's strange that Peres did not understand this as the predictable response from Hamas. He did not understand that by initiating a new round of violence and counter violence, he would be undermining his popularity in the forthcoming elections. Some people argued at the time that the murder of Ayash was an action taken by members of the Mossad who sought to undermine Peres; if that were true, however, Peres could have publicly disassociated himself and criticized the assassination, which he did not.

So Peres's strategy caused Israeli public discourse to once again focus on how to stop Palestinian terrorism (and which party could do so most effectively), rather than deal with terrorism from the Israeli Right.

At this moment, it would have made sense for Yasir Arafat to do what he could to combat Hamas and to prevent it from being able to take steps of violence against Israel. Yet Arafat did nothing to undermine Hamas's ability to deliver retaliatory blows against Israel.

Free to proceed without interference from Arafat, Hamas was given a powerful tactical advantage: a provocative attack on Israel followed by an Israeli retaliation against the entire Palestinian people weakened the credibility of the Fatah elements in the Palestinian Authority who had bet on the Oslo Accords. Hamas continued in March and April with more attacks, guaranteeing a right-wing shift in Israel that undermined the momentary swing toward the peace forces that occurred in the immediate aftermath of the Rabin assassination. Though Arafat finally seemed to understand the disaster that was happening and ultimately arrested Hamas leaders, the switch in Israeli sentiments from anger at the settlement mentality to fear of new violence from Palestinians was hard to overcome.

Even the convening of the Palestinian National Council in April of 1996 and its annulling of the clauses of the Palestinian Covenant that called for the destruction of Israel—a move that would have been seen as a significant step toward peace in a different environment—were not sufficient to alter the mood of despair that had been caused by the killing and wounding of large numbers of Israelis by what the media constantly described as "Palestinian terrorists" rather than "Hamas terrorists."

Israeli politics moved quickly from the hope of the Rabin years to a new despair about peace. This helped create a very narrow electoral margin for Likud, making Benjamin Netanyahu, an opponent of the Oslo Accords, the new prime minister in the election of June 1996. Again, Hamas had its strategy rewarded: they drove out the moderates and showed the world that "the true face" of Israel is that of reactionary chauvinism.

Benjamin Netanyahu was under strong pressure from the Clinton administration to show that the change in government in Israel would not destroy the peace process. However, apart from removing IDF troops (but not settlers) in 1997 from most of Hebron, Netanyahu refused to break with the pro-settler policies that allowed more and more of them to move to the West Bank and Gaza.

When he made some concessions to allow the Oslo Accords to be implemented when he met with President Clinton at Wye River, his political base was outraged. Consequently, Netanyahu never actually carried out the three redeployments of IDF troops called for in the Oslo Accords. Netanyahu was abandoned by his right-wing base, and Labor candidate Ehud Barak, whose military credentials helped undermine fears of "selling out" the interests of Israeli security, was elected prime minister in May of 1999. Barak received 56 percent of the vote, compared to Netanyahu's 44 percent.

In the election, Barak raised many hopes for a return to Yitzhak Rabin's legacy of peace. Yet Barak had never been part of the peace wing of the Labor party and had opposed the Oslo Accords in the weeks before it was signed. He was an authoritarian leader; it is a testimony to the desperation of the Israeli Left that they invested so many hopes in him rather than seeking to create a genuine peace party with a genuinely committed peace leadership. But the leftists inside Labor argued against that—it would be, they thought, "more realistic" to get a right-wing Labor general elected than to insist on a principled peace candidate who might lose.

Their calculations proved to be a tragic historical error.

Barak's electoral majority was achieved only through over-whelming support from Israeli citizens of Palestinian ethnicity. The political Right cited Barak's Palestinian Israeli constituency to challenge the legitimacy of Barak's election. Deeply committed to the view that Israel must be a Jewish state, the Right and even nationalists and racists in the Labor Party argued that a prime minister could not claim legitimacy as the leader of the Jewish State if he did not receive the vote of a Jewish majority.

Barak's decision to make his government dependent on religious and right-wing forces with whom he disagreed politically, rather than to ally himself with the Palestinian Israeli parties, was a further extension of the position that it is more important to have peace with the Israeli Right than peace with the Palestinians. The Israeli Right had, in effect, won even when it lost. It had intimidated the so-called Left into making peace with the Right its most important priority.

Given these internal Israeli political dynamics, Barak, who was supposedly the peace prime minister, failed to implement even the terms of the Wye River agreement that Benjamin Netanyahu had negotiated. Understandably, Arafat felt even further betrayed by Israel. The assassination of Yitzhak Rabin, the bus bombings by Hamas, and the subsequent election of Benjamin Netanyahu had all made it understandable why Israel was dragging its feet in implementing the Oslo Accords. But now with a prime minister explicitly committed to fulfilling the terms of Oslo, it was difficult to understand why no progress had been made.

In mid-2000, few Israelis believed their prime minister stood for anything but his own political survival. And that was in danger of immediate collapse. The minority parties on which Barak had allowed his government to depend (in order to not include the Palestinian Israeli parties in the government) had made it clear that they would soon abandon Barak's government and that new elections would be needed. It was at this moment that Barak, desperately needing to pull off something dramatic to win reelection, decided to use the peace issue.

Chapter Six

CAMP DAVID, THE SECOND INTIFADA, HAMAS, AND THE PALESTINIAN AUTHORITY

THE ILLUSION OF BARAK'S "GENEROUS OFFER"

AFTER HAVING IGNORED THE AGREEMENT to implement Oslo through the steps decided upon at Wye River, Israeli Prime Minister Ehud Barak turned to President Bill Clinton and asked him to convene a meeting at Camp David, where a permanent solution to the struggle with Palestinians would be negotiated.

In the summer of 2000, Clinton had his own political problems. His presidency was severely tainted by his affair with Monica Lewinsky. One of the most hopeful moments in his presidency had involved the Oslo Accords. Now, with Oslo faltering, he likely hoped that a last-minute success in securing Middle East peace might obscure his other presidential failures and strengthen the electoral prospects of his chosen successor, Al Gore.

Clinton accepted Barak's plan to convene a summit at Camp David, but Arafat was uninterested at first. The Palestinian Authority argued that before a summit could be useful, there needed to be more agreement on critical points. At the very least, something would have to change on the ground (for example, a downsizing of the Israeli Occupation and the removal of checkpoints) so that the Palestinians could trust that they were not being pushed into a meaningless agreement like Wye.

Clinton and Barak, however, faced immediate domestic political challenges that made them anxious to have a victory in the Middle East, and managed to pressure Arafat into coming. Once there, Arafat was confronted with an offer he was told he could not refuse. There is no agreement about what that offer was because it was never put into writing.

In fact, there were two offers being made at the same time.

First, there was an offer put on the table by President Clinton. That offer included a promise to Palestinians of 95 percent of the land of the West Bank and a fund of $30 billion to finance a Palestinian state. Had this been the sole offer discussed, things would have been much clearer. But Ehud Barak, while accepting the Clinton offer as "the basis" of the Israeli position, had many reservations and differences in direction. So one of the things that Arafat was trying to do at Camp David was to clear up what part of Clinton's offer was really being accepted by Barak. When the Palestinians tried to piece together a coherent picture of what they were being offered, here is what they came up with:

Offered	What Palestinians Needed
1. A state.	1. A state.
2. Somewhere between 85–92 percent of the 22 percent of pre-1948 Palestine that constituted the West Bank and Gaza.	2. 100 percent of the West Bank and Gaza, constituting 22 percent of pre-1948 Palestine.

OFFERED	WHAT PALESTINIANS NEEDED
3. Israeli control over Palestinian borders.	3. Palestinian control over Palestinian borders.
4. Capital in Jerusalem.	4. Capital in Jerusalem.
5. Incorporation of some sections of Arab Jerusalem into a Palestinian state.	5. All sections of Jerusalem with majority Arab population into a Palestinian state.
6. Free access to holy sites supervised by Israel army as long as there are no security problems.	6. Free access to holy sites without Israeli army given power to determine access on security grounds.
7. Israel retains sovereignty over Temple Mount.	7. Palestinians have sovereignty over Temple Mount.
8. Israel retains military presence in Palestine including checkpoints as it determines them to be necessary.	8. No Israeli military presence and no checkpoints.
9. Palestinians say that this agreement ends all claims on Israel.	9. Since the 3 million refugees remain in refugee camps, there is no way to abrogate future claims on Israel.

When Arafat refused this supposedly wonderful deal, both Clinton and Barak portrayed Arafat's refusal as the ultimate betrayal of the peace process and a sure sign that Arafat had no interest in building peace. This was, both claimed, the best offer that the Palestinians would ever get, and yet they turned it down. What better proof to the world that Clinton and Barak had gone as far as they could on behalf of peace and had suddenly found, as Barak publicly proclaimed, that "there is no real partner for peace." Barak's proclamation became the mantra of the Israeli and American Jewish Right throughout the next twelve years.

From the perspective of Barak and Clinton, Israel had offered a great deal by ceding most of the West Bank to the Palestinians. From the Palestinian perspective, however, the central deal of Oslo in 1993 was that the Palestinians would agree to live in peace with Israel and to accept that 78 percent of pre-1948 Palestine would become part of Israel. In return, the Palestinians could have a state on the remaining 22 percent (the West Bank and Gaza).

That those were in fact the terms promised to the Palestinians was confirmed publicly by Yossi Beilin, one of Israel's chief negotiators at Oslo, who was the justice minister in the Ehud Barak cabinet. Given that promise, the point of future negotiations was solely about the timetable for implementing the withdrawal of Israel from the occupied territories and from the settlements in them. Yet Barak was instead planning to retain between 8 percent and 10 percent of the land that had been promised to the Palestinians just a few years before. That small percentage of land held the vast majority of settlers and Jewish settlements in the West Bank. Nor was the land Barak wished to keep contiguous—instead, it was scattered throughout what would have become the Palestinian state, creating pockets of Israeli control in the middle of Palestinian lands. Israel would continue to rule access to the Temple Mount, potentially continuing the pattern of the past decade in which Israel periodically prevented many West Bank Palestinians from reaching the Al-Aqsa Mosque for prayer, on the grounds that there were potential security risks.

Israel never put a written offer on the table—which is one reason many people coming out of Camp David had different versions of what was actually offered versus what was floated for discussion. But what is not disputed is that Israel planned to retain military roads that crisscrossed the new Palestinian state and checkpoints that would have made passage from one part of the Palestinian state to another very difficult. Imagine this from the standpoint of Palestinians. It was like someone who occupies your home offering to return 90 percent of it but insisting on retaining control of the hallways; you'd need permission whenever you wanted to go from one part of your house to another. It's understandable why the offer was perceived by Palestinians as less than generous.

Yet the absolute deal-breaker of this last set of Camp David talks was the fate of the Palestinian refugees—the nub of the problem for much of the past sixty-plus years. Barak's offer gave them nothing. Though Arafat could have signed an agreement in 1993 leaving the fate of the refugees for later negotiations, no Palestinian leader could have signed what Barak demanded at Camp David: that the refugee issue be ignored and that Palestinians give up all claims against the State of Israel. To thereby abandon the refugees to perpetual refugee status would have been perceived as an unforgivable betrayal by the three million Palestinian refugees, many of whom were living in abysmal conditions.

From the Israeli perspective, the Palestinian people had once again shown their tendency to "never miss an opportunity to miss an opportunity" as Abba Eban, former foreign minister of the State of Israel, put it. In retrospect, many Palestinians share this criticism of Arafat's circle of leadership. But at the time, Arafat was also aware that he was sitting on a powder keg ready to explode. According to Oslo, which was a signed agreement, an interim Palestinian government was supposed to have been established two years earlier. Promises of a return of the land to the Palestinian people had been made and remade and still remained unfulfilled.

The facts on the ground were irrefutable: the peace process created by the Oslo Accords was supposed to end the settlements and return the West Bank and Gaza to the Palestinian people. In 1993 there were 120,000 settlers; in 2000, when Barak met with Arafat, that number had increased to 200,000 settlers.

Barak and Clinton were now faced with a public relations disaster. They had gambled on pressuring a powerless people into accepting a deal at Camp David that they felt they could easily sell to their own electorates as a triumph. Instead, they had come home with nothing. Having created expectations of a miracle, they were shown to be failed magicians. Both were furious. They lashed out at Arafat, blaming him for the failure of the negotiations rather than reflecting on what might have been a more palatable deal for the Palestinian people. Barak proclaimed that "there is no one to talk to" in Palestine who is genuinely interested in peace, thereby giving to the Israeli Right a line to repeat throughout the next decade. In return, Arafat positioned himself as a person who would not trade away any more Palestinian claims to the Palestinian homeland.

People around Arafat made it clear that the Palestinian Authority would continue its role as surrogate policemen for a Jewish state only if Israel produced some dramatic changes on the ground. Palestinian leaders knew that their own people were likely to explode with rage. Indeed, there is evidence that some Palestinian leaders had developed plans to fan such an explosion even before it happened.

Ariel Sharon at the Temple Mount

It was in this atmosphere in 2000 that Ariel Sharon, the right-wing militarist who had assumed leadership of the Likud Party after Netanyahu's electoral defeat, decided to make a symbolic visit to the Temple Mount. This was a way of demonstrating that Israel had no intention of giving up power over it.

The Temple Mount has symbolic importance for both Jews and Muslims. Muslims have taken a provocative stand in relationship to the Jewish historical claim to the Mount, both by excavating and removing historical relics that may have religious significance for the Jews, and by denying that Jews ever had a legitimate claim to the Mount. On the other hand, a Zionist yeshiva in the Old City, supported directly by Ariel Sharon, had been making preparations to tear down the mosque and restore Temple worship. This assumed that Jews would soon reoccupy and rebuild their ancient Temple.

Most religious Jews do not follow that path, and in fact many will not go to the Temple Mount because it once contained the Holy of Holies; this is the sacred place inside the Temple where entrance was forbidden to Jews except for the High Priest once a year on Yom Kippur, the Day of Atonement. For religious Jews, it would be a desecration to walk on that holy ground; since we do not know exactly where that ground was on the Temple Mount, some believe it's best to stay off it entirely. Many religious Jews will go to the Temple Mount only once the Temple is rebuilt, and for most religious Jews, the Temple can be rebuilt only when the Messiah comes. Until that day, Jews pray at the Western Wall located below the Mount. For this reason, Israel's continuing insistence on sovereignty over the Temple Mount has no practical correlate for most religious Jews. The function of the demand to sovereignty is instead to deny Muslims the power to control access to their own holy site and to symbolically show who has most power (a point also made by some Israelis who argue that the decision to build a mosque on the Jewish Temple site was a way for Muslims to make that same point to Jews in the past).

Some of us in the religious peace camp have suggested that Israel offer to lease the Temple Mount for the next two thousand years or until the lion lies down with the lamb and the messiah arrives—whichever should come first. In exchange, Muslims would offer protection and unimpeded rights to those Jews who do wish to visit and pray on the Temple Mount or at the Western Wall. So it was a provocative and arrogant act for Ariel Sharon, accompanied by hundreds of policemen, to go to the Temple Mount and proclaim that it would always remain in Israel.

Some people have asked why Palestinians should riot when a Jew comes to visit his ancient temple. However, Sharon was not acting as an individual Jew interested in connecting to Jewish history. He was the new leader of a political party that never accepted the legitimacy of the Oslo Accords and that supported expansion of West Bank settlements. Sharon's visit was an ultra-reactionary action that sought to dramatize Palestinian powerlessness.

Predictably, the visit set off Palestinian rioting and stone-throwing. Then Israel met the stone throwers with guns and killed rioters. Thus began the Second Intifada. The riots spread throughout the West Bank and Gaza as young men picked up rocks and were met with bullets. And this pattern continued for several months. Many Palestinian teenagers were killed, as were far fewer Israelis.

There were two important incidents that further froze both sides into anger and despair. In the early weeks of October 2000, some Palestinian Israelis protested the shootings of Palestinians in Palestine, and some young Palestinian Israelis set up blockades and threw rocks at passing cars suspected of carrying Jewish Israelis. These were citizens of Israel, and their behavior was not significantly more threatening than the behavior of, say, American college students during militant anti-war demonstrations in the 1960s, or of Israeli rightists in the months before Rabin was assassinated. But these Palestinian Israelis were met with overwhelming force from the Israeli police. Thirteen Palestinian Israelis were killed, and many more were wounded. But more deeply wounded was the sense of unity that

Palestinian Israelis and many Jewish-Arab dialogue groups had sought to create for many years. The growing frustrations among Palestinian Israelis and Palestinians in the West Bank and Gaza, fueled by the broken promises of the Oslo Accords, finally could no longer be contained.

It was in the aftermath of what was perceived by many Arabs as bigotry-motivated assaults—Palestinian Israelis were citizens of the State of Israel, so under any non-racist logic they should have been protected rather than treated as enemy targets—that another ugly incident occurred. Two Israeli soldiers wandered into a West Bank town in early October. They were grabbed by an angry mob and lynched, and their bodies were mutilated and dragged through the streets to the cheers of angry Palestinians.

The bloodthirsty cheers of a civilian Palestinian town restimulated Israelis' fears of their continuing vulnerability to seemingly unrestrained Palestinian hatred. There was little Israeli media attention given to the idea that the assault on Palestinians in northern Israel might have given Palestinians a similar feeling of vulnerability. And Palestinians who were disgusted and horrified by what happened to the murdered Israeli soldiers likewise found their voices largely ignored in the Israeli media.

This lynching struck a deep chord of fear in the Israeli population, who felt that the sheer brutality and dishonoring of the dead shown by this Palestinian mob revealed "the true desires" of the Palestinian people. It supposedly showed that Barak's interpretation of the failure of Camp David was correct: that there was no one to talk to because the Palestinian people didn't really want a solution. They only wanted the destruction and murder of the Israeli people. So the mainstream Israeli media taught.

Like Bill Clinton throughout most of his presidency, and then Barack Obama throughout much of his presidency, Ehud Barak did not understand that liberals' attempts to appropriate the discourse of the Right might provide short-term benefits but would ultimately strengthen the Right. So Barak was surprised when Arab voters refused to vote; peace-oriented voters felt little enthusiasm for a faux-peace candidate. Instead, Ariel Sharon was swept to victory in February 2001.

THE RISE OF THE MILITARIST RIGHT: ARIEL SHARON AND "BIBI" NETANYAHU

The election of Ariel Sharon dramatically accelerated Palestinian despair about the possibility of peace and reconciliation. Sharon had been removed from his cabinet position as defense minister after an independent inquiry concluded that he bore indirect but significant responsibility for the Christian Phalangist massacre of more than 300 Palestinian civilians in the Sabra and Shatila refugee camps of Lebanon. Those with a longer memory knew that Sharon was a major figure in the slaughter of Palestinian civilians in the early years of the State of Israel. Some Jewish peace forces had called for Sharon to be tried as a war criminal and human rights abuser. Now he was Israel's leader.

Sharon proved to be every bit as hard-nosed as had been anticipated. He escalated the military struggle against the Palestinian people, and they in turn responded by using the weapons that they had been allowed to import under the Oslo Accords. Of course, there was no equivalence in military might—the Israeli army was the most powerful military force in the region, and the Palestinians had only small police units with light arms. But the Second Intifada scared many Israelis and led to a consolidation of right-wing support in Israel.

In the first years of Sharon's tenure as prime minister, the Palestinians retained control over their cities while Israel imposed blockades and began sieges that cut off food and water for various periods in response to terrorist attacks against Israeli targets. In addition, Sharon relied upon targeted assassinations of Palestinian leaders who were accused of being militants or terrorists.

Since then, a pattern developed in which Hamas or Islamic Jihad, another anti-Palestinian Authority group, made an attack against an Israeli target and then, "in retaliation against terror," the Israeli army struck Palestinian Authority targets. The Palestinian Authority had not been involved in the attack and usually condemned it, although there are some reasons to believe that privately Yasir Arafat may have given signals that seemed to encourage it. From the standpoint of some observers, it appeared as if Ariel Sharon and Hamas were involved in a de facto alliance against the Palestinian Authority. Both wished to see it overthrown.

The escalating violence brought huge amounts of suffering on both sides. Morally outrageous acts of violence by Islamic Jihad and Hamas were met not with attacks on Hamas and Islamic Jihad but rather with attacks on the entire Palestinian people. IDF troops rolled into West Bank cities, imposing twenty-four-hour curfews that lasted for days (or in some cases, weeks), bulldozing buildings, destroying the electricity and water systems for urban populations, and engaging in acts of vandalism and terror that provoked an international cry for impartial observers to investigate (a process thwarted by Israel). In addition, the IDF arrested thousands of people; they typically rounded up all boys and men from ages fifteen to forty-five in a given area. Israel released some prisoners after brutal treatment and kept others without charges and without the normal human rights promised to prisoners of war.

The treatment of Palestinians was so horrendous that some of the more morally conscious Israelis called to serve in the West Bank formed an organization called *Ometz le Sarev* (Courage to Refuse). They issued a public statement saying that though they would continue to serve in the IDF and defend Israel against attack from other states, they would refuse orders to serve in the West Bank to enforce the Occupation. Hundreds of soldiers signed this statement; while some were simply reassigned by sympathetic military leaders, many others were sentenced to jail terms. By the middle of 2003, the IDF reported that a full 30 percent of young men called to serve in the army were finding ways to get out of service. This overturned decades in which such national service was considered the highest act a young man or woman could undertake.

On the other hand, a stream of terror attacks on buses and cafes created widespread fear and despair among Israelis. So while some resisted the Occupation once they observed what it was actually doing, many others developed strong anti-Palestinian sentiments. To this day, the brutality of these attacks remains firmly embedded in the minds of Israelis. Attacks on Israeli civilian targets continue today—who could forget the brutal murder in March 2011 of a family in the West Bank settlement of Itamar? This included the stabbing to death of their three children (Yoav, age eleven; Elad, age four; and Hadas, age three months). Terrorist attacks on civilians stoke the underlying fears embedded in Jews' collective memory, culture, and institutions and empower rightists who believe that it's impossible to make peace with Palestinians.

When a "separation fence" was proposed, many Israelis welcomed what we in the peace movement call "the Wall." Israelis argued that this wall would reduce the number of violent incidents and even, some argued, increase the long-term possibility of a two-state solution. But Israeli peace forces pointed out that such a wall should be built on the pre-1967 borders of Israel. Instead, the Wall cut into the West Bank and in some places ran through the middle of Palestinian villages—effectively cutting farmers off from their own land. Public demonstrations

by Palestinians, pro-peace Israelis, and internationals have frequently been met with violence from Israeli border police and the
IDF. Far from promoting peace, the Wall has become an eyesore
and a daily reminder of the oppression of the Palestinian people.

Why is it that so many Israelis cannot grasp that their much
greater political, economic and military power—coupled with the
checkpoints, the Wall, and the oppressive reality of daily life for
most Palestinians living under occupation—leads to the response
of terrorist violence? Some Palestinians have said clearly, "Give
us the most modern and powerful tanks, missiles, and airplanes,
and we will completely give up the tactic of terror." They make
this point to highlight the fact that terrorism against civilians is
often the only tactic the powerless have to use against an occupation. This is a tactic that we spiritual progressives reject both on
ethical and strategic grounds. Similarly, though we can understand the outrage that Palestinians feel when their demonstrations are met with overwhelming force and violence, resorting to
violence is always a mistake. But there is little "understanding"
from most Israelis. In fact, the moment anyone dares to say that
they "understand the anger or frustration of the Palestinian people," they are accused of covertly approving of Palestinian acts of
violence. The majority of Israelis are not able to place themselves
in the mindset of the occupied—even though Jews for 1800 years
have often been powerless in the face of overwhelming and hostile power from non-Jews. Why not?

The least charitable explanation is that Israelis are bent on
conquest and have the same mindset as colonial and imperial
powers throughout history. A more charitable explanation is that
terrorist violence reignites feelings of powerlessness and helpless-
ness that are part of the psychic legacy of the Jewish people. This
legacy, which I sum up by using the term Post-Traumatic Stress
Disorder (PTSD), makes it very difficult for Israelis to think outside of the box of being victims. As a result they are unable to

recognize their own superior power or to act from the place of confidence and generosity that such power should enable. And some have suggested that the truth may be a combination of both of these factors: that some Israelis are, in fact, bent on conquest because of their sense of victimhood and their PTSD.

Some of the most outspoken Israelis and members of the Likud, the Russian émigré parties, and other right-wing political movements may fit the less charitable explanation, but most Israelis are in the second category. It is for this reason that I believe it a mistake to look at Israeli responses to Palestinians as primarily a manifestation of fundamental insensitivity. One should give at least equal weight to the notion that Jews suffer from a self-destructive PTSD.

PTSD factors also helped shape the consciousness of Palestinians living in horrific conditions in refugee camps throughout the Middle East; of Palestinians experiencing Al-Nakba through stories told by their relatives; of Arabs who have been held in Israeli prison camps; of families whose homes have been demolished (with Caterpillar bulldozers designed for home demolition); of Palestinians whose lives have been terrorized by curfews that sometimes last all day for days on end; and of Palestinian families whose children have been killed, maimed, or shot with live ammunition. PTSD may help explain why many Palestinians find it hard to imagine the possibility of living in peace with a State of Israel that condones or actively endorses all of these horrific acts.

THE FAILED ROAD MAP AND THE SECOND IRAQ WAR

For a brief period in the spring of 2002, the United States sought to restrain the Israeli reoccupation of Palestinian cities and the destruction of the Palestinian Authority's infrastructure. Then, in a sudden turnabout, the George W. Bush administration backed off, apparently deciding that it would need Ariel Sharon's cooperation (in the form of noninvolvement) in the war against Iraq. The Bush administration began to echo Sharon's argument that peace could not be accomplished until the Palestinians replaced Yasir Arafat with a more responsible and democratic leader who was willing to provide security for Israel by repressing the Palestinian armed struggle for statehood.

Sharon won a landslide victory in new elections held in early 2003, reaping ordinary Israelis' anger at Palestinian violence, which had reached new levels of intensity during the course of the two-year Second Intifada. Labor candidate Amram Mitzna, under constant assault from the Labor Party's right wing, was unable to project a clear and consistent alternative worldview. He could not counter the growing popularity of the hawkish path to homeland security that had become the common sense of much of the Western world (particularly Israel's main ally, the United States) in the aftermath of the 9/11 attack on the World Trade Center. The Labor Party's embrace of this "peace can be achieved only through domination" worldview eventually led Labor members of the Knesset (MKs) Yossi Beilin and Yael Dayan to switch parties and align with the peace party Meretz. It also led former MK Avrum Burg to retire from politics and write a series of books; these books reflected a spiritual progressive perspective that was very far from the perspective he articulated while serving as chair of the World Zionist Organization.

Facing this reality, the Palestinian Authority responded to U.S. pressure by creating the position of prime minister and selecting Mahmoud Abbas, who, in turn, agreed to suppress violence to the extent that he could. However, the Israeli government's escalation of targeted assassinations and home

demolitions, its long-term enforcement of twenty-four-hour curfews, its occupation of major Palestinian cities, and its increased
use of checkpoints and roadblocks between cities had further
weakened Palestinians' belief in and commitment to the peace
process. These factors, along with the absence of an effective
Palestinian police force, made it extremely difficult for Abbas to
rally many Palestinians around the task that the United States
and Israel had demanded as proof of his seriousness: rooting out
Hamas.

In the spring of 2003, shortly after the United States over-
threw the government of Saddam Hussein in Iraq, President
Bush announced the commencement of the Road Map for
Middle East Peace, a three-year process to create two states liv-
ing in peace with each other. Jointly developed with Russia, the
European Union, and the United Nations (together called the
Quartet), the Road Map detailed a series of steps that would lead
to this outcome.

Two Flaws in the Road Map

It immediately became clear to the Israeli peace movement that
this Road Map was fatally flawed in two ways. First, the Road
Map did not present a clear vision of what either side would
achieve by following it—the same problem that had weakened the
Oslo Accords. Without a clear definition of the outcome, neither
side had strong motivation to take seriously the intervening steps
outlined by the Road Map. Partisans on both sides legitimately
asked, "Road Map to where?" The plan called for the Palestinian Authority to police the West Bank and Gaza against terrorists,
yet it presented little incentive for ordinary Palestinians to feel
that such measures would achieve peace and justice for their own
people.

The second flaw in the Road Map was that it empowered the extremists. Both Israel and the United States interpreted the Road Map's performance-based process to mean that if there was violence, the next steps on the road couldn't be taken. Yet, as we understand, there are forces in both Israel and Palestine that oppose the outcome of a Palestinian state living in peace with an Israeli state. To those forces, the Road Map seemed to give a message similar to that given during the Oslo process: "All you have to do is engage in acts of violence to derail the Road Map, and you'll thereby ensure that a two-state solution will never happen." In short, the Road Map was a perfect incentive for violence.

Answers to these problems emerged with "the Geneva Accord," a document negotiated by former Israeli Justice Minister Yossi Beilin with one of Arafat's top advisers, Yasir Abed Rabo, who had been the Palestinian Authority's Minister of Information. The Geneva Accord, issued at the end of 2003, was a plan detailing what a final settlement agreement would be, based on a two-state solution that included mutual recognition, economic and security cooperation, a multinational force to assist with security, both states having Jerusalem as their capital, compensation for refugees, and much more. Here was the detailed plan that, if adopted by both sides, could have ended the conflict. I'll present my own variant of that plan and some other possible plans in the next chapter.

Ariel Sharon reacted by denouncing the Geneva Accord as "subversive," and two cabinet ministers called the Israeli negotiators "traitors ... a crime punishable by death." Yet polls showed substantial support for the Geneva Accord in Israel. This support grew when, in the months after the signing, several million copies of it were mailed to Israeli citizens. Here was a reasonable plan, and many Israelis responded with serious interest in it.

Sharon was put on the defensive; he had to explain why the Occupation continued to be necessary. Some of the leaders of the

Labor Party came to his rescue. While Amram Mitzna, Labor's candidate for prime minister in the 2003 election, had publicly spoken in favor of the accord, Ehud Barak, who had been preaching that there was "no partner for peace" ever since the failed Camp David negotiations, opposed it. Meanwhile, Arafat, who had been consulted at every stage of the negotiations and on the final product, which almost certainly represented what he really wanted, refused to publicly endorse it. He reportedly felt that if he did so, the concessions made in the Geneva Accord would become the new starting point for future negotiations with Israel, and that he would be pressured to compromise further.

Withdrawal from Gaza

By the end of 2003, Sharon came up with a brilliant political move to reduce pressure on Israel to withdraw its hundreds of thousands of settlers from the West Bank: he would unilaterally withdraw Israeli troops and the 8,000 settlers from the Gaza Strip. The Occupation of Gaza had been for most Israelis one of the least popular parts of Israel's occupation strategy. Gaza is one of the most densely populated areas in the world and is filled with refugees who fled or were forced to leave their homes in the years since the creation of the State of Israel. The Gaza Occupation cost Israeli lives and seemed to offer little that was desirable for most Israelis. By de facto giving Gaza to Hamas, Sharon could undercut pressure to withdraw from the far more politically valuable West Bank. But to do so, Sharon would have to ignore the Palestinian Authority, which was in charge of Gaza even though it had less supporters there than Hamas.

Sharon's announcement of withdrawal from Gaza (he called it "disengagement") was accompanied in subsequent weeks by a clear statement that there was no one to talk to among the

Palestinians—despite the existence of the Fatah-dominated Palestinian Authority—and that therefore the disengagement had to be unilateral. Both the PLO and some sections of the Israeli peace movement denounced the move as an attempt to retain control over the rest of the occupied territories. That perception was reinforced when one of Sharon's top advisers, Dov Weinglas, publicly told West Bank settlers that the withdrawal from Gaza was a stratagem aimed at reducing international pressure on Israel to end the Occupation and dismantle West Bank settlements.

The Sharon/Weinglas stratagem worked amazingly well. It handed Gaza over to Hamas, thereby dividing the Palestinian movement in two—a West Bank Palestinian entity governed by the more peace-oriented Fatah and a Gazan entity governed by Hamas. It took the steam out of the Geneva Accord and out of demands for an immediate end to the Occupation. It rendered the Palestinian Authority more powerless than it had already been by refusing to negotiate with its leaders or to give them the ability to run Gaza once Israel withdrew. And it created a marvelous opportunity for Israel to say: "We already tried to get out of Gaza, and all we got was 'Hamastan,' a Hamas-ruled entity based on Islamic fundamentalism and rejection of Israel's right to exist. So no wonder we can't risk that with the West Bank, which is just miles away from Israel's heartland."

Gaza settlers fought the IDF and received international attention as the government of Israel proclaimed that it was making "huge sacrifices" for the sake of peace. Watching the conflict, many Israelis concluded that, without full-scale civil war against the settlers, it would be impossible to dismantle all the West Bank settlements.

Why were Hamas, the Palestinian Authority, and even some in the Israeli peace movement not thankful for what Israel had "given" them? From their perspective, the IDF never granted

Gaza actual freedom. Instead, the IDF remained on the borders of Gaza and worked out an arrangement with the Egyptian dictator Hosni Mubarak to ensure that Gaza's border with Egypt was closed and carefully restricted. Similarly, the Israeli navy prevented ships from entering or leaving Gaza's waters; Palestinian fishermen were restricted to coastal waters and had great difficulty earning their living or providing adequate fish for Gazans. In short, Gaza became an open-air camp that no one could enter and no one could leave except by permission of Israel. Israel retained control over Gaza's airspace and continued to control Gaza's access to water, electricity, and telecommunications networks. Gaza was effectively occupied even though IDF troops had retreated to the borders. Israel repeatedly used this power to punish the entire population of Gaza by periodically restricting or cutting off food, medicine, electricity, and sanitary facilities.

Imagine if some people invaded your home, then proclaimed they were leaving but instead stayed outside and prevented you from going in and out most of the time. Well, you might be happy that they were no longer inside, but you'd hardly celebrate this as "freedom." Nor would you understand how the invader could possibly claim credit for having "given" you back your home.

Hamas responded with rocket attacks on the nearby Negev town of Sderot; these attacks were later described as a war crime by international human rights expert South African Justice Richard Goldstone. The attacks rarely hit targets but nevertheless caused the people of Sderot to live in constant fear, often running to bomb shelters. Israelis pointed to the attacks as proof that giving up settlements would not bring peace.

Politics took a new turn after Yasir Arafat died and Ariel Sharon suffered an incapacitating stroke. With Mahmoud Abbas as Arafat's successor and Ehud Olmert as prime minister

Rusty Stewart

Israeli paramedics evacuate wounded people after a suicide bombing on a Jerusalem bus on August 19, 2003. Hamas and Islamic Jihad claimed responsibility for this attack, which killed 20 people.

of Israel, there was much hope that a new period of peacemaking might begin. But instead Olmert squelched that possibility. Hoping to prove his toughness before making concessions to Palestinians, Olmert used a border attack by the Lebanese movement Hezbollah against two armored Israeli Humvees on the Israeli side of the border as the pretext for a full-scale invasion of southern Lebanon and a massive bombing campaign throughout that hapless country.

The ensuing war was perceived by many Israelis as a debacle, in part because Hezbollah survived and grew in prestige for having survived the Israeli assault. The war caused great suffering. A million Lebanese were displaced, much of Lebanon's civilian infrastructure was damaged or destroyed, and 1,200 Lebanese people were killed. Hezbollah's rockets also proved more effective than had been suspected previously: 300,000 Israelis were displaced, and 121 IDF members were killed, including the son of Israeli novelist and peace advocate David Grossman, who had at first supported the invasion of Lebanon. "And all for what?" asked many Israelis.

Ehud Olmert's popularity sank dramatically and never really recovered. Meanwhile, the Palestinians held open elections in early 2006 in response to demands from the United States and "the international community" (most importantly those promising to fund the Palestinians' attempt to rebuild after the Second Intifada) for proof of the Palestinian Authority's commitment to democracy. Observers from other countries sent to monitor the process reported that it had been totally clean, legal, and peaceful. Unexpectedly for many, Hamas won a majority in the Palestinian parliament. Israelis proclaimed this outcome "proof" that the Palestinian people desired the full destruction of Israel. However, Hamas had not called for the destruction of Israel during its election campaign. Rather, Hamas drew upon its reputation for integrity in using funds to help the poor and to provide social services. Hamas emphasized this integrity in contrast to the corruption that many moderate Palestinians associated with the Fatah-dominated Palestinian Authority, which often allowed money donated by the international community to line the pockets of Palestinian elites.

The United States and Israel both cried foul and refused to accept a Palestinian Authority run by Hamas. One month after the elections, Hamas made a dramatic effort to appease Israel and the United States. It offered Israel a ten-year truce in return for a complete Israeli withdrawal from the occupied Palestinian territories—the West Bank, Gaza Strip, and East Jerusalem—and recognition of Palestinian rights including the right of return. However, Hamas leader Khaled Mashal added that Hamas was not calling for a final end to armed operations against Israel and that it would not impede other Palestinian groups from carrying out such operations. This, of course, was not likely to reassure those who worried that a Palestinian state would soon become the launching pad for yet another war to eliminate Israel—this time with the combatants particularly well positioned to deliver a huge loss of life to Israelis.

In turn, the Quartet of countries that had proposed the Road Map (the United States, Russia, the European Union, and the United Nations) stated that assistance to the Palestinian Authority would continue only if Hamas renounced violence, recognized Israel, and accepted previous Israeli-Palestinian agreements. Hamas refused to abide by these terms. The Quartet then imposed a freeze on all international aid to the Palestinian territories; this lent credence to the view that Western governments supported democracy only when the outcome of a democratic process was the outcome they wanted.

Faced with this reality, tensions grew between Fatah and Hamas. Hamas had won the election, but Fatah sided with the international community in order to continue to receive needed international financial support for the many who were suffering under the Occupation.

In retaliation for the abduction of Israeli soldier Gilad Shalit by Hamas operatives, Israel staged a raid of its own; it arrested and abducted eight Palestinian Authority cabinet members and twenty members of the Palestinian Legislative Council, effectively blocking the Hamas-dominated Palestinian parliament from meeting. Israelis staged a global campaign to release Gilad Shalit, who was held in unknown locations for the next many years, and denounced his capture as an act of "kidnapping." Hamas supporters, however, pointed out that Shalit was an enemy combatant, not a civilian, and that Israel regularly "kidnapped" Palestinian civilians and held them without trial for months or sometimes years. To make its point more clearly, Hamas offered an exchange of prisoners: Gilad Shalit would gain his freedom if all Palestinians held in Israeli jails were also released. Israel refused, pointing out

Flickr/Cau Napoli

Palestinian civilians run for cover from an Israeli missile that landed in Gaza's Nusseriat refugee camp on May 25, 2007.

that some subset of these prisoners had actually committed acts of violence. Most had not.

In June of 2007, fighting broke out in Gaza between Hamas and Fatah, and Hamas emerged the winner; in the process, Hamas killed, maimed, or tortured several hundred Gazans suspected of being loyal to Fatah or to Israel. The ruthlessness of Hamas's repression of its Fatah opponents stood in strong contrast to the democratic values that had almost always prevented political parties in Israel from jailing their political opponents, much less killing them (although phony charges were sometimes raised against outspoken Palestinian Israelis).

At this point, Israel declared the Gaza Strip "hostile territory" and created a blockade that periodically denied Gazans food, water, fuel, electricity and other goods and services. Israel also dramatically reduced economic activity within Gaza by cutting off all exports; this in turn caused widespread unemployment in Gaza. Israel's collective punishment of Gaza was purportedly designed to weaken Hamas's hold on power. An advisor to Ehud Olmert, Dov Weisglass, seemed to regard Gazan civilians as subhuman as he justified the blockade. "The idea is to put Palestinians on a diet, but not to make them die of hunger," he said.

Like so much of the story, the narratives from Israelis and Palestinians diverge radically in describing what caused Operation Cast Lead, Israel's massive assault on Gaza in December and January of 2008. From the Israeli perspective, there had been periodic though largely ineffective mortar and shell attacks coming from Gaza and falling on or near the Israeli town of Sderot. Hamas argued that those attacks were a response to Israel's collective punishment of Gaza.

What both sides do agree on is that there was a massive military operation that was conducted largely by Israeli air strikes on Gaza; this protected Israeli army members, since fighters would be far less vulnerable in the air than on the ground. The Israeli government emphasizes that the IDF sought to focus on military-related targets and warned Palestinian civilians to seek shelter elsewhere before targeting their neighborhoods. Palestinians challenge that narrative, pointing out that many targets were clearly civilian and that the warnings were useless since there were no safe place to go.

Palestinians reported the deaths of as many as 900 civilians and about 600 Hamas combatants; thousands more were wounded. Traveling through Gaza in the aftermath of this assault, observers could see that much of Gaza's infrastructure and significant amounts of civilian housing had been destroyed. Israel, on the other hand, maintained that most of those killed or wounded were enemy combatants. As occupying powers have done in situations like this throughout the colonial period, Israel claimed that many of these combatants intentionally located themselves in civilian areas for protection. Conversely, the Palestinians pointed out that the struggle against the Occupation was being conducted not by an army with uniforms, tanks, and airplanes, but by a rebellion of ordinary citizens against their occupiers. So of course those citizens would be located where citizens are, not in non-existent army camps.

In response to an international outcry against the bombings of civilian homes and schools and the high number of Palestinian deaths and casualties, the United Nations Human Rights Council (UNHRC) set up a fact-finding commission chaired by Justice Richard Goldstone, former judge of the Constitutional Court of South Africa and an important ally to Nelson Mandela during South Africa's transition from apartheid to democracy. Goldstone had previously served as the UN Security Council-appointed prosecutor of the International Criminal Court tribunals for the former Yugoslavia and Rwanda. Goldstone had been a lifelong Zionist, a respected member of the Jewish community of South Africa, and a member of the board of trustees of the Hebrew University in Jerusalem.

Unfortunately, Israel refused from the very start to cooperate with the UN-sponsored investigation. Israelis had derided the United Nations since 1975, when the UN General Assembly passed a resolution that proclaimed, "Zionism is racism." Palestinian supporters successfully made subsequent international conferences on racism focus on the crimes of Israel; many of the countries taking pious stands on Israel's racism arguably had significant racism issues of their own that deserved attention at least as much if not more. The destruction of Tibetan society and culture by China, the genocide in Darfur, the many racist struggles against minorities in Asia and Africa, the genocide in Rwanda, the incarceration of hundreds of thousands of African Americans in the United States—all these were given scant attention compared to the focus on Israel.

The cumulative effect of this perceived disproportionate focus on Israel has been to diminish the United Nation's ability to offer moral suasion in the Arab-Israeli conflict or to garner U.S. support for many other far less prejudicial activities of the United Nations. So when Goldstone approached Israel for cooperation with his inquiry, he was greeted not as a loyal Zionist with an unimpeachable record of judicial fairness but as an irreparably biased representative of the United Nations. Goldstone tried unsuccessfully to convince Israel that this approach would make it difficult for him to present Israel's own case and integrate its perspective into his findings.

The Goldstone report documented a wide array of human rights violations by Israel and Hamas that had occurred during the period of Operation Cast Lead. For example, in regard to Palestinian actions during Operation Cast Lead, the Goldstone report says:

> Palestinian armed groups have launched
> thousands of rockets and mortars into Israel
> since April 2001. These have succeeded in
> causing terror within Israel's civilian population,
> as evidenced by the high rates of psychological
> trauma with the affected communities. The
> attacks have also led to an erosion of the social,
> cultural, and economic lives of the communities

in southern Israel, and have affected the rights
to education of tens of thousands of children
and young adults who attended classes in the
affected areas. Between 27 December 2008 and
18 January 2009, those attacks left four people
dead and hundreds injured.

The report also concludes that Israel was involved in many
human rights violations:

Israeli armed forces, like any army attempting
to act within the parameters of international
law, must avoid taking undue risks with their
soldiers' lives, but neither can they transfer
the risk onto the lives of civilian men, women,
and children. The fundamental principles of
distinction and proportionality apply on the
battlefield, whether that battlefield is a built-up
urban area or an open field. The repeated failure
to distinguish between combatants and civilians
appears to have been the result of deliberate
guidance issued to soldiers, as described by
some of them, and not the result of occasional
lapses.... Some of those killed were combatants
directly engaged in hostilities against Israel, but
many were not. The outcome and modalities
of the operations indicate that they were only
partially aimed at killing leaders and members of
Hamas, Al-Qassam Brigades, and other armed
groups. They were also to a large degree aimed
at destroying or incapacitating civilian property
and the means of subsistence of the civilian
population.

The report adds:

> The destruction of food supply installations,
> water sanitation systems, concrete factories, and
> residential housing was the result of a deliberate
> and systematic policy by the Israel armed forces.
> It was not carried out because those objects
> presented a military threat or opportunity, but
> to make the daily process of living, and dignified
> living, more difficult for the civilian population....

> Allied to the systematic destruction of the
> economic capacity of the Gaza Strip, there
> appears also to have been an assault on the
> dignity of the people. This was seen not only
> in the use of human shields and unlawful
> detentions, sometimes in unacceptable
> conditions, but also in the vandalizing of houses
> when occupied and the way in which people
> were treated when their houses were entered.
> The graffiti on the walls, the obscenities and
> often racist slogans, all constituted an overall
> image of humiliation and dehumanization of the
> Palestinian population.

> The operation was carefully planned in all
> their phases. Legal opinions and advice were
> given throughout the planning stages and at
> certain operational levels during the campaign.
> There were no mistakes made according to the
> Government of Israel. It is in these circumstances
> that the Mission concludes that what occurred
> in just over three weeks at the end of 2008 and

in the beginning of 2009 was a deliberately
disproportionate attack designed to punish,
humiliate and terrorize a civilian population,
radically diminish its local economic capacity
both to work and to provide for itself, and
to force upon it an ever increasing sense of
dependency and vulnerability.... The systematic
and deliberate nature of the activities described
in this report leave the Mission in no doubt that
responsibility lies in the first place with those
who designed, planned, ordered and oversaw the
operation.

Among its other conclusions and recommendations, the
Goldstone Report urged the Security Council of the United
Nations to require the Israeli government to "take all appropriate steps, within a period of three months, to launch appropriate
investigations that are independent and in conformity with international standards, into the serious violations of international
humanitarian and international human rights laws" uncovered
in the report. It adds:

Israel should immediately cease the border
closures and restrictions on passage through
border crossings with the Gaza Strip and allow
the passage of goods necessary and sufficient to
meet the needs of the population for the recovery
and reconstruction of housing and essential
services, and for the resumption of meaningful
economic activity in the Gaza Strip.... [Israel]
should cease the restrictions of access to the
sea for fishing purposes imposed on the Gaza
Strip and allow such fishing activities within

the 20 nautical miles as provided for in the Oslo Accords…. Israel should release Palestinians who are detained in Israeli prisons in connection with the Occupation. The release of children should be an utmost priority.

The recommendations go on for many, many pages of this 324-page report. It includes recommendations that the Palestinian Authority and Gaza authorities "should release without delay all political detainees currently in their power and refrain from further arrests on political grounds and in violation of international human rights laws," and that Palestinian armed groups should "undertake forthwith to respect international humanitarian law, in particular by renouncing attacks on Israeli civilians and civilian objects, and take all feasible precautionary measures to avoid harm to Palestinian civilians during hostilities." Moreover, it recommends that Palestinian armed groups should release Gilad Shalit on humanitarian grounds.

But the most important recommendation was that if the parties fail to engage in good-faith independent investigations in conformity with international standards, then the situation in Gaza should be referred to the prosecutor of the International Criminal Court. Presumably the prosecutor would then determine what crimes against humanity or violations of international law had taken place and who should be put on trial or otherwise sanctioned in the international community.

Neither Israel nor Hamas convened a credible independent investigation. Instead, Israel immediately launched an international campaign to discredit the messenger rather than to investigate what had gone wrong. This *hasbara* (public relations) campaign replicated Israel's standard reaction to charges of human rights violations: it attempted to discredit and demean the organizations or individuals who made these reports, including members of the IDF and other Israelis who shared information with the Goldstone investigation. Wild stories circulated alleging that Goldstone had supported apartheid, that he was an anti-Semite or a "self-hating Jew," and that he had intentionally set out to hurt or even destroy Israel. Jewish newspapers and magazines around the world engaged in a systematic and vicious attempt to hurt Goldstone's reputation and deny his integrity. In Jewish religious terms, it was a campaign of *lashon ha'ra* (destructive and hurtful language), which is explicitly forbidden in Jewish traditional texts.

At one point the hatred reached such a crescendo that Goldstone was told by leaders of his own Jewish Community in South Africa that he ought not attend his grandson's bar mitzvah because the community, having heard so many death threats against Goldstone, could not ensure his safety. As rabbi of the Beyt Tikkun Synagogue here in California's San Francisco Bay Area, I immediately contacted Goldstone to offer our synagogue as an alternate location for his grandson's bar mitzvah. I also told him that *Tikkun* magazine had recently decided to offer him the Tikkun Award for his courageous role in South Africa, Bosnia, Rwanda, and now in Gaza. This award had previously gone to other political and cultural notables including Allen Ginsberg z"l, Shulamit Aloni, Grace Paley z"l, Senator Paul Wellstone z"l, Alfred Kazin z"l, Irving Howe z"l, Howard Zinn z"l, Cornel West, Rabbi Marshall Meyer z"l, Rabbi Zalman Schachter-Shalomi, Marge Piercy, Yehuda Amichai z"l, David Grossman, Benedictine Sister Joan Chittister, Art Spiegelman, Pete Seeger, Tony Kushner, and Marian Wright Edelman. (Z"l is a Jewish way of giving praise to the dead—*zichrono l'vracha*, may their memory be a blessing.)

There were some credible critiques of the Goldstone Report, most notably from Hartman Institute scholar Moshe Halbertal; he pointed out that the Israeli army took some significant steps to protect civilians, notably measures to scare civilians off the roofs of their buildings so that they would not be hurt when the IDF bombed those buildings. Moreover, Halbertal argued, the Goldstone Report failed to acknowledge the "asymmetrical" nature of modern warfare in which the terrorists "use the civilian population as human shields" by refusing to wear uniforms, hiding among the civilians, and firing weapons deliberately placed in densely populated areas. Halbertal's critique and others' responses to it can be read in *The Goldstone Report: the Legacy of the Landmark Investigation of the Gaza Conflict* edited by Adam Horowitz, Lizzy Ratner, and Philip Weiss.

As Jerome Slater said in responding to Halbertal in *Tikkun*, "asymmetrical warfare" is "merely the current jargon for age-old guerrilla warfare, in which poorly armed insurgents rise up against much more powerful state armies. Guerrillas, by definition, do not make themselves easy targets." That does not give the occupying power the right to attack civilian targets. Jews celebrate on Chanukah the victory of such an asymmetrical guerrilla force against the occupying power of Antiochus's Hellenist armies.

Slater also challenges another argument raised by critics of the Goldstone Report: that it seems unfair to single out Israel and that Israel's crimes were not as bad as those of the United States and its allies in Serbia or Afghanistan. Goldstone pointed out to me that this was also an argument used by Milosevic in Serbia to defend his regime's slaughter of civilians in Bosnia. Slater argues that it is a non sequitur:

> You are not absolved from war crimes even if it's true that your crimes were not as bad as someone else's. Secondly, unlike Israel's purposes in Gaza, no one has suggested that the allies deliberately killed civilians, and still less that they sought to

colonize and repress the people of Serbia and
Afghanistan. Rather, they had a legitimate just-
war argument: humanitarian intervention in
Kosovo and, in light of Al-Qaeda's presence in
Afghanistan, self-defense in Afghanistan.

The complaint that the report reflected selective prosecution
has some legitimacy—at least, each side has a good case on that
question. Israel is not the biggest human rights violator in recent
world history: its crimes pale in comparison to what the Chinese
Communist Party under Chairman Mao did during the Great
Leap Forward and the Cultural Revolution, what the United
States did in Vietnam, what Russia has done in Chechnya, what
Sudan has done in Darfur, what Myanmar has done to its own
people, what Iran has done to its own people, and more.

But here the argument gets more complicated. There is a
persuasive case for claiming that the creation of a special investigation of Israel by the United Nations may reflect a general
bias against Israel—though based in part on the long history
of Palestinian dispossession and the growing global outrage
at Israel's behavior and not on a long history of global anti-
Semitism. Most of the countries of the world that today reflect
bias against Israel do not ground their criticism in Christian
or Muslim religious foundations. Indeed, one would be hard-
pressed to find significant evidence of a deep-rooted historical
bias against Jews in most of Africa or Asia or in many other
areas where Jews didn't live and where Christianity had not
shaped the dominant culture. It is, rather, the anger that Israeli
behavior in the past sixty-plus years has generated that creates
this contemporary bias and leads many nations to take stands
against Israel that are out of proportion to Israel's crimes.

However, at least some of this bias is based on a view of Israel
that is far less nuanced than the view I've been trying to develop

in this book. Many contemporary nations see Israel as nothing more than a colonial power and an extension of Western domination. I hope that the argument of this book has evoked a far more complex reality. Moreover, the United Nation's failure to confront even bigger human rights violators like the United States, China, and Russia represents a craven attitude in which the big powers sometimes get a "pass" for actions for which the less powerful State of Israel gets criticized.

But this contention, while correct, does not prove that the actual findings of the Goldstone Report are illegitimate. Israel may indeed have been singled out for prosecution for bad reasons, but the prosecution may still be legitimate. If some corporate bigwigs in the United States quietly get away with embezzlement because of their elite clout, does that mean that no common thieves should be prosecuted? If you believed that some crimes should be prosecuted even if other crimes were not being prosecuted, then you would not exonerate Israel on the grounds of selective prosecution.

The weakest part of the Goldstone Report was its claim that the top leadership of the Israeli political and military establishments had intended to kill civilians as a way of punishing the people of Gaza for the sins of its Hamas leadership. It would have made much more sense for the Goldstone Report to focus solely on the human rights violations that occurred rather than speculate on their cause. It will take decades, if it will ever happen, to open the archives of the present leadership of Israel and examine the relevant evidence. The Goldstone Report was convincing and significant enough without giving its enemies the opportunity to jump on this claim, which could not be definitively substantiated. That charge allowed many right-wing Zionists to switch the debate away from what was substantiated by the Goldstone Report to what was merely speculation based on the Israel's "course of conduct" in the past. It would have been entirely sufficient to have kept the charges focused on what legal scholars call "the reasonable and expectable consequences" of Israel's bombing of the targets it chose, rather than to have attributed motives.

Having studied the mindset of many of the civilian and military leaders who were in charge at the time, I tend to believe that their motive was to prove that Israeli power should not be taunted or played with; that Israel's determination and willingness to use force was as strong as ever; that Hamas would have to pay a price for its continued imprisonment of Gilad Shalit; and that the people of Gaza should have to pay a serious price for supporting or not rebelling against Hamas.

Unfortunately, some of the formulations of the report made it read more like a conviction than an indictment. This made it easier for supporters of the current Israeli government to focus on that point rather than on the huge amount of evidence that Goldstone unearthed, and also to focus on the fact that one of the members of the Goldstone Commission acknowledged having been convinced of Israel's wrongdoing even before she received the evidence. These errors of the Goldstone Commission made it easier for fair-minded people to avoid reading the full Goldstone Report, most of which remains as important and relevant today as it was when it was first compiled.

The U.S. Congress, urged on by the right wing of pro-Israel forces in the U.S. (AIPAC, Christian Zionists, and the many corporate forces invested in or economically benefiting from trade or research with Israel), passed a resolution condemning the Goldstone Report with 343 yes votes and 36 opposition votes. The resolution urged President Barack Obama and Secretary of State Hillary Clinton to unequivocally oppose any endorsement of the report. The Obama administration had already claimed publicly that the report was flawed but did not respond to Justice Goldstone's request that they cite specific flaws. House Democrats led the assault on the report. The report "paints a distorted picture," said House Majority Leader Steny Hoyer. It "epitomizes the practice of singling Israel out from all other nations for condemnation." The National Jewish Democratic Council urged Democrats in Congress to support the resolution and denounce the Goldstone Report.

Almost two years later, in March 2011, Justice Goldstone published an op-ed in the *Washington Post* acknowledging his mistake in attributing intentionality to Israel's killings of civilians. This was a courageous act and a reflection of Goldstone's integrity—few justices ever publicly acknowledge their mistaken judgments. Unfortunately, the op-ed also contained a one-sided (though correct) critique of Hamas's behavior subsequent to the release of his report. Goldstone said, "If I had known then what I know now, the Goldstone Report would have been a different document."

Because Goldstone did not specify what parts of the report remained valid and why, his op-ed was seized upon by the Netanyahu government and portrayed as a total repudiation of all the charges in the report. Right-wing media published demands on me at *Tikkun* and Jeremy Ben Ami at J Street to publicly repudiate the entire report, even though most of the Goldstone Report's charges have not been investigated by an authority with the power to subpoena documents and testimony from relevant actors. Goldstone never intended to issue a blanket retraction of his report; he still stood behind most of his report, but the U.S. media obscured this point. What upset him and led him to write his op-ed was that his report was being used by those who sought to delegitimize Israel's existence as a state. Goldstone sought to repudiate those who had misused his original report, and he tried to show that he still felt far more connection to Israel than to Hamas. Unfortunately, the way he did it failed to communicate the nuances of his position. The op-ed became fodder for right wingers in the Zionist world, while seemingly repudiating the peace movement members who had originally welcomed Goldstone's work.

The assault on Gaza did not end the shelling of Sderot, nor did it free Gilad Shalit. Israel soon returned to its policy of cutting off the import of food items, medical supplies, and other necessities—particularly anything that could be used to help Gazans reconstruct the homes and apartments that had been destroyed by the Israeli assault. Israel also continued to fly drones and helicopters over Gaza, from time to time killing people identified as suspected militants. Often, these strikes killed innocent bystanders.

Meanwhile, in the years after the Gaza War and the Goldstone Report, increasing numbers of people around the world became more aware of the plight of the Palestinian people. Some began to imagine ways to break the blockade of Gaza in order to bring food, medicine, and other supplies to the Palestinians living there. Israel did its best to block these supplies; it argued that the supplies were rarely delivered to the people who actually needed them, but instead were appropriated by Hamas to be used as rewards for those in Gaza who supported Hamas. Israel's blockade was made more effective because the Mubarak regime agreed to enforce the blockade on its borders with Gaza. In turn, Gazans built hundreds of tunnels into the Egyptian desert, from which they were able to smuggle in many of the needed goods. The tunnels have provided as much as 80 percent of Gaza's imports, and the United Nations referred to the tunnels as a "vital lifeline." Some tunnels also bring weapons that are used against Israel.

In the spring of 2010, a group of yachts and small ships sailed toward Gaza filled with humanitarian volunteers who sought to break the blockade. This flotilla was forcibly stopped on the high seas by the IDF, which killed nine of those aboard the biggest ship and wounded many others. The incident reminded the world media of the deplorable conditions still facing the people of Gaza. To many in the United States, however, when a problem has been brought to light there is a sense that it has been addressed. Surely now, people imagine, the children of Gaza are no longer facing malnutrition? A second flotilla in July of 2011 tried to once again bring the world's attention to the suffering of the Palestinian people; this time, the Israeli government was able to prevent the ships from sailing. When protesters arrived from abroad as part of a "flytilla," they and some of their Israeli supporters were arrested for the "crime" of displaying signs calling for an end of the blockade. Some Israeli civil libertarians questioned how Israel could expect to be treated as "the only democracy in the Middle East" if it prevented citizens and visitors from peacefully expressing their political opinions.

It remains unclear whether the new regime emerging in Egypt will, as some of its leaders have promised, truly keep the border between Gaza and Egypt open. This would mitigate the impact of the Israeli blockade. Hamas offered to allow monitoring to prevent the import of heavy weaponry and has also agreed to work with Fatah to bring forth a united Palestinian people for negotiations with Israel. It is unclear whether this Fatah/Hamas reconciliation will hold and whether it will lead to a more hopeful outcome. But one thing should be clear: any peace agreement negotiated with the Palestinian Authority that does not have the approval of Hamas will not achieve lasting legitimacy. Hamas is one of the chief antagonists to Israel; if it is not included in negotiations and agreements, it will feel little moral pressure to live by those agreements.

THE SETTLEMENTS: DRIVING A POLICY OF CONQUEST

The expansion of settlements in the West Bank from the mid-1980s to the present, coupled with the construction of a "separation wall" and the imposition of hundreds of checkpoints, has created a wide range of problems for the Palestinian people. The settlers have sometimes grabbed land from Palestinian farmers, sometimes claiming that the land was empty, not owned, or legally sold to them by Palestinians (even though the Palestinian Authority has made such sales illegal). The details of these illegal and immoral land grabs are detailed in the book *Lords of the Land* by Tel Aviv University historian Idith Zertal and *Ha'aretz* columnist Akiva Eldar. A central element in this process was the decision by the Israeli government to declare West Bank land "state land" that does not belong to the Palestinian people. As described earlier, a substantial number of Israelis have long disputed the notion that there is a Palestinian people. Thus the march of folly continues in our time.

The same picture emerges from the monthly reports from Israel's Shalom Achshav and from the periodic reports on human rights in the occupied territories by the Israeli human rights organization, B'Tselem. According to B'Tselem,

> Using a complex legal-bureaucratic mechanism, Israel took control of some 50 percent of the land of the West Bank, primarily for establishment of the settlements and preparation of land reserves for their expansion. The main means used for this purpose is declaring and recording the land as "state land." This procedure, which began in 1979, is based on the manipulative application of the Ottoman Land

Israeli settlements in the West Bank

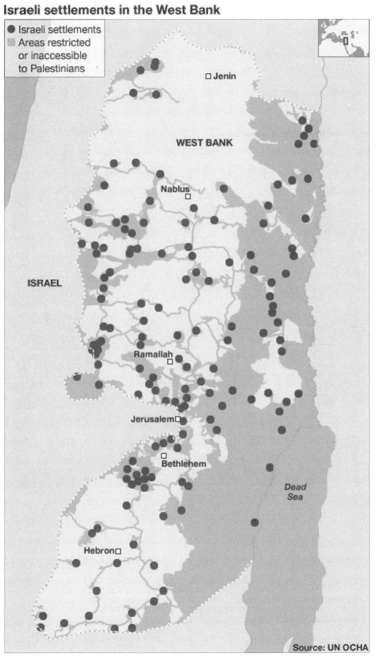

● Israeli settlements
▨ Areas restricted or inaccessible to Palestinians

□ Jenin

WEST BANK

Nablus □

ISRAEL

Ramallah □

Jerusalem □

Bethlehem □

Dead Sea

Hebron □

Source: UN OCHA

Law of 1858, which was in force on the eve of
the Occupation. The mechanism resulted in the
declaration, mostly between 1979 and 1992, of
913,000 dunams as state land, which comprise
16 percent of the West Bank. The other methods
used, each based on a different legal basis, were
requisition for "military needs," declaration of
land as "abandoned property," and expropriation
of land for "public needs." In addition, Israel
has aided citizens in purchasing land on the
"open market." Simultaneously, in many cases,
settlers independently seized control of private
Palestinian land, while Israeli officials failed in
almost all cases to enforce the law and return the
land to its lawful owners.

The system of two sets of laws, one applicable to the settlers
and other Israelis and another applicable to Palestinians, has led
some to describe the reality of the West Bank as "apartheid." This
term describes the government policy of segregation and discrimination formerly used by the minority white population in South
Africa to oppress the country's black majority. But this is a rather
inexact analogy. Discriminatory policies in the West Bank are
based on a national struggle, not on racial or religious grounds.
So, while there are two sets of roads in the West Bank—one for
the settlers and their visitors and another for Palestinians—a
Muslim Palestinian Israeli has the same rights to use the Israeli
roads or even to settle in the West Bank as a Jewish West Bank
settler. However, prejudice makes this hypothetical unlikely; almost none of the Jewish settlements would allow a Palestinian
Israeli to move in or marry someone living in the settlements.

There are frequent and well-documented attacks by settler
groups on Palestinian olive trees and agricultural and grazing

lands, as well as direct attacks on settlers' Palestinian neighbors, including on Palestinian children. The IDF sometimes intervenes to protect Palestinians, but most often it doesn't. The authorities enforcing the Occupation rarely step in to prosecute the settlers involved, or do so with such light sentences that the settlers are encouraged to keep at their violence. B'Tselem summarizes it this way:

> Israelis, individually or in organized groups, carry out the attacks on Palestinians and Palestinian property to frighten, deter, or punish them, using weapons and ammunition they received from the IDF. The settlers sometimes act in retaliation for violence committed by Palestinians, and sometimes not.

> The actions against Palestinians include blocking roadways, so as to impede Palestinian life and commerce. The settlers also shoot solar panels on roofs of buildings, torch automobiles, shatter windowpanes and windshields, destroy crops, uproot trees, and abuse merchants and owners of stalls in the market. Some of these actions are intended to force Palestinians to leave their homes and farmland, and thereby enable the settlers to gain control of them.

> During the olive-picking season, when many Palestinians are at work in the orchards, settler violence increases. The violence takes the form of gunfire, which sometimes results in casualties among the Palestinian olive-pickers, destruction of trees, and theft of Palestinian crops.

While most of the issues raised above are built into the very structure of the Occupation, the settler violence is not—it is a choice made by some settlers. I want to emphasize again, however, that most settlers, while quick to deny the reality of settler violence and to minimize the suffering that the Occupation causes to Palestinians, do not themselves participate in or condone that violence.

Most settlers are, like most Israelis and most Palestinians, decent human beings who did not create the existing system. They might be willing to leave were they offered housing of comparable worth inside the Green Line. On the other hand, the periodic outbreaks of Palestinian fury at the settlers, sometimes resulting in honoring the "martyrs" who had engaged in immoral acts of terror, contributed to a feeling of isolation and fear on the part of many settlers—a feeling that eventually coalesced into overt racism toward Palestinians.

This racism, which has increasingly pervaded the entire Israeli society, may be based not only on fear but also on a deep, unconscious feeling of guilt and shame for the suffering of the Palestinian people and the continued theft of their land. Perhaps Israelis' conscious demeaning of those whom they are oppressing is an effort to keep those feelings at bay. "They deserve it" is the instant answer that many settlers (and increasingly, members of mainstream of Israeli society) give when questioned about Palestinian suffering.

Inside the State of Israel, racism and discrimination against Palestinian Israelis is rampant. This comes most dramatically in the unequal allocation of funds to towns with a predominantly Arab population or to the Arab section of East Jerusalem. However, it bears more resemblance to the discrimination currently practiced in the United States against African Americans and the poor (e.g. in the unequal financing of education in poorer cities and richer suburbs or in the unequal enforcement of drug laws) than to the legally imposed discrimination enforced by South Africa's apartheid laws.

This distinction has been less clear, however, in the second decade of the twenty-first century. Benjamin Netanyahu and his foreign minister Avigdor Lieberman, who represent the unapologetic racism that is growing among the Israeli political right, have encouraged overtly discriminatory legislation that has the distinct flavor of apartheid. One such move is to grant extensive benefits to those who serve in the IDF, which does not accept Palestinian Israelis into its ranks. A new law passed in 2011 makes it a crime for Israeli individuals or organizations to organize economic boycotts of Israel or Israeli settlements. Another proposed law forbids any references to "Al-Nakba" (the Palestinian word for the 1948 "catastrophe") in school textbooks. These restrictions on free speech again call into question Israel's claim to be "the only democracy in the Middle East" or a representative of Western values.

Racism in this struggle is never one-sided. Racism against Jews flourishes in the West Bank and Gaza. But this racism is not based on deep cultural tropes of anti-Semitism. Though demeaning of Jews exists in some strands of Islamic thought and these themes are drawn upon occasionally by some Arabs and Muslims, Jews have previously lived peacefully as a minority within Muslim lands. It is primarily in the modern period that Muslim anger toward Jews has congealed—as Jews became allies to French and English colonizers, as Jewish settlements expanded, as the State of Israel was established and Palestinians were expelled, and as Israel occupied the West Bank and Gaza.

There are Palestinians under the age of forty who have never met a Jew or an Israeli except when the Jews were carrying weapons and enforcing curfews, causing blackouts, denying food, breaking into apartments to find "suspects," or otherwise acting in ways that terrorized the population. The resulting prejudice or anger toward Jews or Israelis most closely resembles the contempt many Jews developed for *goyim* (non-Jews) when it was Jews who were being oppressed for no plausible reason in Europe and Asia. And just as that prejudice and anger has dramatically declined among American Jews who have experienced sixty-plus years of being treated with respect and equality in the United States, the same could happen to Palestinians if they are treated by Jews with respect and equality.

OCCUPATION, BLOCKADE, AND ASSASSINATIONS

In the early days of the Obama administration, an effort was made to push the newly created Israeli government of Benjamin Netanyahu to temporarily stop the creation of new settlements and expansion of existing settlement activity in Arab East Jerusalem. Many in the Israeli peace movement questioned the demand, arguing that the United States should use its power not to achieve a temporary halt in construction but rather to articulate a clear vision of a proposed settlement and then push Israel to accept its terms. A newly formed pro-Israel but also pro-peace lobby, J Street, sought to mobilize American Jews to support Obama in his call for a settlement freeze. The Palestinian Authority, believing that Obama was serious about using American power to achieve a lasting peace agreement, accepted U.S. pressure to abandon efforts to get the United Nations to follow up on the recommendations of the Goldstone Report. Instead, they focused on the settlement freeze.

For the Fatah-dominated Palestinian Authority, it wasn't too difficult to shift focus away from the suffering in Gaza. After all, Gaza was still run by Hamas, which had brutally kicked Fatah supporters out of Gaza. The Palestinian Authority instead embraced the Obama administration's demand that negotiations begin as soon as a settlement freeze could be achieved. However, the Netanyahu government, itself filled with ultra-right-wing elements—including a foreign minister who had proposed transferring Palestinian Israelis to an Arab state—refused to compromise even enough to give Obama any of what he had asked for.

Humiliated, Obama shifted focus away from the Palestinian issue. The Palestinians who had followed Obama's call to make the restart of negotiations contingent on a settlement freeze refused to resume negotiations; the very thing that was to be negotiated—how much of the West Bank would be available for a Palestinian state—was being resolved by the aggressive building projects of right-wing Israelis aided by the Israeli government. Most American Jewish institutions refused to criticize Netanyahu's policies and many Jews on the political right sought to portray Obama as "anti-Israel" for having tried to get Israel to agree to a three-month settlement freeze during which negotiations could resume.

And so the cycle of repression, targeted assassinations, and blockade—followed by outbursts of anger and a return to terrorism—continued.

The Palestinian people have shown remarkable resilience in the face of oppression, creating a rich cultural life that includes theater and cinema, poetry and literature, education and high-quality university training, and of course personal and spiritual/religious lives. Some have even labeled Palestinians "the Jews of the Middle East," likening Palestinian resilience to that of the Jews who developed a rich culture despite living in repressive regimes for much of the past 1,800 years. Some Western observers claim that Palestinians are more fully "developed" (read "Westernized") than other segments of the Arab peoples of the Middle East—an ironic consequence of being in such close touch with the Western-oriented culture of Israeli society. Palestinians are hence well positioned to make good use of their freedom should they ever be free of Western and Israeli domination. Others argue that it will take many decades for Palestinians to recover and heal from the psychic consequences of the Occupation.

In the spring of 2011, many Israeli writers suggested that Israeli compromises on behalf of peace were unlikely because the U.S. administration would not dare to try to impose anything on Israel. The United States had already backed off its demand for a settlement freeze, and the Obama administration was consistently boxed in by forces in the U.S. media and Congress that consistently portrayed Israel as the innocent victim and Arabs as the evil Other. The Obama administration even went so far as to veto a proposed UN Security Council resolution that simply quoted the words of U.S. Secretary of State Hillary Clinton when she had condemned the building of new settlements during the first year of the Obama presidency. In these circumstances, Israeli writers alleged, most Israelis simply lost touch with what was happening on the West Bank and Gaza. Life seemed to be working well for Israelis who were able to simply shut their eyes and ears to the suffering of the Palestinian people. For years, the Palestinian Authority had renounced violence, condemned every act of violence committed against Israel, cooperated with the Israeli intelligence forces to stop potential assaults on Israel, and proven their commitment to a peaceful path. However, as Hamas continually pointed out, they never got anything substantial in return from the Israeli government beyond calls for further repression of potential Palestinian militants.

It was in this context that violence resumed in 2011 in Jerusalem; a bomb was detonated near a bus stop, killing one person and wounding thirty others. Israel then bombed Gaza in retaliation for the firing of rockets. Yet what truly struck horror in the minds of Israelis and Jews around the world was a terrorist attack against Itamar, a West Bank settlement known to be one of the most violent and hateful toward Palestinians. An independent Palestinian terrorist group claimed credit for the attack, which was denounced by the Palestinian Authority. In the attack, a family of five, including a three-month-old baby, was knifed to death. For many Jews, the barbarism of this attack brought back stories of Nazis killing Jewish babies during the Holocaust, and for some, ancient stories of the killing of all male children by the Egyptian Pharaoh. It mattered little to Israelis that most Palestinians responded with the same shock and horror as Jews—the incident resurrected primal fears and the desire for immediate revenge on Palestinians who had nothing to do with the assault. This same cycle of violence repeated itself in August of 2011 when Israeli bus-riders near Eilat were killed and wounded by another Palestinian attack.

Yet, the democratic revolutions sweeping the Arab world in 2011 raised the possibility of a brand-new dynamic: a democratic Middle East. In such a context, Arab states might be willing to take much stronger steps to reassure Israelis that they are not about to face a second Holocaust and that they are not as isolated as their psyches might lead them to believe. Similarly, democratically reconstituted Arab states might create the context in which the people of Gaza could feel empowered to challenge the "wipe Israel out" mentality of many who lead Hamas. Yet the most powerful challenges will not go away until both Palestinians and Israelis feel so embraced by the peoples of the world that they can begin to dismantle the mass psychology of trauma that has turned them toward revenge and hatred as a core psychic strategy for maintaining a sense of inner safety.

Some have suggested that the Arab Spring (as the 2011 revolutions have been dubbed) will introduce a new dynamic in which Arab democracies will at once reassure Israel that it can have a warm peace if it ends the Occupation. They argue that the Arab Spring could simultaneously push both Israel and Hamas away from resorting to violence. Others, however, fear that Arab democracies, particularly if they become more responsive to the worldview of Islamic fundamentalists, might continue the practice of using Israel as an excuse for their own internal problems. This might resemble the way that "terrorism" became an excuse for the United States to make wars in the Middle East that had little to do with fighting those who had caused 9/11.

The May 2011 reconciliation between Hamas and the Palestinian Authority was interpreted in part as a response to this new situation. Hamas, which had previously depended on support from Syria, found itself in a difficult position in receiving backing from Syrian dictator Bashar Al-Assad, who was involved in the mass murder of nonviolent protesters in his own country. At the same time, the Palestinian Authority found itself without the support it had previously received from ousted dictator Mubarak.

When the Palestinian Authority approached the United Nations in September for membership, partly in acknowledgment that 20 years of negotiations with Israel had yielded little except benefits to Israel, Hamas condemned the effort. Hamas maintained that UN recognition of a Palestinian state on 22 percent of pre-1948 Palestine would de facto recognize Israel as the legitimate ruler of the other 78 percent and de facto give up on the "right of return" for Palestinian refugees. So while Hamas is ready to agree to a twenty-year "truce" with Israel, it rejects any de jure acceptance of Israel's legitimacy. Israeli hawks believe that such a truce would provide Hamas with the opportunity to strengthen itself so that it could accomplish its final goal of destroying Israel completely. Peace movement activists, on the contrary, believe that if a truce with Hamas were accompanied by a peace treaty with the Palestinians, an end to the Occupation, and international recognition of Palestine by the United Nations, the militant factions of Hamas would lose their credibility and popularity with most Palestinians and become a less significant political force.

One thing is certain: the story that I've been telling in this book will go on and on for a long time and will continue to command the world's attention for years to come. Even if there is something resembling a political agreement, the psychological and spiritual legacy of so many years of hatred and mutual demeaning of the Other guarantees that it will take a very long time to heal Israel/Palestine. I cannot predict at this time how the Arab Spring, the efforts through the United Nations, the democratic revolt against Syrian dictator Assad, the role of the Israel Lobby in the 2012 presidential elections, or the powerfully hopeful economic justice uprisings of Israelis in the summer of 2011 will actually play out over the long run. However, I am confident that what is needed in the Middle East is an approach that involves embracing the people of both sides, helping them gain confidence in themselves and in the Other, and helping them overcome all the factors that make them believe that the Other is so intractable that peace is impossible. And that is why the discussion in this book will remain relevant no matter what political developments take place in the coming decades.

Yet I do not want to dismiss the importance of a political settlement. Anything that would stop the violence would be an important contribution to creating the possibility of both sides embracing each other and the world embracing them both. In a Haggadah commentary by the late Rabbi Tamerat that was put together by the Hartman Institute, God commands the children of Israel to remain in their homes when the angel of death passes over Egypt because even when your cause is just, contact with violence corrupts. Israelis and Palestinians become furious when they are accused of being victimizers because they so deeply see themselves as victims. They do not realize that one can be a victim and victimizer at the same time and that the difference is less than a hair's breadth. Changing these self-perceptions would be helped dramatically if the violence could be stopped.

Unfortunately, many of those who seek to end the violence are quickly denounced by the Israel Lobby in the United States, by Israeli leaders, and by leaders of Jewish establishment organizations around the world as anti-Semites, self-hating Jews, or enemies of Israel—precisely mirroring the Hamas voices that see Palestinian efforts toward peace and reconciliation as selling out the Palestinian people.

CRITICISM OF ISRAEL IS NOT ANTI-SEMITISM

For most of Israel's existence until the emergence of an extreme right-wing government under Benjamin Netanyahu in the period after 2008, one of the most commendable aspects of Israeli democracy had been its tolerance of dissent. While Israeli television and radio have always tended to reflect the perspective of the government, Israeli newspapers have frequently reflected the intense debate that has always been a hallmark of Jewish culture. ("Two Jews, three opinions," the old Yiddish saying goes.) The ferocity of debate and mutual denunciations in the Israeli Knesset reflected the intense divisions about Israel's treatment of Palestinians within Israeli society and was not silenced. It was only in the last few years that the Knesset and the Israeli government have sought ways to intimidate, publicly discredit, or even silence groups like the New Israel Fund, B'Tselem, and other Israeli groups working for peace and human rights.

Until then, the debate was much more vigorous in Israel than was possible for peace-oriented Jews living outside Israel, who have long suffered from overt attempts to prevent free speech in the diaspora Jewish communities. To some extent, this stems from a self-policing. Jewish communities around the world have been fearful of reflecting divisions that might weaken the support of their own countries for the policies of Israel. So Jewish critics of Israeli policies have often been labeled "self-hating Jews" or even overt anti-Semites. Similarly, non-Jews who have entered into these debates have often found that expressing the slightest sympathy for the plight of Palestinians earned them the label of being "anti-Israel" from many diaspora Jews.

These charges have some credibility among Jews because of the Left's rather ambiguous history in regard to anti-Semitism. Karl Marx's 1844 essay "On the Jewish Question" cast "the Jew" as a symbol of what was worst in capitalist society; this continued and strengthened a long tradition in European countries of blaming the Jews for being both the most oppressive capitalists and also the most dangerous revolutionaries.

In 1991, I wrote a short book on this topic, *The Socialism of Fools: Anti-Semitism on the Left,* in which I summarized some of the information that is still not widely understood in some progressive circles about how the Left has ignored or sometimes even participated in anti-Semitic behavior. It even turned out that Jews themselves, seeking respectability within Western societies or in leftist circles, sometimes embraced (or more often, failed to challenge) these ideas and behavior. That the political Right has been far more enmeshed in compromises with or active sponsors of fascist anti-Semitism in the past 150 years has not been lost on diaspora Jews, who disproportionately give their votes to left-leaning political parties.

Yet Jewish suspicion of the Left has persisted. This has accelerated in the last thirty years as a growing percentage of diaspora Jews began to find their economic interests more aligned with the policies of right-wing parties than with the relative altruism of many on the Left. Though they've remained a solidly liberal/progressive voting block, some Jews' distrust of the Left has grown, particularly as the Left articulated criticisms of Israel that were lacking in nuance. (By the Left, I mean those involved in anti-war movements, human rights movements, civil rights movements, the liberal wing of the Democratic Party, the Green Party, and those who identify with the politics of publications like *The Nation, In These Times, The Progressive, Mother Jones,* and others.)

Nevertheless, the vast majority of Jewish and leftist critics of Israel in Western societies in the past thirty years are neither anti-Semitic nor "self-hating" Jews. Few Jews in the Left have encountered overt anti-Semitism from their non-Jewish colleagues. They've rarely encountered anyone on the Left who espouses conspiracy theories about Jews controlling the economy or the media, which have thrived in anti-Semitic rhetoric for the past hundred years. Nor do they find covert hostility to the Jewish community, Judaism, or the Jewish people. Overwhelmingly, what they do encounter is what they perceive to be legitimate anger at the policies of the State of Israel—anger that they themselves frequently share.

If at times Jews in these movements tend to be supercritical of Israel, it is most often because they feel a special responsibility to a country that consistently (and without ever seeking their democratic approval of this designation) calls itself "the state of the Jewish people." And when they have encountered what appeared to some to be anti-Semitism, they have found that most of their non-Jewish comrades felt similarly uncomfortable.

Religious Christians who are not part of the right wing's brainchild, the "Christian Zionist" movement, often find themselves under attack the moment they raise issues about the morality of Israeli policies. Jewish friends who are liberal or even progressive on every other issue under the sun will frequently and unexpectedly react with anger and hostility toward these criticisms; often, they suggest that the Christians involved might unconsciously be anti-Semitic.

For many of the most sensitive Christians, this criticism is enough to silence them. Well aware of the terrible way that Christian political parties, churches, and individuals either collaborated with or at least failed to defend Jews during the Holocaust, the most sensitive Christians often feel that they ought not challenge their Jewish friends when it comes to Israel. They might think: "Perhaps I really am ignorant on these issues? And do I have the moral standing to get involved in this super-contentious struggle?"

The upshot of this dynamic is that liberal or progressive Christians often try to avoid dealing with the Israel/Palestine issue, effectively abandoning those Jews who have taken the risk of challenging the dominant "Israel is always right" mantra in the Jewish community. I'm hoping that many Christians who read this book will spread the word that Jewish progressives are begging ethically sensitive Christians to get involved on the side of peace, justice, and love. You're welcome to use the approach I'll present in the next few chapters. You're also welcome to join the Network of Spiritual Progressives, our interfaith pro-peace and pro-justice movement. The message progressive Jews want ethically sensitive Christians to hear is this: "You are not being respectful or helpful to Jews by allowing those of us on the Jewish Left to have little Christian support while those on the Jewish Right get lots of Christian support. We've created interfaith organizations and invited you to join us. Please do so!"

Jewish critics of Israeli policies toward Palestinians in much of the post-1967 period have found themselves under increasing attacks by organizations or individuals in the Jewish community. The most prominent Jewish peace and reconciliation activists have frequently found themselves boycotted in the Jewish media, then heavily criticized when they brought their criticisms into mainstream media. Then even the mainstream media began to be attacked as "anti-Semitic." The *New York Times*, which has many Jewish journalists and is owned by a Jewish family, was dismissed by some in the Jewish world as a hotbed of "self-hating Jews." Similar accusations have been lobbed at the Israeli newspaper *Ha'aretz*.

Television news organizations that showed horrific footage of the damage done by Israeli attacks on Lebanon, the West Bank, and Gaza were similarly assaulted by Israeli lobby organizations and by campaigns of protesters insisting that the footage must have been doctored or misrepresented. The result was that over time major media became much more timid about presenting information that was unfavorable to the Israeli government. Major critics found themselves less able to present their message in the media, much less in the synagogues and community centers of the Jewish community.

I myself was told by the editor of one of the major Jewish newspapers that the owners had ordered that my op-eds no longer be printed. I was also told by the editor of a major American mainstream newspaper that he had been ordered by his publisher to not allow op-eds critical of Israeli policy. When critical comments were published, the media in question saw themselves as being "courageous," given the internal demands to stay away from anything that might incite more pressure from the pro-right-wing-Israel forces. (I do not use the word pro-Israel, since in my view many of those who criticize Israeli policies are just as pro-Israel as the right wingers who have tried to appropriate the title of being "pro-Israel.")

Diaspora critics of Israeli policies sometimes find themselves faced with serious threats to their careers or, among those who are most well known and outspoken, even their lives. Whether in a law firm, a medical practice, a university, a news organization, Hollywood, or American politics, many of those who question the morality of Israeli policies have come to believe that their well-being dictates that they hide these disagreements or risk serious loss to their careers. *Tikkun* was a widely known intellectual voice articulating these criticisms; as editor of *Tikkun*, I often found myself counseling or consoling academics, journalists, or other professionals who were facing this kind of challenge and pressure.

Sometimes, those who have achieved power in some other non-political realm can defend these attacks and even force the attackers onto the defensive. In the spring of 2011, the governing board of the City University of New York voted to deny an honorary degree to Pulitzer Prize winner Tony Kushner (author of the play "Angels in America") after one member of the board accused him of being anti-Israel. The outcry in the academic and artistic community about the stifling of free speech forced the board to reverse its decision. But when former U.S. president Jimmy Carter published a book suggesting that unless Israel changed its policies, it would slowly drift toward becoming an apartheid society in the West Bank, his reputation was seriously damaged in many circles by an assault from right-wing Zionists who portrayed him as either ignorant or anti-Semitic. I've heard this from many "middle of the road" Jews who never even bothered to read his book. This was despite his ongoing and quite remarkable work to promote human rights and the alleviation of poverty around the world. I've even been warned by some to not use his endorsement of this book, because doing so would automatically stop many in the Jewish world from reading it. If people with this level of fame and influence can be subject to abuse that actually has an impact, what chance do the rest of us have?

Go one level down in fame to the intellectuals, academics, and social-change activists who have given their creative energies to fighting for the human rights of Palestinians, and you will find right-wing Zionist campaigns against them. People like Noam Chomsky, Howard Zinn, Amira Hass, Uri Avnery, and former MK Avrum Burg have all faced abusive dismissals of their thinking and writing by people who have heard about their alleged anti-Semitism. Go one level down in fame from there to people in the media or academia who are not yet famous or economically secure, and you'll find immense pressure against them if they dare publicly criticize Israel. This pressure is often employment-threatening and is sufficient to keep many people who would agree with the pro-Israel, pro-Palestine perspective of this book to instead distance themselves from any involvement with peace activists or association with *Tikkun*.

In this sense, the anti-communist McCarthyite tactics of the 1950s have been given new life by the Israel lobby in the United States. All too many people have been intimidated by them. Many rabbis have told me privately that they agree with much of what they read in *Tikkun*, but would never dare suggest that their congregants subscribe. Nor would they use my books for study purposes or invite me to be a scholar-in-residence. They literally fear for their jobs. And I've had hundreds of communications or private sessions with non-Jewish as well as Jewish lawyers, city planners, architects, engineers, scientists, high-tech professionals, accountants, small business people, social workers, psychotherapists, school teachers, college professors, corporate and government bureaucrats, liberal candidates for office, and health care professionals who seek my professional counseling on how best to handle the tensions and implicit threats to their careers that arise in their workplaces should they dare to express their genuine feelings of concern about Israel and Palestine. Many of these people have a hard time reconciling their sense of Jews as liberal and fair-minded on almost every topic under the sun—except Israel.

REFLECTING ON THE HISTORY: FROM THEN UNTIL NOW

What I have tried to do in presenting this narrative is show that there is a way to understand this history that avoids the exclusive blaming of one side or the other. Both sides have cocreated the struggle between Israel and Palestine. Each side has acted in ways that are cruel and deny the humanity of the other. And each side has a legitimate narrative that feels persuasive until one tries to see the same events from the perspective of the other.

In the next section of the book, I give specific strategic suggestions for moving from understanding to an actual strategy to bring peace. I emphasize the centrality of overcoming the blame game—because that is a first step in the long march to peace.

It is my firm belief that lasting peace and reconciliation are not only possible but also likely to be achieved in the next twenty years, possibly sooner. The hunger for a world of caring and kindness is a more powerful force than the desire to hold onto anger and nurse old pains. True, it will take the courage to forget—to not focus attention on all the wounds and all the disgraceful actions of the other. There are enough on both sides to give adequate ammunition to those who wish to perpetuate conflict for the next hundred years.

The new consciousness needed will take the discipline and hard work of a generation of healers (medical, psychological, and spiritual), and it will take a sustained challenge to the ethos of cynicism that pervades the media, intellectual life, and all too many religious institutions. But it will happen, and when it does, a new generation will look back on this period and say, "What could those people have been thinking?"

I'm writing this book at least in part to let our own generation and future generations know that there are many people who are thinking, even in the darkest of moments, that love and kindness and generosity will prevail. We will testify to that possibility even when doing so earns us the scorn of the "savvy," the anger of the partisans, and the disdain of the powerful. And that is what it means in practical terms to believe in Spirit or God or Highest Power or however you feel comfortable referring to the Force of Healing and Transformation—the belief that there is a force in the universe that makes possible the transformation from that which is to that which can and should be.

That power is in each of us (or as the religious tradition puts it, we are created in the image of God). If we can overcome our egos enough to find ways to work together effectively, and if we can withstand the anger that gets directed at us when we believe in the possibility of a world based on love, justice, and peace, then we will be able to make a real contribution—right now, in this time and place—to the process by which the world will be healed. Let's turn now to a discussion of how that could happen.

Chapter Seven

HEALING THE TRAUMAS OF
BOTH PEOPLES

IN A REGION AS DAMAGED AS ISRAEL/PALESTINE, a true peace agreement achieved through nonviolent strategies will depend on healing the trauma in the psychological and spiritual life of both peoples who live in that land. My goal is to help everyone realize that we are not really fully human until we are able to humanize the Other. Every time we dehumanize the other, we lose our own humanity. But this understanding has little traction in the minds of people who are psychologically or spiritually wounded. Without being aware of it, those discussing the Middle East often think and speak from a psychology of trauma.

PSYCHOTHERAPY FOR SOCIETAL PATHOLOGY

Throughout this book, I've avoided trying to present either side in the Israel/Palestine conflict as primarily psychologically impaired. Instead I have tried to show that many of the choices made on each side of this struggle make sense when considered from the standpoint of each side's assumptions about the world.

Yet I've also made it clear that the inability to see the Other's point of view is best-understood in terms of what I consider to be a social form of Post-Traumatic Stress Disorder (PTSD). Evolutionary history produced in many animals a fight-or-flight survival response to both perceived and real-world conditions of danger. For humans this included the perception of grave bodily harm, imminent death, or intolerable oppression. The body goes into a hyper-alert state and allows us to manifest momentary strength and resilience that we often didn't realize we had available. Once the danger is past, the body relaxes and returns to its normal condition.

PTSD occurs when for whatever reasons the individual is unable to get back to that normal condition; the person remains in a somewhat decreased but nevertheless heightened state of attention to danger and mobilization of body and mind. The person perceives the dangers as still being present when they are not, or interprets present dangers through the lens of past dangers that were far greater; the person hence imagines, misunderstands, or exaggerates the threats in the situation he or she is facing. Often the person may perceive her or himself to be in the same situation as the original trauma or may feel as if the current situation is so close to the original trauma as to be indistinguishable. Often the person may unconsciously participate in recreating dynamics that do in fact resemble the original trauma. While this may occur in normal life to some degree for everyone, we call it PTSD when this occurs frequently and when it distorts the individual's perceptions in ways that lead him or her to make irrational or self-destructive assessments of his or her life situation or impair his or her ability to function in the family, workplace, or society. What differentiates PTSD from other psychological categories is that here we acknowledge that the original trauma was rooted in a real situation of danger and not primarily a product of an internal distortion of perception or feelings. Most frequently that original trauma was rooted in some act of violence or abuse.

Though the discussion in this chapter emerges from the Middle East struggle, the strategy ideas here are relevant to any society in which a social form of PTSD makes it difficult for people to rationally confront the challenges that they face. I see this particularly in the post-9/11 politics of the United States in dealing with our economic and political challenges. But it applies equally when recognizing that the entire global community is mostly in denial about the ecological disasters the human race has been bringing upon itself in the twenty-first century.

I believe it is helpful to see both Israeli and Palestinian behavior as a product of PTSD. Because I lived and conducted psychological research in Israel, I'm better able to discuss how PTSD plays out among Jews than among Palestinians, so my analysis in this chapter gives more attention to Israeli Jews than to Israeli, West Bank, or Gazan Palestinians.

It is striking to me that the Zionists who built Israel put a great deal of focus on "negating the Disapora," insisting that diasporic conditions created a psychologically inhibited life for the Jewish people by making them dependent on the goodwill of non-Jews. It isolated them from their neighbors and pushed them into conditions of extreme physical and emotional vulnerability, alertness, and fear. Yet the policies of the State of Israel appear to be the "return of the repressed." The policies recreate the very reality that Zionists sought to avoid and escape.

Israel has made itself dependent on the support of the United States, which not only provides first-rate military hardware and economic assistance in the billions, but also runs interference for Israel at the United Nations. (The United States consistently vetoes UN resolutions, supported by most countries of the world, that challenge Israel's Occupation.) Israelis have achieved by far the strongest military force in the Middle East. Yet they see themselves as vulnerable. Perhaps they unconsciously remember that this very strategy of depending on the kings and lords of feudal Europe and Islamic countries, rather than seeking alliances with the people of those countries, eventually backfired in horrific ways. For the average Israeli, this paradox is their reality. It consumes the national consciousness with never-ending emotional contradictions: anxiety and bravado, feeling the strongest in one moment and the weakest in the next.

Israel has chosen occupation over peace year after year by refusing to deal with the consequences of barring Palestinians from returning to their homes and by refusing to accept terms for a peace settlement that would bring normalization to their situation. (This includes embracing the terms of the Geneva Accord, which would have ensured Israeli security while returning to full Palestinian control 95 percent of pre-1967 Palestine and exchanging the other 5 percent for land of equal economic, political, and historic value.) Israel now suffers the vulnerability that faces any occupier anywhere on the globe.

Israel continues to make itself a global pariah; it is perceived in many countries around the world as the sidekick and lapdog for American global imperialism. Jews in the Middle Ages thought that their path to security lay in accepting the role of being the "public face" of the nobility in relationship to the peasantry; in so doing they instead became the target of popular anger at a system in which they were relatively powerless players. Now Israelis and Jews find themselves in a similar situation on a global scale.

Some will argue that Israel has no choice. Yet what they fail to note is that this is not a viable choice either, because even if identification with the largest imperial power offers the Jews temporary protection, it simultaneously increases hostility among the peoples of many other countries and creates the precondition for future persecution of Jews. As the United States global empire begins to decline, the anger that Jews generated through their

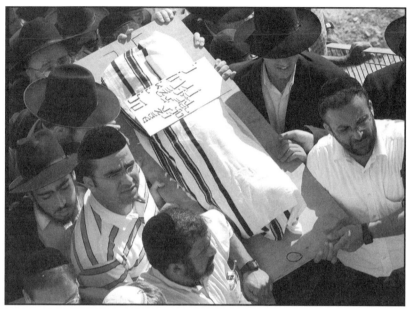

Rusty Stewart

Relatives carry the tiny body of eleven-month-old Shmuel Zargari on August 20, 2003. The infact was one of twenty people killed in a suicide bombing at Jerusalem's Western Wall.

blind support of Israel, combined with their role as public cheerleaders for banking and investment firms, is likely to intensify and once again put Jews in danger.

Psychotherapists have witnessed similar behavior in our clients. It is not uncommon to see survivors of trauma or abuse creating relationships in which they psychically replicate the circumstances of their original traumas. Psychoanalytic theory describes how humans are unconsciously drawn to attempt to redo the situation with the hope of a better outcome, thanks to a mastery that was not there the last time. Indeed, that may work if the patient consciously and intentionally enters the circumstance with adequate support to help them rework their internalized self image. They may emerge with a new, positively modified sense of self-worth and empowerment, and may consequently make fundamentally different choices from those they made when facing the trauma the first time.

Sadly, this making of new choices is not what is happening for Israelis. All too often they experience themselves as having far less power and security than they have. They thereby make public political choices as though they were still weak and vulnerable. I've explored these dynamics in my book *Surplus Powerlessness* (Humanities Press, 1991). While some Palestinians and some of their supporters around the world see Jews' perceived powerlessness as merely a cynical stratagem used by a powerful oppressor to appear to the world as the victim rather than the victimizer, most of us who have lived in Israel and who interact daily with right-wing American Jews know that their fears are real. They are the internalized consequence of a traumatic and painful psychological history, and they call out for compassionate treatment rather than scorn.

Renowned British sociologist Zygmunt Bauman makes a related point in an article in *Tikkun* entitled "The Holocaust's Life as a Ghost—Lingering Psychological Effects" (reprinted in the *Tikkun Reader: Twentieth Anniversary*). Bauman argues that— seeking perhaps to join the "aristocracy of victimhood"—some Jews today who were not themselves even alive at the time of the Holocaust unconsciously strive to assume the moral legitimacy of being victims. As a result they see others around them, particularly the Palestinians, as potential slaughterers, and these "assumed-would-be-persecutors are guilty in advance, guilty of being seen as inclined or able to engage in another genocide."

Yet as Bauman suggests, it is this claim of hereditary victimhood even by Jews who were not alive at the time of the Holocaust and who grew up in a time when Jews had a relatively greater degree of power that gives a sense of meaning to the lives of many Jews. So tens of thousands of American Jews move to the West Bank settlements where they live in beautiful houses with green grass and swimming pools; they are surrounded by barbed wire to keep out their angry Palestinian neighbors whose land has been appropriated to create these settlements and whose water, which is needed for basic family needs, is now diverted. In this situation, settlers certainly can claim a vulnerability and an objective basis for fear of these neighbors.

Why would people who had not themselves been the victims of the original trauma seek to recreate that trauma for themselves? Were Jews feeling left out as liberals and progressives began to valorize the oppressed (women, gays, immigrants, etc.)? Or, as psychologist David Glick suggested to me, is it perhaps a way of unconsciously identifying with our ancestors who perished in the Holocaust and thus continuing a relationship with them out of some combination of loyalty and survivor guilt? That way some Israelis (and some Jews who move from Brooklyn to the West Bank) can, on one hand, share their ancestors' suffering; at the same time, they can prevent themselves from becoming victims by mastering the danger through aggression and power. Hence they put themselves in a dangerous situation but deal with it differently, thus transforming themselves into active choosers of their fate.

Jews have never fully psychologically and spiritually worked through the tragedy, pain, and humiliation of 1,800 years of exile culminating in the Holocaust. In part because of the need to find a homeland for hundreds of thousands of survivors after the Holocaust, and in part because Zionist ideology sought the power they believed was needed to survive and despised the powerlessness of the European ghetto existence, the psychic energy and focus of intention that was needed to go into mourning was never created.

From this Jewish perspective, we have never completed the psychological work needed to recover from our profound experience of humiliation and suffering so that we can instead experience righteous indignation at anyone who turns the powerless Other into a victim. This may be part of the reason that the new addition to the Jewish calendar, Holocaust Memorial Day, is called the day recalling "Shoah and Gvura" (Holocaust and Strength/Courage); mourning without jumping to the category of courage and strength, really allowing ourselves to feel deep grief and powerlessness, seemed too emotionally dangerous and too out of sync with the new mythology of Jewish power promoted by the Zionists. Many Jews who obsessively talk about the Holocaust have never actually allowed themselves to feel the pain, to grieve fully, and then to be able to heal from it.

Carrying that burden of pain has led to some very self-destructive behavior both for Israeli Jews and for American Jews—behavior that has begun to recreate a world of hostility toward Jews. And while many Jews respond by saying, "nothing new there—they always hated us," the truth is that to the extent that the people of the world accept the Zionist claim that Israel is the major contemporary manifestation of the Jewish people and hear Jews around the world saying "amen" to that claim, they end up becoming angry at Jews for Israeli government actions that would anger them no matter who was doing them, Jews or non-Jews.

My colleague Peter Gabel, in his *Tikkun* magazine article "The Meaning of the Holocaust: Social Alienation and the Infliction of Human Suffering," argues that the paranoid sense of meaning described by Bauman is a special case of a deeper search for meaning that is largely frustrated in most societies:

> That need for meaning emerges from a desire
> that is at the heart of our very social existence—
> the desire for a mutual recognition through
> which we become fully present to each other as
> social beings in connection, fully confirmed in
> the relation Martin Buber called "I and Thou."

In the un-alienated social existence to which we
aspire, meaningfulness is the realization, through
a potentially infinite number of particular
cultural embodiments, of the I and Thou of
mutual recognition. That is why movements
for social justice are inherently meaningful—as
they 'rise up,' these movements generate the very
experience of becoming present-to-each-other
through a confirming recognition that grounds
the call for correction of injustice, which is always
manifested as a denial of this I-Thou relation in a
particular historical context.

Because we have not yet achieved a society that validates this
yearning, every time we reveal ourselves as seeking this deeper
connection, we simultaneously reveal our own vulnerability and
set ourselves up for rejection and humiliation. We construct what
Gabel and I call "pseudo-communities" (our nation, our race, our
corporation, our football or baseball team) in which we momentarily allow ourselves to experience ourselves as part of something larger. We hope thereby to escape the feeling of emptiness
and hurt that might come were we to reveal (to ourselves as well
as to others) how alienated we are from our deepest desires. So
we cling to these constructed groups even though they embody
some level of phoniness because of their refusal to seek real human connection and their willingness to substitute superficial
forms of connection (like fundamentalist religious or ultranationalist beliefs) because these are the best outcomes we believe
can be achieved. After the patriotic parade, the public celebration
of our race, the holiday partying of our corporation, the victory
celebration of our local team ("We won! We are number one!"),
we return to lives that are still governed by the dog-eat-dog logic
of the capitalist marketplace. The "we" that we had celebrated

disappears into the competitive and often unsupportive realities of daily life in advanced industrial societies.

Yet, Gabel points out, our deeper desire for loving, unalienated connections with others is always in danger of "breaking through" into consciousness. The terror of reexperiencing humiliation leads us to project onto an external Other (the "enemy") a set of negative views about who they are, or to treat them in ways that are mechanical and leave little space for genuine encounter—lest we make ourselves vulnerable to them and their potential rejection of us. As Gabel concludes, "The ethical call that the future makes upon the present, that God's universe makes upon its current manifestation, is to strive to become present to the Other as a Thou and to make visible the unity and sacredness of all Being."

When psychotherapists see clients who are acting self-destructively, their task is to help them figure out why this is happening and then help the clients feel sufficiently safe and understood so that they will try different behaviors that are healthier and more life-affirming.

Usually, psychotherapy clients make a voluntary choice for therapy because they know that in some way or another their lives are not working and they need help. Or they are so self-destructive that others have locked them in a mental health facility and they are forced to accept help (not something I advocate except in the case of suicidal or homicidal activity). But that doesn't work when a whole society or nation needs psychological healing. We can't incarcerate a society into a hospital, and its members are usually in total denial about the need for society-wide therapy. What do we do then?

This, of course, is a dilemma for all liberals and progressives as we face the far more self-destructive behavior of Western societies; they proceed to destroy the life-support systems of the planet while ignoring the pleas of the scientific community to reverse the damage already done, and they continue to engage in wars and economic systems that generate hatred, anger, and revenge. There is little hope for solving the world's environmental crisis as long as we in the advanced industrial societies and emerging societies like China and India are unable to recognize that our well-being depends on the well-being of everyone else on the planet. We need to approach each other in a spirit of caring and generosity. Without this, no one is going to be willing to engage in the sacrifices needed to transform our global economic arrangements in ways that replace the frenetic commitment to "growth" with a commitment to genuinely protecting the planet, even at the price of reducing our level of consumption. This will not happen unless we can stop seeing ourselves through the distorted lens of past traumas.

SPLITTING

A common way that those who suffer from PTSD protect themselves from the pain that they've experienced is the process called "splitting." Faced with feelings of fear, abandonment, and shame for not having received the respect and caring due to valued human beings, many people split their perceptions of self or other into two parts. The parts of the self that are perceived as good are held onto and sometimes even romanticized or seen as larger than they really are; the parts of the self or a valued other that are perceived as "bad" are split off, disassociated from the self or valued other, and then projected onto some other being who is perceived as being the embodiment of bad or evil. The person cannot recognize that which is good and valuable about this Other. Though this dynamic is very complex and would require a separate book to fully unpack, a short summary follows.

Children born into psychologically damaged families or into groups that have been systematically degraded by the dominant culture (e.g., Jews, Palestinians, people of color living in a pre-dominantly white society, women, homosexuals and transsexu-als, people living under occupation, working-class or poor people living in a "meritocratic" society that blames them for their social or economic status, etc.) tend to lose contact with what is most beautiful and holy about themselves. They internalize negative views of themselves that have been transmitted to them by par-ents (who have themselves lost contact with what is most beautiful about themselves), teachers, friends, and the dominant culture of the society. Unable to see themselves as beautiful manifestations of the divine, they develop a core inner belief that they are being treated poorly by others because they somehow deserve that, ei-ther because of their presumed inadequacy or because they have done something bad. This self-punishing feeling is difficult to live with, so they then develop a compensatory external personality in which they attempt to cover up the "bad self" that they perceive themselves to be with a good self. They present this good self to themselves and the world even though they don't really believe that that good self is their true, deepest reality.

When, however, the troubling bad self that they have tried to repress threatens to break through into consciousness, they split that part of themselves from their external personality and project the bad self onto some other person or group. Their own person or group becomes the embodiment of the good self, and the bad self or parts of self that they actually believe to be who they "really are" are now externalized onto some evil Other that can be denounced, fought against, punished, or even killed. It is important to understand that this splitting is held onto because the person or group involved needs to do this in order to ward off the feeling that it is they themselves who are bad. So it is never sufficient to break through this dynamic by simply tell-ing them, "Hey, you are wrong about the alleged evil Other (e.g., Palestinians, Israelis, homosexuals, immigrants, people from blue states, people from red states, religious people, atheists, fundamentalists, liberals, etc.), and let me show you why they really are not so bad."

That information is useful, but it cannot be assimilated as long as the people engaged in splitting need this defense to not feel terrible about themselves. Instead, what is needed is to develop a public awareness of the fact that everyone on the planet is fundamentally a decent person; their distortions are a product of complex psychological, social, economic, and religious factors that have kept them from being the fullest embodiment of the goodness that pervades the universe. This is what we mean by saying that people are created in the image of God and are fundamentally deserving of respect. So part of the task of healing from PTSD is to help people reconnect with their most beautiful and holy parts that they've not believed in. But this is no easy task.

In order for them to get to the point of really believing that they are deserving of love and capable of it, they need to be able to recognize and overcome this tendency toward splitting and connect to a more dimensional understanding of reality. From that perspective, they will be able to see what is really and truly beautiful about themselves.

Those of us who want to bring healing to the world have to be attuned to this dynamic and develop mass psychological interventions that facilitate the overcoming of splitting. And there will be no one strategy or methodology that works for everyone, because each strategy will speak to some in a given population and be less effective with others.

The good news is this: when people can actually see how they've come to unfairly blame themselves for the distortions in their lives and recognize how they have developed a toolbox of psychological defenses that inhibit their true capacities, it becomes very easy for them to see that same dynamic working in others. They can unravel their own previously existing tendencies to use splitting as a defense.

Once people are able to acknowledge that they have some hurtful and destructive tendencies but also some very loving and caring tendencies, and once they can accept that this complexity is true about themselves and about everyone else, they can begin to see previous enemies as people who have lived through lots of pain, have not yet overcome that pain, and hence are momentarily stuck in distortions. And our task as healers seeking peace and reconciliation is to help people make this transition—starting with ourselves.

Needless to say, this is a difficult challenge. Moreover, we will face enormous resistance from those who are most distorted in these respects. They will dismiss attempts to educate people about these issues as psychobabble or as totalitarian mind control. Unconsciously fearful of being pushed to confront the terror inside themselves, they will do everything they can to demean those who seek society-wide transformations of the pain that keeps people from recognizing their common bonds with one another.

THE ISRAELI FEAR OF BEING A FREIER

Freier (pronounced fry-er) is a popular pejorative word used by Israelis to describe people who are suckers, fools, easily taken advantage of, easily manipulated, or easily dominated. In "Thou shalt not be a freier," a 2006 article published in the Israeli newspaper *Ha'aretz*, Shahar Ilan points to Israeli researchers who have noted the way the fear of being a freier plays a larger role in Israeli culture than in many other cultures. She writes:

How has such a great fear of being a freier
developed in Israel, of all places? [Dr. Linda-
Renee Bloch of Bar-Ilan University] explains that
this is due, among other reasons, to a desire to
be free of the image of the Jew in exile. She says
there are five attributes of Israeli character that
come together to create the culture of "just don't
be a freier": a particularly strong ego and sense of
honor, avoidance of law and rules, individualism
without responsibility, competition, and
machismo. There are some people, she adds, who
are prepared to kill in order not to come out as
freiers. She cites examples of murders for purely
negligible reasons, like a fight over dogs or an
argument over a lounge chair on the beach.

A more sympathetic reading of this reality, I believe, would
see the excessive fear of being a freier as a manifestation of the
impact of what I've described as cultural PTSD among Jews in
general and Israelis in particular.

Avoiding being seen as a freier may be a universal dynamic—
it's certainly prevalent in American teens and many adults—but
it is particularly intense in Israel where the cultural assumption
is that it was this freier consciousness that allowed Jews to trust
their non-Jewish neighbors enough to believe that they would be
safe in Europe. This delusion cost the lives of millions of Jews.
So the freier toughness and cynicism may be a defense, a protection, and a counter to the shame of being descended from a people who throughout much of the past 1,800 years were victims
of abuse, theft, rape, and murder. The shame that Jewish men
could not defend their own wives or children often gets internalized into feelings of being weak and fundamentally inadequate;
Israel and Zionism erected a counterculture that celebrated the

Flickr/ISM

A Gazan family sits together in the rubble of their home on January 20, 2009. Their home was destroyed during Israel's Operation Cast Lead.

cynical, tough guy who would never be vulnerable again to this "ghetto mentality."

This has been the repeated history of the Jews over thousands of years; it should come as no surprise that the result is a deep "never again" mentality that carries not just the pain of the Holocaust, but also the pain of being the target of historical anti-Semitism around the world. And Palestinians, in sometimes describing themselves as "the Jews of the Middle East," have at times written their national story in ways that similarly portray themselves as powerless victims.

These psychodynamics enable both Israelis and Palestinians to close their ears to the reasonable parts of peace offers made by the other side and to ignore the large majorities on both sides who want nothing more than to live in peace and pursue their own lives without worrying about violence. And it is these psychodynamics that lead so many to show how "tough," "realistic," and "powerful" they are by rejecting any compromise that requires trusting the humanity of the Other.

These kinds of issues, of course, are not unique to Israelis and Palestinians; they are universal in a world where the dynamics of fear and domination have become "common sense." They shaped the recent rise of the Tea Party in American politics and the strange situation in which middle-income working people vote for the very politicians who have undermined their economic well-being and sense of solidarity with each other. These dynamics have spread worldwide and often seem almost intractable. How could one possibly hope to change them?

Socio-Cultural PTSD Explains Why Imposed Solutions Will Backfire

In Chapter Eight I will propose a variety of possible political solutions. But the problem remains: if people are so traumatized that they cannot make a rational choice in their own self-interest, what can the rest of the world do to help? I talk of trauma here not to give Israel a pass on the inhumanity of the Occupation or to give Palestine a pass on the inhumanity of terror against civilians, but to recognize that we need something that transcends the normal limits of politics as understood in the West. We need to put to rest the debate about which side is the righteous victim and which side is the oppressive aggressor.

The typical mindset of the peace movements in Israel, Palestine, and the United States is that once a political solution is achieved, healing can come as a second or third step in the process. This would be ideal. However, given the foreseeable conditions of the next ten years, simply waiting for that political solution to happen or expecting it to emerge in negotiations with the current leaders is likely to lead to greater misery for both Israelis and Palestinians.

Many otherwise peace-oriented people believe some form of coercion is needed to push both sides into a rational agreement to end the violent part of the struggle and make it possible for psychological and spiritual therapies to be applied. We at *Tikkun* have suggested that after a peace settlement, a truth and reconciliation process should be created, modeled on what partially worked in South Africa but with elements specific to the Israeli and Palestinian situation. Such a truth and reconciliation process would make a huge amount of sense. That process, however, took hold only in South Africa after the world and the internal militant struggle of the black African majority had convinced the Afrikaners that they had to give up apartheid. So in the case of Israel/Palestine, could coercion work?

The toughest kind of coercion would be this: the United States and other major powers, through either the UN or an independent coalition, tell Israel and Palestine that they have 120 days to accept the specific terms of a two-state solution (Chapter Eight details my proposed solution) or the world will impose an economic boycott and a no-fly zone. They would commit to preventing any goods from arriving from any neighboring states or from the air or sea until both sides have accepted and begun to implement the peace agreement. An Israeli government faced with this threat would certainly fall. Israelis would demand and win a new election, which might put into power the peace forces that have advocated a generous and openhearted two-state solution. Such an election could lead the Palestinian people to likewise embrace this solution.

Though I believe this to be a terrible option, based on the very violence and coercion that I've opposed when it has been used by Israel against Palestinians, others have argued that this path is rational and might even work.

But everything I know about PTSD leads me to believe the opposite. The last thing you want to do with a PTSD client is to restimulate the original trauma. This coercion strategy would do exactly that—accentuate the experiences of powerlessness and humiliation that both Israelis and Palestinians have been attempting to ward off for many decades.

When dealing with extreme cases of PTSD that manifest in murderous or suicidal intentions, we therapists sometimes have to hospitalize the patient so that he does not destroy himself or others. But when it comes to a full society, there is no societal hospital to which people can be sent.

The moment that Israel perceives an imminent threat of military or economic coercion, the most extreme elements in the Israeli population, who unfortunately have been growing in political strength in the past decade, will almost surely start to draw upon the Masada complex. Let me explain.

When young Israelis reach the age of eighteen, they are all required to enter the IDF (except Israeli Arabs and those Jews who are part of an ultra-Orthodox community that has bargained its way out of army service). For many decades, one of the rituals of induction to the IDF had been to climb the steep hills leading to Masada, the ancient fortress where the Jewish revolutionary extremists who rebelled against Rome in 67-70 CE found refuge and later launched new attacks on the occupying Roman forces. When the Romans finally breached the fortress to conquer these zealots in 73 CE, they found close to one thousand bodies—the scene of a mass suicide.

The story may be legendary, but its implicit message has been central to the Zionist ideology of the State of Israel: "Unlike those diaspora Jews who failed to resist and were marched into the gas chambers of Europe singing pious religious songs about the coming of the messiah, we, the new breed of Jews, will never again give up our state. If necessary, we will follow the example of the Masada Jews, who killed themselves rather than let others kill them."

You cannot understand Israel without understanding how deeply this message is embedded in the collective unconscious. And we have to acknowledge that the attraction of Masada as a national narrative reflects a deep respect for the courage and commitment that those ancient Jews manifested by killing themselves. Their act turned them from passive victims into active choosers of their fate.

Of course, not all Israelis think the same way. The upside of the narcissistic culture of global capitalism, with its emphasis on the fulfillment of individual desires, is that it serves as an important corrective to the mass suicidal message of Masada. Yet there are still plenty of people in Israel who have absorbed the Masada complex into their deepest being—such that if faced with a perceived return to the vulnerability of statelessness, they might choose the path of Masada rather than surrender to the overwhelming power of a global coalition. In the process, the world might face grave dangers from a suicidal people with military and nuclear capacities of potentially great destructiveness. While most Israelis would not follow a destructive path, they'd find it difficult to constrain a militant minority who articulated the fear of the majority that the Jewish people were about to once again face a dangerous period of total powerlessness. The dangers to the world, not just to the Middle East, would be immense. So coercion is not a wise strategy to pursue for those who seek peace.

A cautionary note: there remains a danger in always trying to understand and sympathize with this Jewish trauma. The danger is that we are unwittingly strengthening a kind of narcissistic entitlement. This gets Jews and Israelis off the hook for confronting their own aggression and developing a self-awareness that they split off and project onto Palestinians, Arabs, or all non-Jews in order to continue to see themselves as the eternal victim. David Glick put it this way: we risk getting into one of these vicious cycles in which Israelis and Palestinians get caught up in a kind of mutual projective identification. Each denies their own aggression toward the other and then acts in ways that elicit the projection. This then confirms the projection while confirming their own innocence.

Glick articulates why, in my own view, it is completely appropriate to make moral judgments about the Occupation and to not fall into some form of moral relativism.

Each year at Rosh Hashanah, the beginning of the ten days of repentance, we publish articles in *Tikkun* and host presentations in Beyt Tikkun's Synagogue-Without-Walls about how to repent for the sins of the Jewish people in supporting U.S. and Israeli policies that are immoral. We encourage our Palestinian friends to make similar repentance for their sins, and we encourage all Americans to repent for the sins of cooperation with a global system of economic and military domination. We do not believe that PTSD or any other psychological explanation should lead us to abandon ethical categories. The Jewish concept of sin, *cheyt*, denotes an arrow going off course and missing the mark; it does not denote some fundamental evil lurking inside ourselves. Similarly, repentance in Jewish terms really means getting ourselves back onto course so that we can be the fullest expression of the goodness we are at our core. However, it is important not to allow psychological understanding to deflect our realization that certain behaviors are simply unacceptable; we must give attention to rooting them out of our individual or societal lives.

Yet my larger point here is that when dealing with a societal PTSD, ethical categories, while useful, valid, and not to be abandoned, must be balanced with a strategy of healing that does not rely on knocking people over the head with our perception of what they are doing wrong. The goal is not to be "right" and powerless, but to actually change things in the world. This requires a psychological and spiritual sophistication that has been sorely lacking in the social change movements of the past hundred years. Jessica Benjamin suggested to me that we need to change the question, "How can I win?" Instead we must ask, "What is the right thing to do that has the most chance of being good for all concerned?" This kind of thinking requires a context of safety, and one of my central themes is that any viable peace movement must create a sense of safety that allows such a shift to occur. To go this path, the movement itself must feel safe to its own members.

So How Can We Work With Societies Suffering From PTSD?

I've spent my lifetime working on this question, and what I know is how little we all know about this, and yet how very urgent it is. It's urgent, in part, because this same question is central to the advanced industrial societies and those who are seeking to become like them (India and China, for example). Before it's too late, we can overcome our planet-destroying notions about the value of endless growth, expansion, consumption, newness, more, bigger, better, and still more! These values are rooted in spiritual deprivation and the heritage of material deprivation that have combined in the modern world to produce a whole lot of hurtful behaviors that need to be stopped. The only way those behaviors are going to be stopped is if we can help societies heal from the kind of sociocultural PTSD I have described. Even knowing that this is the central question facing us as a human race would be, I believe, a huge advance toward finding a solution.

So let me share with you some of what I've learned that may be helpful. There is no single correct approach to healing, either on the individual or the societal level. In the thirty-three years since I became licensed to do psychotherapy and in the sixteen years that I've also been a pulpit rabbi, I've learned that formulas and theories are helpful, but only when mixed with a whole lot of understanding of the particular details of the person, couple, family, organization, or society. That's why in this book I felt it necessary to tell the stories of each side, rather than rush into strategies of healing.

And this leads me to suggest that a societal PTSD has to be dealt with on two different levels simultaneously. On one hand, we need a massive campaign of consciousness-raising to challenge the dominant worldview that people care only for themselves and will never be there for each other. That campaign is not unlike the campaigns that were waged relatively successfully in the past fifty years against sexism and patriarchal views of women, against homophobia, and against racism. These struggles are not yet won, but have achieved amazing success. On the other hand, we need individual and small group interventions to help people, one by one, overcome the depression and splitting that keep people trapped in self-and-other-destructive patterns of behavior. On this level, the first thing we need to do is create circumstances in which people can feel safe to talk freely about the traumas that they've experienced to someone who will help them feel safe and genuinely heard and who will acknowledge their pain.

Please keep in mind that PTSD is based on a trauma that has led people to not trust, to not feel safe, to not believe that they really could ever have a world that is based on love and generosity. This pathogenic belief must be gently and lovingly challenged and dismantled from their psychic structure. A first step in the process of healing is to give people a chance to tell their stories out loud to others who listen without judgment and sympathetically urge them to fully allow themselves to grieve over their inner pain.

Some elements of societal PTSD can be linked to specific events that have happened to a given society, race, or national/ethnic group (e.g., the Crusades, the Holocaust, the Nakba, the dropping of the atomic bomb, the prelude to the 1967 War, 9/11, the start of the Iraq War, the Second Intifada). Still other elements may be deeply embedded in a given economic, social, or political structure that gets reexperienced every day. The latter may include the trauma of being separated from our own connection to God or Spirit and instead forced (by our family, our psychological and social conditioning, our jobs, etc.) to experience ourselves as alone and separate from everyone else, cut off from the spiritual source of our being and the deepest truth that we are manifestations of God.

This trauma may be all the more marked when individuals have faced abuse from parents, relatives, teachers, bosses, spouses, neighbors, random strangers, or even our grown children as we age. Similarly, we may daily reexperience the trauma of aloneness in a society that sets people against each other in an economy that encourages some to "win" at the expense of many others "losing." Or we may experience a deep depression as we internalize what we perceive to be the almost inevitable death of the life-support systems of the planet; we may experience ourselves and everyone we know as powerless to stop the environmental crisis manifested in, but not exhausted by, global warming, the destruction of so many species, and the conjunction of the seemingly inexorable rising of the global human population and the decrease in adequate food and water supplies. These larger issues provide a background condition that may intensify the forms of PTSD I've been discussing in this chapter.

So a central part of the strategy to overcome PTSD is to build a cultural and political movement that helps people believe in the possibility of a world of love and generosity, of human efficacy, of global and environmental healing, of reconnection to our highest selves—a goal that, if achieved, would not only help transform the dynamics in Israel/Palestine. It would also empower ordinary people like you and me to restore democracy and take power away from the oligarchs and global corporate powers that continue to pollute our food, air, water, and earth. It would enable us to form the kinds of social movements necessary to build a rational economy and political life that served the interests of all.

We already have wonderful ideas about what such arrangements could look like (for starters, read the Spiritual Covenant with America at www.spiritualprogressives.org). What we lack is a populace that believes in itself enough to engage in the struggle necessary to create such a world. And since I am addressing a need that goes far beyond the need to embrace Israel/Palestine, I'm going to talk here in terms that are equally relevant for healing the largest pathology of the Western world: our inability to trust other people and know that they would be capable and desirous of building a world together in which both their needs and our needs could be met. In this world, we would be both safe and capable of realizing our fullest human capacities.

For dealing with individual pathologies, Western societies have trained a corps of psychotherapists. But they do not yet have a corps of society-oriented therapists—let's call them social healers or tikkunistas, based on the Hebrew word tikkun (healing, repair, and transformation). Ideally, we'd have universities training such anti-war therapist professionals, credentialing them, and sending out hundreds of thousands of such people each year to work on the traumas that distort American, Israeli, and most other societies in the world.

Unfortunately, there is no one to employ such people because those who have the power and money in this society are not seeking tikkun; they are seeking to preserve the status quo. We who seek to build peace, justice, and environmental sanity in our world need to create a corps of such people who can do this social healing work on a voluntary basis. As the baby boomers reach retirement age, this may be one important way that they can contribute to the world—becoming tikkunistas. Similarly, we've seen that students, when sufficiently motivated, can find time in their lives to become involved in social change work. As we saw during the 2008 presidential campaign, tens of thousands of us ordinary people got mobilized to donate our time, even taking off weeks or months from work, to participate in a campaign in which we deeply believed. We at the Network of Spiritual Progressives will offer such trainings to help prepare people to do this kind of work, and we will need thousands of other institutions and organizations to be similarly involved in providing such training. If you are one such person or know of others who are, please let me know!

But let's not mystify this whole process. Anyone who wishes to become involved as a societal healer and who shares the commitment to a New Bottom Line of love, caring, kindness, and generosity can make an important contribution to this transformation of culture in a very powerful way: by publicly and consistently affirming your commitment to build a world of love and caring, by refusing to accept the notion that less than that is acceptable, and by supporting the projects, movements, political candidates, and efforts on a local and national level that explicitly talk about these goals and validate them in the eyes of others.

Still, the more we can have a corps of people who have received some relevant training and who are willing to give time, money, or public identification with this movement, the more likely we are to achieve the necessary healing for Israel/Palestine, for the Middle East, for the Western world, and for the whole world.

So here is some advice to people who say: "Yes, I'm ready to be a tikkunista, a healer and repairer of the world. I want a New Bottom Line for our world, and I want to be one of the people who dedicate their time to doing this work." The first thing that you must realize and become deeply familiar with is your own inner resistance to taking seriously the path of love, caring, and generosity as societal path. Throughout all the work that you do on this path, you must continually come back to the task of reminding yourself of the resistance you yourself feel, the doubts you nurture, the fears you yourself have, and the splitting you yourself have at times engaged in. It's not that you should wait to fully overcome those resistances, fears, and doubts; none of us can do that as long as we live in a world in which the dominant ethos is one of fear, distrust of others, and the strategy of domination as the path to personal or homeland security. In a thousand little interactions each day, we are called upon either to affirm the possibility of deeper loving connection or to hide that yearning in ourselves and refuse to recognize it in each other. Many of us routinely and unconsciously choose the latter path, not only because we believe that we wouldn't have enough love to go around if we were to acknowledge our own desires and their desires, but because we do not wish to expose ourselves to the possibility of rejection and the consequent humiliation that has been so painful so many times in the past.

What we can do is make strides in the direction of trusting more, caring and loving more, being more generous, and being more willing to support others who are reaching for these same values in their personal lives and building a movement for social transformation. Keeping in touch with our own fears and doubts can make us much more effective in working with others; it helps us be compassionate toward those who are still most fully dominated by these fears and doubts themselves.

But this is hard work. So we need to train ourselves in the techniques of mindfulness that have been particularly powerful as taught in parts of the Buddhist world. (Here it's useful to consult the works of Jack Kornfield, Sylvia Boorstein, Jon Kabat Zinn,

Flickr/ISM

Palestinians, Israelis, and internationals march together near a military base that Israel erected to protect a settlement.

Robert Thurman, Thich Nhat Hanh, the Dalai Lama, Wayne Muller, Joan Borysenko, Jeff Roth, Nan Fink, Joseph Goldstein, Larry Rosenberg, and Mark Epstein.) Teach nonviolent communication skills as developed by Marshall Rosenberg. Introduce dialectical behavior therapy as taught by Marsha Linehan and use its techniques. Create a twelve step program adapted to the realities of the society you seek to heal. Draw from all healing traditions! I particularly recommend reading Kaethe Weingarten's book *Common Shock* as part of the process of preparing yourself for this work.

A movement of social healers that is in touch with and compassionate toward its own members will be much more likely to attract and be effective with those whose pain sustains their

PTSD. This is why the first step is to connect with others who share this goal of being social healers, and to create a local group of tikkunistas who can meet on a regular basis, share stories of the work they are doing to promote the vision of a world filled with love and generosity, receive supportive advice, role-play difficult situations, and give one another encouragement and love in this difficult work. We need these kinds of groups in Israel and Palestine, but also in North and South America, Europe, Australia, and throughout Africa and Asia.

Now here's some advice for people in these groups: Don't start with the most difficult problems. Instead, build an alliance with the part of your client or subject that most yearns for healing and for a healthy connection to others.

Translation to social situations: Some people ask me, "How do I deal with the most reactionary fundamentalists or ultra-right-wingers on Israel/Palestine? I'm at a family meal, or a Seder, or a happy gathering of people I like, and someone makes some awful comments and I get drawn in and suddenly realize that they really have racist or hateful attitudes toward Palestinians (or Jews, or women, or liberals, or gays, or whatever)—what can I say to change their minds?" My advice: don't bother. Make some general statement like: "Well, I'm someone who wants to live in a world with lots more love, caring, kindness, and generosity, and so I want to do what I can with my life to make that happen. I believe it can, because deep in all of our hearts we share the same human needs and desires. If we have the chance, I'd love to talk with you about our common ground. But if you really want to know what I think, let me recommend some books that provide my perspective." On the other hand, if someone at the table or the gathering seemed to spark up with a little light in their face when you mentioned love, caring, kindness, and generosity, ask them privately if they might be interested in talking to you more at a quieter and less conflicted place and time.

My reasoning is this: There are tens of millions of people who share your desire for a different kind of world, only they often end up thinking that they are the only ones. So start by affirming in them their most hopeful and loving parts. These are the people who can become the center of a global movement that could repair much of the PTSD that emotionally cripples people everywhere.

You could make a great contribution if you could bring together all or many of the people you've met who are already in contact with their most hopeful and loving parts and who might be able to project a message of love, generosity, and caring into the public sphere if they didn't have to do it by themselves and could see that they were part of something larger. You could connect them with each other in a context in which they were going to do some project to bring more of that kind of energy into the world and thereby begin to create the public context within which the various manifestations of PTSD could begin to shrink. If your focus is on Israel/Palestine, then part of the task of such a group is to learn as much as possible about the details of the situation and to discuss with each other ways that you can give encouragement to others in your area who may feel the same way you do but feel scared to get out in public by themselves.

Let them know that you and the people that you've brought together will try to give them whatever support and cover you realistically can give. Build a group of people who understand that affirming your shared values in the public sphere is an extremely important contribution that they can make, particularly if they can do so not just as individuals but as part of a movement. For people who are already part of a movement addressing, let's say, Israel/Palestine issues, help them see that they are part of this larger movement for a world based on love and generosity, and that affirming the existence of that larger movement is a major contribution to making it real. Instead of only projecting righteous indignation at the alleged or real faults of the other side, these movements would become far more effective were they to embody the nuanced, generosity-oriented approach developed in this book.

Put forward a rational plan for what things could look like if people in the society in question were willing to work on getting past their PTSD so that they could act in their own rational self-interest. For Israel/Palestine, I'll do that in Chapter Eight. A rational plan doesn't cure PTSD. But it does speak to the feeling of hopelessness that many people have and from which they retreat into the perceptions of the world they developed when they were originally traumatized.

In the case of Israel/Palestine, if you don't like the plan I put forward, develop your own using my criteria: that the plan be one that would, if adopted by both sides in a spirit of generosity and genuine desire to create a lasting peace and reconciliation, actually make each community feel that its most important needs had been met and that it had also been generous to the other community and its needs. Then, stick with your rational plan. Don't compromise it because someone has told you that it is not realistic. Be strong about building a world of love, caring, and generosity. Those who believe that such a world is impossible are driven by a deep despair—don't let their despair infect you. Instead, insist that what they think is utopian foolishness is actually the only rational way to get the world you want. Let others know that you will not settle for anything less in your life, because the path of love, kindness, caring, and generosity is absolutely necessary for planetary and societal survival in the coming decades.

Be compassionate toward those who disagree. Always see what legitimate needs they have that have been stunted or denied by the kind of childhood, family life, adult life, and intellectual, societal, or religious conditioning they've received, and seek to validate those underlying needs even if the form in which those needs now get expressed is a hurtful or destructive form. Always see the goodness in them. Let them know the goodness you see in them, and allow yourself to actually feel some of the pain that must have been there to lead them to act in hurtful or self-destructive ways now. Be with them in a real way. As you do this, you strengthen the capacity of all members in your movement to work through the parts of themselves that do not yet really believe that love and generosity can triumph. As they learn to accept those parts of themselves and understand their own fears and their own temptations to go back to the Right Hand of God paradigm, they become more effective in helping others move beyond their own fears. Build support groups within your movement to allow people to get feedback and support for their own uncertainties and inner conflicts. And then build a social movement of people who are willing to affirm your rational plan while simultaneously affirming the goodness of the Other.

Seek ways to make it safe for people to "come out" as loving human beings who believe in a world of love and generosity and who insist that those capacities are in everyone. Create a public counter-culture that affirms the possibility of a world based on caring and love. Do public events built around affirming your highest values.

Create a countercultural vision of what it means to be a hero, to be strong, to be a successful human being. Instead of allowing the culture to define that in terms of being the lone individual or the "people who dwell by themselves" and survive despite the obstacles, define strength in terms of the capacity of people to be vulnerable and caring with each other and open to taking care of strangers and people both near and far. Define the hero as the person or people that brings the greatest amount of peace, justice, compassion, environmental sanity, and love into their families, their neighborhoods, their communities, their country, and their world. Define as weak and in need of care those who think that it's cool to be tough and show no emotions, those who can't trust other people, those who are so detached from their emotions that they think it's cool to be cynical and savvy and clever rather than genuine and open and caring for others. Write songs, make movies, and develop television sit-coms and stand up comedies that reflect this different way of thinking. Create a "reality television" show in which Israelis and Palestinians (not the "make nice" people in each community, but the hard-liners) are tasked with the project of getting to know each other and finding common ground. Create dramatic movies that emphasize the struggle against cynicism and the possibilities for loving communities that challenge the status quo.

Remind the public of the destructiveness and futility of the path of domination and power over others. Mourn for the victims of all who have been victimized by the Right Hand of God consciousness: the witches, the heretics, the Jews, the natives, the homeless, the immigrants, the members of the armies and terrorist squads. Mourn for all the victims of a world based on the vision of domination. And mourn for ourselves, for the hurts that we've sustained, for the losses to our families, to our communities, to our own lives for having to twist ourselves around to fit into the mold required of people living in a world of fear and mutual distrust. Allow us to mourn the parts of ourselves that never got nourished, the fears that we felt we had to suppress in order to convince everyone else that we are okay. Allow us to mourn the way that has distorted our relationships, our family life, and the loving connections that might have been.

Make it fun and joyous to be part of a movement for love and generosity. Create lots of ways for people to be together in mutual affirmation of your shared vision—maybe a sing-along at your home or an evening watching a movie and then discussing it? Create a monthly book club to read books that affirm the loving vision you hold or a potluck to hang out and share stories.

Sponsor public talks by visiting speakers or local experts, and try hard to get your friends, neighbors, and others to attend. Thrust into those discussions the worldview of love and generosity. Take care of each other. Help people in this movement feel that they are cared about by the others in the movement. Find out if there are people in their families who are sick and if they need help in caring for them. Then volunteer to help. If they are unemployed, help them find work. If they are single and don't want to be, help them meet potentially appropriate partners. If they are lonely, invite them to dinner or to join you and your family for an outing.

Avoid political correctness. Don't make people feel that they are unwelcome if they don't share every aspect of your own political views or of the movement's political views—as long as they do share the fundamental concern to really care about the well-being of the Other, whoever the Other becomes at any given moment. Help people develop their understanding of the situation in the Middle East by providing internal study groups. But do not be too inclusive—do not have as part of your movement people who really believe that one side has been the good guys and the other side the bad guys; otherwise, you recreate the problem the movement is intended to heal. And feel free to disinvite from your movement people who are disruptive, hurtful to others, demeaning of leadership, demeaning of intellectual life or careful analysis, or have joined your movement in order to recruit people to another movement with different aims.

Create a movement and a new political party that has an appropriate balance between internal nurturing and external challenging of the fears that sustain the traumas that are distorting public policies. Don't allow others to intimidate you into abandoning words like love, caring, and generosity or into feeling that you are on weak grounds because you are recognizing the psychological and spiritual dimension of the Middle East struggle (and of all struggles for peace and social justice).

Build public events that embody and validate the path of love and generosity. Create a public celebration of families in all their diversities. Insist that schools teach empathy as equally important as any of its other subjects, and run people for the local school board with that as their platform. Insist that colleges give scholarships to high school students who have excelled in empathy as often as they give scholarships for those who have excelled in sports. Make empathy and caring for others one of the key elements to be evaluated in college and graduate school admissions processes. Give community awards to those in the community who have been voted by their neighbors to be the most caring people in their town. Create public gatherings in which people write letters of apology to those who have been traumatized by the hurtfulness of your society. (Imagine Americans writing letters to the families in Iraq and Afghanistan whose children were killed or wounded by American bombs. Imagine Israelis and Palestinians sending such letters to each others' families.) Create a public ritual for people coming out of the army to help them heal from the indoctrination toward violence that they've received, and invite army veterans to attend.

These are some of the elements in a strategy to overcome PTSD. They emerge from an analysis of movements that have been successful in challenging racism, sexism, homophobia, and anti-Semitism over the course of the past hundred years (while acknowledging that those movements still have not yet fully won their struggles).

Now in the next few chapters, let me go deeper into a few of these elements and apply them to the issues of Israel/Palestine. First, I'll present what I believe to be the most plausible, rational solution for Israel/Palestine, a solution that could only work if we developed the psychological and spiritual foundations for it. Next, I'll consider the strategies currently being offered by various groups seeking peace and comment on their relative strengths. I'll also provide a strategy of my own: the Strategy of Generosity manifested in a Global Marshall Plan to be launched first in the Middle East. Finally, I'll turn to the spiritual foundations of peace and reconciliation and discuss the changes in Judaism (and by implication in all other religions) that would help inspire the rational solutions I offer.

Chapter Eight

TERMS OF A SUSTAINABLE AND JUST PEACE AGREEMENT

THE PREDOMINANT VIEW AMONG DIPLOMATS and policy-makers in the United States, Europe, Israel, and the Arab world is that what is needed now is agreement on the terms of a final settlement accord. Adherents to this view argue that the international community will implement peace once the diplomats can sit down and work out the terms that are acceptable to both sides. As a result, their main goal is to get the parties to sit down in a negotiating process and work out these terms. Many of U.S. media and public policy discussions of Middle East developments, from the Arab Spring to the reconciliation between Hamas and the Palestinian Authority, get assessed primarily from the standpoint of its impact on the possibility of getting these negotiations to start or continue.

In my view, this perspective is mistaken. No matter what agreement is worked out in such negotiations, it is unlikely to succeed in reality until a dramatic reconciliation of the heart takes place among the various parties to the conflict. Without such a reconciliation, even a globally popular settlement agreement (like the Oslo Accords was when it was first signed) has little chance of succeeding. This reconciliation of the heart is the topic of the next three chapters. In this chapter, I will propose the terms of a true peace agreement that will be possible once there is a transformation of consciousness of the people involved— that is, when they genuinely desire a lasting and just peace for their own community and for the Other. That transformation of consciousness could be facilitated if the United States, European countries, and the peace movements in Israel and Palestine were to popularize these terms.

Tikkun's Proposal for Two States at Peace

Here is what a peace plan must involve for it to have any chance of swaying hearts and minds on all sides:

1. The peace treaty will recognize the State of Israel and the State of Palestine and defines Palestine's borders to include almost all of pre-1967 West Bank and Gaza, with small exchanges of land mutually agreed upon and roughly equivalent in value, historic meaning, and military significance to each side. The peace plan will also include a corresponding treaty between Israel and all Arab states; this treaty will specify recognition of Israel, promise full diplomatic and economic cooperation among these parties, and accept all the terms of this agreement as specified herein. It will also include a twenty-to-thirty-year plan for moving toward a Middle Eastern common market and the eventual establishment of a political union along the lines of the European Union. This could entail building a federation between Israel and Palestine, or between Israel, Palestine, and Jordan—a plan originally proposed by Israel's president Shimon Peres.

2. Jerusalem will be the capital of both Israel and Palestine and will be governed for all civic issues by an elected council in West Jerusalem and a separate elected council in East Jerusalem. The Old City will become an international city whose sovereignty will be implemented by an international council that guarantees equal access to all holy sites. This council's taxes will be shared equally by the city councils of East and West Jerusalem. East Jerusalem and its residents will be part of the Palestinian state and West Jerusalem and its residents will be part of the State of Israel.

3. Immediate and unconditional freedom will be accorded to all prisoners in Israel and Palestine whose arrests are connected in some way to the Occupation and/ or resistance to the Occupation. Those who have been convicted of murder by a jury of their peers will be turned over to the government of their own people for further incarceration.

4. An international force will be established to separate and protect each side from the extremists of the other side who will inevitably seek to disrupt the peace agreement. And a joint peace police—composed of an equal number of Palestinians and Israelis at both personnel and command levels—will be created to work with the international force to combat violence.

5. Reparations will be offered by the international community for Palestinian refugees and their descendents. The amount should be generous so that, within a ten-year period, Palestinians will be brought to an economic level equivalent to that enjoyed by Israelis

with a median income. The same level of reparations will also be made available to all Jews who fled Arab lands between 1948 and 1977.

6. A truth and reconciliation process will be created, modeled on the South African version but shaped to the specific needs of these two cultures. In addition, an international peace committee will be appointed by representatives of the three major religious communities of the area to develop and implement the teaching of a) nonviolence and nonviolent communication, b) empathy and forgiveness, and c) a sympathetic point of view toward the history of the other side. The adoption of this curriculum should be mandatory in every grade from sixth grade through high school. The committee should be empowered to ensure the elimination of all teaching of hatred toward the other side. It should also be empowered to stop teaching against the implementation of this treaty in any public, private, or religious educational institutions, media, or public meetings. (A similar strategy was pioneered by the United States in Japan and Germany after the Second World War.)

7. Palestine will agree to allow all Jews living in the West Bank to remain there as law-abiding citizens of the new Palestinian state, as long as they give up their Israeli citizenship and abide by decisions of the Palestinian courts. A resettlement fund will be created for the following purposes: a) to help West Bank settlers move back to Israel if they wish to remain Israeli citizens, and b) to help Palestinians move from the lands of their dispersion to Palestine if they wish to be citizens of the new Palestinian state.

8. In exchange for Palestine's agreeing to allow Israelis to stay in the West Bank as citizens of the Palestinian state, Israel will agree to let 20,000 Palestinian refugees return each year for the next thirty years to the pre-1967 borders of Israel and to provide them with housing. (This number—20,000—is small enough to not change the demographic balance, yet large enough to show that Israel cares about Palestinian refugees and recognizes that they have been wronged.)

9. Full and equal rights will be afforded to all minority communities living within each of the two states, and independent institutions will be funded in each state to vigorously enforce minority rights. All forms of religious coercion, religious control over the state, or religious control over personal status issues like birth, marriage, divorce, and death will be eliminated. Each state, however, will have the right to give priority in immigration and immigrant housing—but not in any subsequent benefits—to its own leading ethnic community (Jews in Israel, Arabs in Palestine) for as long as either community faces substantial discrimination or violent assaults in other countries of the world.

This agreement, while involving substantial compromises from both sides, provides the minimum terms to satisfy both Israelis and Palestinians who truly desire peace.

TWO STATES WITH OVERLAPPING ELECTORATES: AN ALTERNATIVE SOLUTION

A plausible objection made to the two-state solution is that it leaves too many Israelis and Palestinians deeply unhappy; they may really want to be part of their own ethnic community's state, yet be unable to if they are Palestinians living in Israel or Israelis living in Palestine. In particular, Israeli settlers might not be willing to either leave their homes in the West Bank or to give up their Israeli citizenship.

In the past years, a new proposal (one that involves overlapping electorates) has begun to emerge. Its critical element is this: where you live would no longer determine your national identity. Any Israeli living in the area of what was once the British Mandate of Palestine would remain a citizen of Israel, and any Palestinian living in the territorial area of the State of Israel would nevertheless be a citizen of the State of Palestine. Both states would be required to supply recruits for a jointly-run army to protect these two states from external enemies. All other relevant parts of the two-state solution suggested in the two-state peace plan I outlined previously would be incorporated into this plan, including vigorous enforcement of minority rights.

In this arrangement, Israel would remain a Jewish state— that is, a state of and for the Jewish people. Palestine would be a state of and for the Palestinian people. All Palestinian Israelis would be required to transfer their citizenship and national voting rights to a Palestinian state, and all Israeli Jews would be required to be citizens of the Jewish State. Anyone else would be free to choose citizenship in either of these two states. Both legal and informal arrangements preventing Jews or Arabs from living anywhere they chose in the land of Israel and Palestine would be deemed illegal in both societies. Local municipalities in both Israel and Palestine would be required to serve the local residents in their vicinity who might be citizens of either state. Citizens of both states could vote to elect the leaders of municipal and regional governments that would allocate funds for schools, transportation, energy, water, police, community centers, and any other local social or communal services.

The details of this proposal are still being developed. But its essential features are these: a Jew could live in any part of Israel/Palestine without giving up her/his Israeli citizenship, and a Palestinian could live in any part of Israel/Palestine without giving up her/his Palestinian citizenship.

With this arrangement, the fear of Israel losing its Jewish identity disappears, thus rendering obsolete the primary argument against the Palestinian "right of return." Israelis have argued that if they admitted Palestinian immigrants, those Palestinians would quickly overwhelm the democratic mechanisms of the State of Israel, especially if demographics shifted to make Palestinians the majority. They worry that in a standard two-state situation, demographic factors such as the higher growth rate of Arab families would eventually turn Israel into yet another Arab-and-Muslim-majority state.

This plan, on the other hand, would guarantee that as long as there are states, there would still be one state in the world committed to protecting Jewish interests and providing a place of refuge and escape for the world's Jews. Similarly, Palestinians would no longer need to worry about whether Israeli settlers would overwhelm or distort the operations of a Palestinian state, since those settlers would not be forced to move or to become citizens of a Palestinian state.

The overlapping electorates plan also offers distinct advantages for Palestinians; Israeli settlers are not an element Palestinians would want represented in their parliament in the early, fragile years of the new Palestinian state. Just as Israel kept Palestinians out of its political process by putting Palestinians under martial law without voting rights in the first decade of Israel's existence, Palestinians will likely want to keep Israeli settlers out of their political process as well.

Working out the details of this overlapping electorates plan should provide a serious challenge for peacemakers in the coming years, but it deserves to be fleshed out and assessed for viability.

THE ONE-STATE SOLUTION

This plan calls for uniting both Israel and Palestine into a single, secular, democratic state. By eliminating privileged status for any ethnic or religious group and creating a secular democratic process on the model of the United States or the United Kingdom, the single state of Israel/Palestine would provide a homeland for all its citizens. Moreover, the single state would no longer be attached to its various diasporas and their fantasies, but would instead serve its actual residents.

Advocates for the one-state solution point out that Israel is rapidly creating the infrastructure and reality of one state. With settlers and Palestinians living next to each other throughout the area that the British once defined as Palestine, Israel has created this de facto reality on the ground. All that is needed now is to create democratic elections for the merged communities that already exist. To split these two societies apart, many argue, would be virtually impossible and would certainly produce a civil war. The former deputy mayor of Jerusalem, Meron Benvenisti, nicely sums up this line of thinking when he says, "The question is no longer whether [Israel/Palestine] will be binational, but which [one-state] model to choose."

Professsor Tony Judt suggested that "a legitimately constituted binational state would find it much easier policing militants of all kinds inside its borders than when they are free to infiltrate them from outside and can expect to appeal to an angry, excluded constituency on both sides of the border."

If Israel/Palestine is, as some peace activists allege, already de facto one state—albeit a state that denies equal rights to one of its larger ethnic groups—a one-state solution could come about through a campaign for equal rights that would challenge the current unfair distribution of power between Israelis and Palestinians. "One person, one vote" is a demand that could resonate deeply with the global community and even with American Jews. This may be what Palestinian leaders had in mind when they warned at the end of July 2011 that if Palestine did not become a recognized separate state soon, the Palestinian Authority might dissolve itself and let Israel take responsibility for the West Bank directly. In such a situation, a campaign for equal rights could gain substantial support both inside Israel and worldwide.

But there is also a short-term downside for Palestinians if Israel accepts the one-state proposal within the next decade: why should Palestinians want to instantly become a dispossessed, impoverished minority in an Israeli-dominated culture and economy? Israelis would still outnumber Palestinians, at least for another decade; moreover, this new democratic society's Knesset might easily pass legislation renouncing forever the notion of compensation—much less the right of return—for refugees. Remember, Israel is not South Africa, where a minority of whites ruled over a majority of blacks. If one state were established today, Jewish Israelis would still far outnumber all the Palestinians in Israel, the West Bank, and Gaza combined.

On the other hand, many progressive Israelis and peace movement activists in both Jewish and Palestinian communities see the possibility of a secular, democratic Israel as the best solution. They note that most Israelis have deep ambivalence about Judaism and would easily accommodate to a state that

Flickr/Cau Napoli

A Palestinian man walks beside the separation wall.

no longer gave the religious Jews special power over daily life. A secular, democratic Israeli state could still retain major Jewish holidays as special occasions and days off work and school, but would accord the same status to major Muslim and Christian holidays. Instead of basing itself on Jewish culture, such a state, they argue, would develop an Israeli identity that incorporated Arab and Jewish cultural and religious inheritances. Israel would no longer claim to be "the Jewish State" but rather the state of the people who live in Israel, which would include millions of Muslims and Christians as well. The flag would no longer reflect only Jewish identity, and the national anthem would articulate the vision of Jews, Muslims, and Christians living in peaceful harmony.

Some will object: "But won't such a state soon have a majority of Palestinians? What about Israel as the place of refuge for the Jewish people?"

The one-staters have a possible response: "Israel may well have been necessary and justified as a place of refuge in the immediate aftermath of the Holocaust. We can honor those Zionists who sought to create a place of safety and an army to defend Jews. But by trying to be a Jewish state that discriminates against its own Arab minority and occupies and oppresses Palestinians in the West Bank and Gaza, Israel has done more in the past thirty years to endanger Jews around the world than anything anti-Semites could have possibly accomplished on their own. And Israel is not a safe place for Jews—they are far safer in many other countries than they are in a Jewish state continuing an occupation. So if Jews need a place of refuge, they'd be better off in New York and California than in a Middle East still angry at them for what the self-proclaimed Jewish State is doing to Arabs."

Unfortunately, one-state solutions to communities with strongly-opposed factions have not had a great track record in the past several decades. The fighting among Sunnis, Shiites, and Kurds in Iraq, Hutus and Tutsis in Rwanda, the many factions in the former Yugoslavia, Muslims and Hindus in Kashmir (and the list goes on) suggests that forced marriages are not always the best solution unless all relevant communities feel a truly enthusiastic desire to be together. This shared enthusiasm is far more likely to emerge from the two-state solution based on the terms outlined above than from trying as a first step to create one state. However, the one-state solution might eventually become plausible after the two-state solution works effectively to create good relations.

At the moment, however, most Palestinians are committed to finding a path to establishing their own Palestinian state. And few Israelis could be convinced that a one-state solution would be safe for them, at least not until the PTSD in both communities has been mostly cured.

Ironically, one way that a two-state solution might be achieved more quickly would be for Palestinians to demand a one-state solution and "one person, one vote." The fear of losing the Jewishness of their state might be precisely the thing that would lead many middle-of-the-road Israelis to quickly seek a reasonable two-state solution.

A global campaign for equal rights inside the de facto one state that currently exists, coupled with a commitment to nonviolence by Palestinians, would quickly change the political dynamics within Israel and could lead to the Israeli right wing deciding to embrace a two-state solution—not just rhetorically as Prime Minister Netanyahu has already done, but in substance. For that reason, it would be strategically smart for the Palestinian people to embrace the demand for "one person, one vote" inside Israel if Israel continues to reject the kind of terms that are outlined above for a two-state solution.

Any lasting solution to the struggle between Israel and Palestine would take major changes of consciousness in our world, but the changes needed for the one-state solution are so much greater and would take so much longer to achieve. In the short run, I see the two-state solution and the overlapping electorates solution that I outlined above as more achievable.

The No-State Solution

Our most urgent goal should be to end the suffering of the Israeli and Palestinian people that is caused by this conflict. The full implementation (carried out by liberal and progressive forces in Israel, Palestine, and the United States) of the peace movement strategy I propose in the next chapter could achieve either the two-state solution outlined above or the overlapping electorates solution within ten to twenty years. Because such an achievement would immediately and dramatically relieve the suffering of my own people and the suffering of the Palestinians, I feel morally obliged to support that path.

However, if I were to focus on a longer-term strategy and actually articulate my own highest vision, I would not move from my support for a two-state solution to a one-state solution. Rather, I would advocate for a no-state solution. While maintaining the rich diversity that exists in national, ethnic, and religious cultures, I'd separate that from political national entities. Instead, we need to create ecological districts that can work with other such districts around the world to provide a rational plan for producing and distributing goods and services, for reducing population growth, and for eliminating practices that threaten the survival of the planet. While I believe that some existing states might actually be able to work in tandem with these environmental districts, most of the nations of the world have embraced narrow forms of nationalism that are based on an "us first" ethos; this stands in marked contrast to the world's need for a "humanity and the earth first" ethos in the twenty-first century.

A brief explanation: The major challenge facing the human race in the twenty-first century is to save the planet from environmental destruction and to save the human race from obliteration. We are facing the consequences of a few hundred years of environmental insanity and about ten thousand years of human brutalization of one another and of other animals. At the core of that human self-destructiveness is the triumph of an ethos of materialism and selfishness—an ethos that the prophets of ancient Israel railed against when they condemned idolatry. For them, recognizing God as the force of healing and transformation entailed also recognizing the way that every human being is created in the image of God.

Idolatry manifests in our blindness to God and hence our willingness to treat other human beings as instruments of our own selfish needs. That same ethos is now fully embedded in and manifested through the daily operations of global capitalism. Capitalist economies reward those who seek to maximize their own advantage without regard to the consequences for others. As a result, it tends to produce people who believe that being rational is "looking out for number one."

This kind of consciousness, so prevalent today, has produced a media monolith that glorifies those who are "the winners" in whatever form of competition the media can invent—from sports to "reality shows" to elections. Long-term relationships feel less secure while divorce rates surge; many people feel lonely, alienated, and afraid of being tossed aside by their employers, by their friends, and even by their own families once they are no longer "productive" or "useful." Take this consciousness to a global level, and it often yields an ultranationalism; this is actually a manifestation of this same ethos of selfishness and materialism dressed in the garb of the "higher purpose" of serving one's clan, tribe, race, religion, geographic area, state, or nation at the expense of the others.

We need to transcend the currently dominant view that nations and individuals must look out for themselves rather than care for others. By the middle of the twenty-first century, we will need to replace nation states with regional environmental districts that are constituted around the ecological survival needs of the planet and set up to maximize our capacity to care for everyone else on the planet. Even sooner, we need to shape our production of food, housing, communication technologies, and transportation infrastructure—not to mention our practices of education, celebration, and joyful play—around humanitarian and ecological needs. I believe that regional environmental districts have a greater chance of preserving democratic processes than any currently conceivable form of international government. In short, we all need a no-state solution.

Or to put it another way, both the Israeli people and the Palestinian people have to learn a lesson that everyone on the planet has yet to learn: our individual and communal survival and well-being depend on the well-being of the planet earth and the well-being of everyone who lives on it. We do not need nation states; indeed, they may be a major obstacle to planetary and personal survival. What we do need is a new global ethos that I call the Caring Society—caring for each other and caring for the planet.

If nation-states continue to squabble and use violence against one another, they not only sin against humanity, but also divert the needed energy and resources that must be directed to saving our planet from environmental disaster. So it is time to start moving in the direction of transcending states rather than thinking of one state, even a secular, democratic state of Israel/Palestine, as a long-term solution to the problems of the Israeli and Palestinian peoples. If a one-state solution were an immediate possibility, that would have some genuine attractions. But since it is not, we need to give our energies in the short run to a two-state solution and in the long run to a no-state solution.

It is time for people involved in the Israel/Palestine struggle to recognize that our peoples are part of the human race, that there is a much larger drama going on that involves the very survival of the human race in the twenty-first century, and that we need to stop being one of the many distractions that keep the human race from dealing with the global challenges it faces. These challenges include the environmental crisis, the threat of global nuclear war, growing poverty and division between rich and poor, and growing psycho-spiritual alienation, depression, and despair.

THIS PEACE DEPENDS ON TRANSFORMED CONSCIOUSNESS

At this time, we do not need "a peace process" in the form in which it has operated in the past. We need agreement on these nine points. Increasing numbers of people on all sides of this conflict are recognizing that "the peace process" and "negotiations" have little to do with achieving peace and much to do with political theatre aimed at creating the impression that some progress is being made. The "winner" in these negotiations is the side that escapes blame for the failure of the peace process. We've seen this go on for decades, and meanwhile the situation on the ground only gets worse.

Too often the debates over the terms of a peace agreement focus only on political and geographical considerations. The real peace process we do need, however, is a process of transformation in the way that each side views the Other. Any peace treaty that does not generate a campaign in each of the communities (including their respective diasporas) to understand the legitimacy of each side's historical narrative and their own needs for security and justice is bound to be a failed peace treaty.

In the final analysis, we at *Tikkun* and the interfaith Network of Spiritual Progressives believe that peace can come only through a fundamental transformation of consciousness. People on each side must begin to abandon the worldview that their own security depends on dominating the other side, which is construed as the "evil other." Only an openhearted reconciliation based on a newly developed capacity to see former enemies as real human beings—sharing similar needs for peace, security, dignity, and recognition—can produce lasting peace. The implementation of these formal proposals would not necessarily be sufficient to create that change of heart. Yet the step of envisioning this process may itself contribute to a thawing of the icy rejection of the Other—a thawing that is the precondition for developing the consciousness that is needed. For that reason, articulating this vision may itself be a step toward its achievement.

This kind of transformation of consciousness was already commanded in Torah: "If you see your fellow's ass or ox fallen on the road, do not ignore it; you must help him raise it." (Deuteronomy, 22.4) The Torah's supposition is that we might ignore him, but we must not. Instead, we must stop and give that person what she or he needs in the way of assistance. Our first response to a situation is not our last one; we can change our response through a process of ethical/spiritual work and transformation. We need this transformation not only in regard to our neighbor, but in our dealings with all the people on our planet—because they are equally precious and equally created in the image of God and because our well-being depends on the well-being of everyone else on the planet. This is the lesson of Torah, Moses, Isaiah, Jesus, Muhammad, Buddha, Krishna, Marx, Gandhi, King, and all other great teachers of spiritual and political social healing for the twenty-first century. This is precisely what is needed in Israel/ Palestine.

Chapter Nine

STRATEGIES FOR ACHIEVING PEACE

P EACE, JUSTICE, AND RECONCILIATION for Israel and Palestine are possible.

Yet the cycle of violence manifested once again in the Second Intifada, the wars with Lebanon, the Gaza invasion, the recommencement of rocket attacks from Gaza, and targeted assassinations by Israel have shattered so many lives on both sides of the struggle that there is little willingness to convince the other side that peace remains a possibility.

Palestinians point to the Israeli army offensives that leveled apartment buildings and buried people alive under wreckage in Jenin, southern Lebanon, and Gaza—not to mention the weeklong curfews imposed on the Palestinian people—as proof that Israel has lost its moral compass.

The combination of outrage and powerlessness in such circumstances has made suicide bombings a continuing threat to Israeli civilians. I and most others in the peace movement see terror as morally unacceptable. In turn, the suicide bombings have given strength (though not moral validity) to the growing call of some on the Israeli Right to use this moment to begin the process of transferring Palestinians.

It is this continuing violence that made it hard for many Israelis to take seriously the offer developed by the Saudis and ratified by all the Arab states at an Arab summit in the spring of 2002. The offer, which was repeated again in 2007, promised that the Arab states would finally grant full recognition and normalization of relations to Israel if Israel would return to the pre-1967 borders and allow the return of refugees to their homes. This offer was almost entirely ignored by Israel, most of whose citizens no longer believed or trusted any Arab voices.

Many in the Arab world have pointed out that the Saudi plan offered Israel everything it said it wanted in the first nineteen years of its existence: peace, normalization of relationships with its neighbors, and a whole new start. But for most Israelis, the notion of trusting a return of what had become several million refugees (including refugees' children, grandchildren, and great-grandchildren) was a nonstarter. It provoked fear that those refugees would bring with them generations of anger and hatred that would guarantee civil war, not peace. Nor do most Israelis trust the intentions of Arab states.

Yet it is Israeli violence toward Palestinians on a weekly and sometimes daily basis—reframed by Israeli public relations (*hasbara*) as merely fighting terrorism—that makes it so hard for Palestinians to trust that talk of peace is anything other than a stalling tactic for Israel to consolidate its hold on the West Bank. What Palestinians see in their day-to-day life is Israel seizing yet more West Bank land to expand settlements; building "Israeli-only" highways direct from the settlements to Jerusalem or Tel Aviv; tearing down Palestinian homes; shooting, maiming, or killing Palestinian nonviolent demonstrators; jailing thousands without charges or trial by jury; and carrying out "targeted assassinations" against "suspected terrorists."

Violence is not a strategy that can lead to peace. To the extent that either community embraces or even tolerates (worse, sometimes celebrates) its violent actors and violent public discourse, it gives the other side not just an excuse for violence, but actual fear that it has no choice but to resort to violence.

Peace activists must be on guard against any form of violence, including violent speech, cheering on of others' acts of violence, and even the psychological and spiritual violence of seeking to coerce one side into a peace agreement that does not seem to them to serve their interests.

In this light, let's consider some of the strategies that could be embraced by some in the Israeli and Palestinian peace movements.

STRATEGY ONE: NONVIOLENCE AND THE PALESTINIAN PEACE MOVEMENT

The emergence of a nonviolent Palestinian peace movement has been one of the most hopeful signs of the past decade. A younger Palestinian generation that no longer wishes to threaten Israelis with acts of terror has allied with Israeli supporters to engage in nonviolent confrontations at the Wall and in Palestinian neighborhoods of East Jerusalem where families are being evicted from their homes so that Jewish settlers can move in. Nonviolent protesters have also sought to break the blockade of food and other necessary supplies to the people of Gaza. And they have demonstrated at spots where Israeli soldiers or border police are tearing down Palestinian homes for the alleged offense of being "illegal" for "security reasons." Their actions have taken on symbolic meaning and generated great moral authority for the cause of peace.

Unfortunately, it is not easy to keep these demonstrations nonviolent. Israeli troops, border police, and settlers show up at these scenes and start shooting at the demonstrators—sometimes using rubber bullets, sometimes using live ammunition, and frequently using heavy doses of tear gas. Peaceful protesters have been killed, wounded, injured, and emotionally trauma-tized. Palestinians often respond by picking up rocks and throw-ing them at the Israelis. In these cases some still insist that their demonstration is nonviolent because it doesn't involve using weapons as lethal as those of the settlers and the Israeli forces.

Yet Israelis watching the news perceive the scenes of Palestinians throwing rocks as violence, so they scoff at the no-tion that Palestinians have adopted a nonviolent strategy. Most of the time the demonstrations are not covered by the news at all, so most Israelis have no clue that they are taking place, much less what settlers and soldiers did to provoke the rock throwing. Israelis sometimes say, "If you don't live here, you don't really know what's happening here." They are apparently oblivious to the government censorship of news it considers related to na-tional security. For many Israeli citizens, the truth is that they don't know what is being done in their name by the settlers and the government.

Moreover, the Israeli media and government present acts of terror by fringe Palestinian groups as if they represent the main-stream of Palestinians, particularly when one or another of the "liberation" groups takes credit for such terror attacks.

We must strongly support Palestinian nonviolence and call for it to be led by activists who preach nonviolence not as a momen-tary strategy but as a principled commitment of the Palestinian national liberation struggle. Like the Anti-Apartheid Movement in South Africa and the Civil Rights Movement in the United States, a Palestinian liberation movement will have to use schools, mosques, and churches to train tens of thousands of Palestinian Muslims and Christians in the philosophy and practice of nonvio-lence. And just as civil rights activists faced considerable opposi-tion, so too will Palestinian peace activists face opposition. But with the moral discipline and force of nonviolence at their dispos-al, they will draw a great deal of support from around the world.

Flickr/Jillian

Nonviolent protesters sit in front of IDF soldiers in the West Bank village of Bil'in. After these activists dodged tear gas and rubber bullets every week for two years, the Israeli Supreme Court ordered the IDF to reroute the Wall so that it did not prevent farmers from sowing their land.

This movement must necessarily be accompanied by a systematic teaching of nonviolent communication to reorient the media, the churches and mosques, and the school systems of Palestine to no longer demean Israelis. There are some courageous Palestinians already engaged in this project, but to portray them as having already succeeded in changing the character of the Palestinian struggle would be wishful thinking. The victory that the residents of Budrus and Bil'in achieved against the Wall, which had been built right through their farmland, took many years of massive weekly protests and a leadership unequivocally opposed to violence. However, that model has not yet become the dominant reality of Palestinian resistance to the Occupation.

At the same time, we recognize the imbalance of power. After all, there is no corresponding nonviolence from the Israeli government. The Occupation is inherently violent—imposing curfews, restricting freedom of movement, expropriating land and water supplies, and relying on the acts of the Israeli army to protect the 400,000 settlers who now occupy land that once belonged to the Palestinian people. Nor have tens of thousands of peace-oriented Israelis mobilized to create nonviolent civil disobedience campaigns challenging the expansion of settlements, the destruction of Palestinian homes, the creation of the Wall, or the systematic governmental acts of violence against the Palestinian people.

Nevertheless, those who genuinely care about the well-being of the Palestinian people should encourage a nonviolent struggle as well as a discourse in Palestinian schools and media that reassures Israelis that Palestinians no longer seek to push the Jews into the sea.

It may not be "fair" to put this task on the Palestinian people, but it is smart; if they follow a path of principled nonviolence, they will open up new possibilities for consciousness-change among Israelis by making it far harder for the Israeli elites to sell the notion that Palestinians are a threat. To the extent that the Palestinian movement articulates the kind of vision that affirms the humanity of the oppressors, as Martin Luther King Jr. did so eloquently in the struggle against segregation, it will thaw some of the frozen-in-fear consciousness of Israelis and make it easier to overcome the irrational elements in their thinking.

This is the special privilege of the oppressed—that they are able to see the nature of reality more clearly than the oppressors. They see how the oppressors have lost their ethical moorings and have distorted their own consciousness in order to perpetuate whatever perceived privileges they receive from the oppressive order they have created.

And this is what the Israelites meant when, after having been liberated from slavery in Egypt, they perceived themselves as having been "chosen" to spread the message that liberation was really possible for all people. So they built their religion around retelling the story, by reading the Torah portion every week and retelling the full story every Passover.

That same sense of obligation to spread the message that every human being is created in the image of God is the first ethical teaching of the Torah in the first chapter of Genesis. In framing the story of human creation in this way, the liberation struggle of the Jews becomes simultaneously a vision of the equal worth of all human beings and a message about the potential liberation of all humanity.

When such a movement calls for our support, there is no ethical path but to support it with all our heart, our soul, and our very being. Today, all such struggles for peace and justice must be explicitly and unequivocally nonviolent. To the extent that they are, they manifest God's spirit in the world and command the respect and support of all humanity.

Strategy Two: Creating a Spiritually Oriented Peace and Justice Movement in Israel

Israeli peace activists struggle against almost overwhelming odds given the combination of fears generated by terrorism and Jews' unresolved traumas (detailed above in Chapter Seven) that continue to shape Israelis' perceptions of the Palestinian people. Those peace and human rights activists deserve our respect and support.

And there is something more that is needed. Although most Israelis are not religious in the sense that the Orthodox parties

Flickr/theroadisthegoal

A soldier reads from his prayer book while guarding the Wailing Wall.

are, many consider themselves "traditional" (*mesorti*). They see themselves as part of the Jewish people and its several-thousand-year-old traditions; many justify the sacrifices they make to stay in Israel in terms of that tradition. Despite the efforts of religious peace organizations, many Mesorti Israelis have not yet encountered a peace and justice movement that speaks the language of the Jewish tradition and emphasizes its loving, compassionate, and generous themes.

Yet that is exactly what is needed to break through the current dichotomy between the ultranationalist Right Hand of God discourse and the human rights-oriented universalism of the Left. What they haven't yet heard is a Jewish spiritual movement that affirms Judaism and the historical experience of Jews, that acknowledges the complex reality that Judaism has within it both a Right Hand of God discourse and a Left Hand of God discourse, and that unequivocally embraces the latter. With this embracing of the Left Hand of God comes a commitment to social justice for the poor (among Western industrialized nations, Israel has one of the largest income gaps between rich and poor) and reconciliation with the Palestinian people.

Many leftists in Israel would find this strategy distasteful because they have developed a strong phobia of religion based on what they perceive to be the selfishness and power-hungry attitudes of the religious parties in Israel. They have never encountered the love-oriented Emancipatory Judaism of which I speak and which I'll discuss in the next chapter. Fostering such a Judaism in Israel could have a dramatic impact in breaking through the fears and frozen attitudes toward Palestinians.

The other element desperately needed by the Israeli peace activists is a similar intensity in struggling for the well-being of poor and middle-class civilians who are struggling to keep afloat. The upsurge of Israeli energy to fight economic oppression in the summer of 2011 was, unfortunately, not led by the peace movement.

Instead, it was led by many who felt that their "legitimacy" would be compromised if they identified with those who wished to end the Occupation. Yet peace movement people rightly pointed out that much of the money that could be used to provide help for poor and middle-income people is instead being diverted to the needs of the settlers and the Occupation. Though this has been said by peace activists for decades, it has not been said in a way that actually is heard by those facing economic hardships. The peace movement could give equal emphasis to social justice and to peace. If it did so and partly used the language of a Jewish spiritual and religious consciousness to show how its message was an outgrowth of genuine Jewish values, peace activists might gather the kind of popular support that would position them to change Israeli policies.

STRATEGY THREE: WEAKENING AIPAC AND THE "ISRAEL LOBBY" IN THE UNITED STATES

AIPAC, the American Israel Political Affairs Committee, working informally with a series of pro-right-wing political action committees, has become one of the most powerful and influential lobbies in Washington, D.C. Using this power, it has supported the U.S. invasion of Iraq and has pressed for more powerful military action against Iran. It has vigorously championed the policies of the Occupation and the consequent repression of the Palestinian people.

Instead of recognizing that Israel has been hurting itself by its harsh treatment of the Palestinian people, AIPAC has become a cheerleader for the most reactionary governments that Israel has ever had. In so doing, it has seriously damaged Israel's best interests and the best interests of Jews around the world; Israel would be far better served by identifying Jews with the traditional Jewish values of justice, peace, compassion, repentance, forgiveness, and generosity. And AIPAC has helped move a section of American Jews toward supporting the most right-wing elements in American politics on the faulty grounds that right wingers are "good for Israel." In short, AIPAC has been bad for the United States, bad for Israel, and bad for the Jewish people.

Ironically, though AIPAC is strongest in its ability to mobilize the grassroots to put pressure on elected officials, many of those mobilized do not share the right-wing politics of their leadership and are often surprised to learn that their own organization is really siding with the political Right in Israel. They have accepted AIPAC's claim that it is merely a pro-Israel lobby that will support any and every Israeli government without regard to its political orientation. Former Minister of Justice Yossi Beilin pointed out in *Tikkun* magazine that when he was assigned by Prime Minister Rabin to build support for the pro-peace policies of the Rabin government after the Oslo Accords, he was stymied by AIPAC, which actually was supporting policies opposed by the Rabin government. Thus the claim that AIPAC was politically "neutral" was proven false when Israel for a short time elected a government seeking peace and not endless domination of the Palestinian people. Imagine how the American people would react if the United States set up a supposedly pro-American lobby and public relations firm in other countries to rally support for the United States and that organization taught the worldview of George W. Bush and Dick Cheney—but refused to teach the worldview of Bill Clinton and Barack Obama.

There have been brief moments when a U.S. administration has tried to push Israel toward a more rational and less fearful approach to Palestinians, only to find itself pushed by AIPAC to back down and accept Israeli policies. At this point in the discussion, increasing numbers of Americans are asking the question: "Why is the United States willing to subordinate its own interests to those of Israel?"

The Israel Lobby is one of the most powerful and effective lobbies in the United States, capable of intervening in congressional and presidential campaigns and perceived as effectively blocking the futures of any who are deemed to be "anti-Israel," which they often equate with being anti-Semitic. AIPAC is the most significant voice of the Israel Lobby, and many of the major Jewish institutions in the United States can be counted on to walk lockstep with AIPAC; they will define as "delegitimizing Israel" any organization, newspaper, magazine, columnist, or individual that exposes or challenges unethical behaviors of the Israeli government toward Palestinians or that criticizes the Occupation or the Gaza blockade.

When people point out the vast power of the Israel Lobby to shape American policy or show how it stifles American interests (as John Mearsheimer and Stephen Walt demonstrated in *The Israel Lobby*), they are immediately labeled anti-Semitic by many in the Jewish world. The argument is that these critics are reactivating traditional anti-Semitic stories that exaggerate "Jewish power" in order to mobilize hate campaigns against Jews.

This criticism might make more sense if in fact the Israel Lobby was exclusively or primarily Jewish. But the truth of American politics is that while Jews may be most prominent in this respect, the blind loyalty toward Israel in the U.S. Congress is at least as strong in congressional districts where Jews play a very small role in local politics. The reason: Christian Zionists. These are people whose evangelical Christian beliefs have led them to become strong advocates for any policy supported by the Israeli government.

For some, Christian Zionism is a product of a justified guilt at the history of Christian oppression of Jews, which then gets misdirected into blind support for the Israeli government. For others, it is a product of a particular version of Christian fundamentalism that preaches the notion that Jesus will return to earth and provide redemption to all true Christians only after the Jews have returned to Israel and engaged in a final war between Gog and Magog. Being nice to the Jews and helping Israel is seen as an integral part of working out this Christian scenario, which, interestingly, also envisions and hopes for the conversion of Jews to Christianity.

When Jewish leaders in the United States are asked by the Israeli peace movement how they can make common cause with Christians who believe that, once Jesus returns, all Jews will either convert or go to Hell, their cynical response often goes something like this: "We take our help where we can get it. We'll worry about eternal damnation once Jesus actually returns to earth, which we don't believe is going to happen very soon."

Put together the Christian Zionists, AIPAC, and many from the older generation in the Jewish community who feel a blind loyalty to Israel, and you get a powerful political force. To say so is certainly not anti-Semitic. In fact, AIPAC has boasted about this power as a way of convincing Congress and various administrations that they ought not buck the Israel Lobby.

Acknowledging the power of the Israel Lobby does not, however, lead me to believe that it is the decisive element shaping American foreign policy in the Middle East. U.S. foreign policy is decisively shaped by what President Eisenhower warned about when he retired as president: our military-industrial complex. Today, we should probably add to that the "intelligence" and "security" institutions of the United States. These are not some hidden or conspiratorial elements—they conduct public discussions and debates among themselves, rely on policy experts in universities and Washington think tanks, consult with elites in countries they consider our allies, and together shape the fundamentals of American foreign policy.

For the past several decades these elites have come to believe that Israel serves American strategic interests; they see Israel as a potential threat to those in the Middle East who might be tempted to challenge American oil interests, and they believe Israeli technology is useful to American corporations and the U.S. military. If, however, those elites should ever decide that the alliance with Israel no longer serves their interests, the power of the Israel Lobby would decrease dramatically. So although the Israel Lobby is one dimension of the problem and challenging it can be an important element in a strategy for seeking peace and reconciliation in the Middle East, it is only one of the dimensions of the problem we face.

The most effective group doing this work right now is J Street and its chairman, Jeremy Ben Ami. Ben Ami's strategy is to show that ending the Occupation is the best path for Israel's future security. This strategy has major limitations. It means that J Street rarely emphasizes to Jewish audiences or to the media anything about the suffering of Palestinians under the Occupation. Its bottom line is "credibility" among those who believe that the only important reason to end the Occupation is to strengthen Israel; this narrows its discourse away from ethical and even Jewish prophetic concerns. As a result, others like Jewish Voices for Peace (JVP) continue to build lobbies that are more focused on the hurtfulness of the Occupation, even as they seek to weaken the Israel Lobby (though so far with far less inside-the-Beltway effectiveness than J Street). I'm wholeheartedly supporting J Street, and I understand and appreciate the subtlety of its strategy. But I also believe in supporting JVP and other strategies that more directly and unequivocally challenge the Israel Lobby and highlight the immorality of the Occupation and its inconsistency with fundamental Jewish religious and spiritual values.

At the same time, and not in contradiction to supporting J Street and JVP, I'm continuing to build our interfaith Network of Spiritual Progressives for those who seek to draw from biblical and prophetic discourse that unequivocally champions the powerless, to study the wisdom of all the religious and spiritual traditions of the human race, to apply that wisdom to the Israel/ Palestine struggle, and to highlight the pain in both Israel and Palestine. It is my view that healing Israel and Palestine will require not only Jews, but many, many non-Jews to give this their priority attention. So having the Network of Spiritual Progressives as an intentionally interfaith organization pursuing a "progressive middle path" that is both pro-Israel AND pro-Palestine gives an appropriate context for pro-peace and pro-reconciliation Jews, Muslims, Christians, Buddhist, Hindus, secular humanists, atheists, and others. They can work together not only to challenge the inside-the-Beltway discourse of AIPAC and the Israel Lobby, but to build a mass grassroots base for the dramatic turn in U.S. policy described below in Strategy Six.

STRATEGY FOUR: UN RECOGNITION OF PALESTINE

The decision to recognize Palestine as a state and a member of the United Nations could be an important step, if done in the right way. Flying the flag of Palestine at the United Nations and around the world should send an important message to Palestinians that their long struggle for respect and acknowledgment of their suffering has taken a giant step forward. And peace efforts would be strengthened if the resolution recognizing Palestine also included acknowledgment of Israel as an affirmative action state for Jews and Palestine as an affirmative action state for Palestinians; each would have the right to give priority in immigration matters to the communities they were set up to serve, but both states would be required to adhere to full and equal human rights in employment, housing, travel, education, freedom of religion (and freedom from religion). Both states would also maintain the right to protect themselves from terror and military interventions or conquest. Recognition by the United Nations would have far greater meaning if the General Assembly simultaneously set up a fund to provide reparations to both the Palestinian people and Israelis who fled Arab lands.

Yet UN recognition may also prove to be an obstacle to peace to the extent that it reinforces Israelis' perceptions that they face a hostile world and can only depend on their own strength. The United Nations has been largely discredited in Israel because of its "Zionism is racism" resolution (even though that was eventually retracted under pressure from the United States) and because the UN Human Rights Committee has passed condemnatory resolutions against Israel while ignoring the far greater human rights repression in China, Iran, the United States, and other nations.

UN recognition of Palestine, however, could have a positive impact on Israeli consciousness if the General Assembly also passed a set of resolutions that acknowledged the two-sidedness of the Israel/Palestine struggle, condemned violence against Israeli and Palestinian civilians, expressed sympathy for the suffering of the Jewish people, and expressed the right of Israel, like any other sovereign state, to take actions it deems necessary for its own self-defense—as long as that does not include continuing the Occupation of the West Bank and Gaza. It would also help for the United Nations to acknowledge that both sides have contributed to the current mess, that both sides have acted in harsh and cruel ways, and that both sides have a legitimate claim on the land of Israel/Palestine.

Doing this does not require the United Nations to deny the inequalities of power between Israel and the Palestinians. Nor should it lead to the United Nations accepting as legitimate Israel's policy of blockading Gaza. But a difference in tone and respect could have an impact on Israeli consciousness. Moreover, a UN General Assembly convocation in Israel and

Palestine, if done in a way that conveyed genuine caring for the well-being of both sides, might be an important step in this direction. Done without this spirit of compassion for Israel and Israelis, the recognition of a Palestinian state by the General Assembly could have great symbolic but little on-the-ground impact on the Israel/Palestine struggle.

President Obama assured AIPAC and Israel in the spring of 2011 that the United States would continue to veto full membership of Palestine; without the Security Council's acceptance of Palestine and simultaneous reaffirmation of support for Israel's security and Israel's right to exist as an affirmative action state for Jews, the General Assembly resolution will have little impact in changing Israeli policy on the ground.

Yet this necessary compassion, expressed in a UN resolution embracing both Palestine and Israel, is unlikely to be supported by the Arab states, by most UN members, or by the pro-Palestinian forces in Europe, North America, or Palestine. Their need to express their righteous indignation will likely trump their ability to see that their own goals and interests would best be served through a spirit of generosity and caring for the Israelis—precisely that which is also absent in Israel's treatment of Palestinians.

STRATEGY FIVE: BOYCOTTS, DIVESTMENT, AND SANCTIONS AGAINST SETTLEMENTS—NOT AGAINST ISRAEL

There are two very different kinds of Boycotts, Divestment and Sanctions (BDS) proposals that are being debated by peace movement activists.

The first kind I'll call "coercive, non-targeted BDS" and label it BDS1. It aims to change Israeli policy by creating strong external pressure until Israel capitulates to the demand to end the Occupation. Its proponents focus on Israel as a society, arguing that one must challenge Israeli society as a whole since the country has democratically elected governments that imposed and continue to tighten the knots of oppression on the Palestinian people.

The second kind I'll call "targeted, moral-witness BDS" and label it BDS2. It seeks to provide a way for those who oppose the Occupation to take actions in their own personal lives that reflect their ethical outrage at Israeli policies and at the settlers. It does not target Israel as a society; it targets only the Occupation itself and the settlers.

BDS1 is a nonviolent yet coercive strategy that involves economic pressure rather than military confrontation. Its advocates imagine a huge global movement of people who will refuse to buy products from Israel, get major investors to divest from firms that do business with Israel, and/or get governments to put economic sanctions on Israel. (This includes refusing to sell weapons to Israel, eliminating Israel's status as the largest foreign aid recipient of U.S. largesse, and perhaps refusing to sell Israel oil or other energy supplies.) Some advocates of BDS1 urge universities and cultural or scientific institutions to refuse any collaboration with Israel; they urge organizations not to hold conferences in Israel, musicians and literary figures not to appear at public events in Israel, and ordinary Western civilians not to vacation in Israel.

What I like about BDS1 is that it's something that people can do besides helplessly look on and wait for negotiations that never happen, drag on endlessly, or produce technocratic solutions that do not dispel the anger on both sides. True, boycotts don't always work directly, but they sometimes are able to generate a shift in consciousness and a higher level of awareness; that is a first necessary step in this situation.

Nevertheless, I do not advocate the BDS1 strategy. The first and most important reason is that BSD1 is likely to produce (and has already produced) a defensive and paranoid response in Israeli PSTD victims, which is most of the society. It elicits the exact opposite outcome from what is needed to move toward ending the Occupation. The feeling that "the whole world is against us" leads people to support right-wing politicians and self-destructive policies rather than opening their hearts to the Palestinians and seeing them as potential allies and friends.

The second reason I do not currently embrace BDS1 is that as a worldwide movement it has not articulated what it really wants for Israel and Palestine. Some people say that the goal is "the end of the Occupation." However, it turns out that for at least a significant element of the BDS1 movement in Europe and in Palestine, "the Occupation" does not mean what happened in 1967 but what happened in 1948 (the creation of Israel itself). For many of these people, it is the very existence of the State of Israel that is "the Occupation." I do not support or want to be associated with a movement that seeks to end Israel's existence. So until the BDS1 movement unequivocally commits to supporting Israel's existence, even while seeking to change its policies, I can't sign up.

The third reason I do not support the BDS1 strategy at this time, even though I have great admiration for some of its activists whose moral courage impresses me more than their strategic choice, is that it is wildly premature politically. BDS1 supporters often point to the role of BDS in overturning apartheid in South Africa. I was part of the U.S. branch of that anti-apartheid movement. When it first became a significant force on U.S. campuses in the early 1980s, the Civil Rights Movement in the United States had already created a mass understanding of the evils of anti-black racism.

So when ultra-conservative President Ronald Reagan took power in the 1980s, he never disputed that apartheid was an evil system that needed to be replaced. Almost everyone across the political spectrum in Western countries agreed that it was evil. Instead, Reagan argued that the most effective way to eliminate the apartheid system was through what he called "constructive engagement." We in the anti-apartheid movement argued that this was unlikely to have any impact on the South African government; over the course of the next ten years, we managed to convince universities, churches, and eventually the U.S. Congress and major corporations to divest from and boycott South Africa until it ended apartheid.

But nothing like this consensus exists today in the United States about the evils of the Occupation, and even less consensus exists about what might be wrong with the current manifestations of Zionism in Israel. BDS works when a majority of the population already supports the goal (e.g., the end of the Occupation). In a 2011 Gallup poll, 63 percent of Americans indicated that they sympathized with Israel more than with the Palestinians; this was the highest rating of support for Israel since 1991. American Jews make up only 2.2 percent of the United States. Until Americans reject the very notion that they must choose between support for Israel and support for Palestine, and until they can tell the pollsters that the well-being of each depends on the well-being of the other, there is no chance that BDS can be an effective strategy.

However, I do support BDS2, a softer version that carefully and publicly affirms its support for the State of Israel's existence and yet urges people not to buy from companies that produce consumer goods in the West Bank settlements or produce weapons or other equipment for the Israeli military to use in the West Bank and Gaza. BDS2 may be summed up in the following pledge: "I do not now, nor will I ever consciously, buy or allow for the sale of products that have been produced by West Bank settlers. Nor will I buy or allow for the sale of military equipment to Israel that is used primarily to enforce the Occupation of the West Bank or to build settlements. I will do this until a just and sustainable two-state solution is firmly in place and is building reconciliation of the heart between Israel and Palestine."

BDS2 focuses on the Occupation, not on the existence of Israel, and thus has far greater moral authority. But that doesn't make it any less scorned by much of the American Jewish and Israeli establishment. In July 2011, the Israeli Knesset passed a law that effectively made it a crime to publicly support a boycott against Israel—including a targeted boycott of Israeli settlement products. Human rights organizations were even joined by the pro-settlements Anti-Discrimination League in emphasizing that Israel was suppressing free speech and destroying its own democratic values. Nevertheless, the Knesset's law will allow Israelis to sue any individual or organization that publicly advocates for BDS1 or BDS2, and the complainant need not prove any personal damages to win large material compensation.

I also oppose coercive tactics to push Palestine toward a peace agreement, for many of the same reasons. Just as it is unlikely that coercion would generate a change in consciousness of those Israelis who wish they lived in a world without Palestinians, so it is unlikely that coercion would change the minds of Palestinians who wish they lived in a world without Jews. When a large-scale Palestinian peace movement emerges that supports reconciliation of the heart with Israel, I will rejoice. But I do not believe that any set of coercive tactics is likely to move us closer to that time, as decades of violence and coercion by Israel have proven. In fact, coercion moves us much further away from the goal and makes people more intransigent.

STRATEGY SIX: A GLOBAL MARSHALL PLAN FOR ISRAEL/PALESTINE

Hundreds of millions of people around the world have begun to realize that our well-being as individuals and the well-being of the planet depend on the well-being of everyone else. We are fundamentally interconnected. This message, embedded in almost all of the world's spiritual and religious traditions and in most forms of secular humanism, is precisely the recognition that we at *Tikkun* and the Network of Spiritual Progressives (NSP) believe is necessary to reshape the political, economic, social, and spiritual dynamics in the United States, the West, and the Middle East.

To turn that insight into action, we at the NSP developed our campaign for a Global Marshall Plan (GMP). The GMP is a plan for all of the world's people to work in solidarity to eliminate poverty once and for all and to heal the environmental crisis. The GMP takes its name from the post–World War II Marshall Plan, a massive and successful project to provide aid to Western European countries—including Germany, which had been our antagonist in the war. Similar steps were taken by the United States to support the rebuilding of Japan.

We believe the Middle East could become the first location for implementing such a plan. It could play a major role in changing the dynamics between Israel/Palestine if (and only if) it was implemented in a spirit of genuine caring, generosity, and openheartedness. It would need to include atonement for the ways that we (whoever that we is, including at least the United States and the Western powers) have failed to adequately care for the well-being of others and express a genuine desire to repair the damage we've done to the planet and its people in the past several hundred years. The GMP could defeat terrorism and violence more effectively than any strategy of domination, militarism, "savvy" public relations, and self-interested global corporate manipulations. And it could undermine the depressive certainty that everyone is only out for themselves and will take advantage of others when given the chance. It would be a major blow against PTSD and the fear of being a freier—psychological forces that otherwise are likely to undermine any peace agreement.

Historians have debated how altruistic the original Marshall plan was. Some argue that a large part of the motivation for the plan was to strengthen capitalist economies in Europe to prevent them from becoming communist. A similar motive to prevent the world from devolving into terrorist-generated chaos might inspire some who will join our efforts for a GMP. But other historians point to the strong strands of generosity that were tapped when Americans embraced rebuilding the devastated lives of the defeated nations against whom they had just waged war. This was enlightened self-interest; it can ally with strong altruistic and empathic tendencies that persist in Americans and many others around the world. This time, it could be mobilized to combat the suffering of humanity that leads to destructive wars, violence, and ecological irresponsibility.

Here are the key components of the plan (a full version of which you can read at www.spiritualprogressives.org/GMP):

1. Use between 1 percent and 2 percent of the U.S. Gross Domestic Product (GDP) and the GDP of other advanced industrial countries to once and for all end both domestic and global poverty, homelessness, hunger, inadequate education, and inadequate health care, as well as to repair the global environment.

2. Create local, national, and international boards composed of the poor, NGOs serving the poor or struggling for social justice, and cultural, spiritual, intellectual, and religious leaders with a proven history

of commitment to social justice struggles. These boards will employ economists, social planners, and experts in health, education, and welfare who are committed to the goals of this project to ensure that the funds do not get siphoned off to the government, to elites, or to projects that do not deliver education, health care, and elimination of poverty.

3. Change all global and regional trade agreements so that they no longer primarily serve the interests of the advanced industrial countries or local elites in poorer countries. These agreements should aid the reestablishment of local, ecologically sensitive farms and support the provision of free, high-quality water.

4. Implement this plan in a spirit of ecological and cultural sensitivity and humility. Cultural sensitivity means that we must make sure that the GMP is implemented by the people who are receiving whatever we have to offer in the way of goods or services in a way that affirms and respects their own cultural heritage. Humility means that people in advanced industrial countries must recognize that our greater wealth has not necessarily been accompanied by greater wisdom or spiritual depth and that other nations' poverty has often been a result of the way the West has exercised its global power.

5. Fund this plan through cutbacks in military expenditures, through a 1 percent tax on all global financial transactions of over one million dollars (often labeled a "Tobin tax," after the economist who first suggested this approach), and through taxes on the super-wealthy. This includes anyone owning more than

100 million dollars in assets and oil companies making after-tax-profits of more than a billion dollars, excluding those profits reinvested in developing sustainable public transportation and alternative energy sources.

Where aid has failed to work as expected or hoped, it is not mainly because funds have been siphoned off or misused, but because they have not been part of a comprehensive plan to end both domestic and global poverty. Imagine that you wanted to end malaria, but instead of draining all the swamps in your area, you drained a few at a time, often with inadequate funds to even do that effectively. Then, after some time, people in your society said, "Let's stop draining the swamps—after all, that hasn't had much of an impact on malaria, but meanwhile it's costing us higher taxes." They'd be right. The partial steps have not worked and will not work.

These next decades are likely to be the last in which U.S. economic and military power decisively shapes the world. As China, India, and other countries become more powerful, they will likely draw upon the precedents we've set as a world power. If we could dedicate our next two decades to showing how a world power could transcend us-versus-them thinking, we could be proud of the American legacy. And that legacy could dramatically affect the "common sense" that leads Israelis and Palestinians to believe that they must protect themselves against the dangerous Other.

To make the global change in consciousness, people in the United States might stop talking about keeping America "number one" and stop ignoring the suffering of billions on this planet. We in Western societies could show that world powers can act in ways that seek the advantage of all people on the planet. Too many otherwise decent people shrug their shoulders in despair about achieving this kind of consciousness in America. They tell themselves that to be realists, they must accept the current way that the capitalist system functions, with its unrelenting struggle for wealth and power at the top. If we want to promote an ethos of generosity and caring for others, we need to help people become aware of every aspect of our lives in which the dominant ethos of selfishness and materialism is being reinforced, and then argue for our version of the Global Marshall Plan as part of the strategy to heal our society of these distortions.

Many people try to make this change in their own lives, or they find a religious or spiritual community in which generosity trumps selfishness. To change the world in a significant way, these inclinations toward a different way of being in the world need to find political expression in an explicit public challenge to the dominant ethos. The GMP provides a vehicle for making that challenge heard. Generosity and genuine caring for others can be a much more effective and morally coherent approach to human safety, "homeland security," peace, and development. We call this approach the Strategy of Generosity.

Building the Strategy of Generosity requires that we reconnect with our human capacity to recognize others as embodiments of the sacred or, in the secular language, as fundamentally worthy because of who they are and not just because of what they can do for us. This profound and intuitive connection among people must become the center of our campaign for peace and environmental sanity. The bonds of caring among human beings can and must be fostered and nurtured by our policies. Otherwise, they are often undermined by economic and political arrangements that make these fundamental human ties seem unrealistic and even threatening.

The key to our Strategy of Generosity is our commitment to cultivating trust and hope among the peoples of the world so that we might begin to reflect and act effectively to end world poverty in our lifetime and save the global environment from almost certain destruction. We at *Tikkun* offer this plan with a commitment to humility and the conviction that the GMP must derive from our commitment to the well-being of everyone on the planet and not primarily from a self-interested motivation to advance American or Western world power and influence. However, we of course know that this is actually a far better way to achieve homeland security than spending trillions on arms, military assaults, and "defense."

We must also make clear that although the West has superior technology and material success, we do not equate that with superior moral or cultural wisdom. As described earlier, our approach must reflect a deep humility and a spirit of repentance for the ways in which Western dominance of the planet has been accompanied by wars, environmental degradation, and a growing materialism and selfishness. We have much to learn from non-Western cultures, from their spiritual and intellectual heritage, and from their ways of dealing with human relationships. That insight must guide the kind of Global Marshall Plan that the NSP supports, so that this doesn't end up being a new installment of "the ugly Americans" pushing our agenda around the world.

The GMP can work only if it is perceived not as a new way for the West to dominate the world or fund further penetration of Western corporate and media dominance around the planet, but primarily as the manifestation of a new awareness that has grown in the Western world of our interdependence with and caring for everyone on the planet. Even domestic support for the GMP will grow to the extent that people perceive it as a manifestation of genuine caring rather than primarily as a smart and savvy way to protect the United States (which it also is) or as a way for some smart liberal and progressive politicians to gain greater public support (which it also is). For us, the GMP is worthy not only because it serves the biblical imperative to care for the poor and the downtrodden, but also because the very debate around the idea of a Strategy of Generosity will be empowering.

If the campaign for a GMP adheres to the approach we present here, it will help many people recognize their deeply held (but sometimes denied) desire for mutual recognition, genuine caring, and love. Insisting on values like generosity, repentance, humility, and the transcendence of selfishness and materialism provides a language to challenge the one-dimensional, technocratic rationality that is often presented as the only form of respectable thinking in our society. Our language seeks to support the reemergence of a heart-centered rationality that involves responding to others with overflowing generosity and responding to the universe with radical amazement at the grandeur of all that is.

Though it's likely to take a long time for our version of the GMP to be adopted by the United States and other world governments, the campaign for it has an intrinsic value because it brings fundamental, long-ignored human needs into public discourse, challenging the widely held notions of "what is realistic" that have constricted our imaginations and crippled our politics. We need to advocate for love, generosity, respect, and caring in a strong way, not defensively or as if we suspect that they are secondary measures to integrate only if we can "afford to." The truth is that the advanced industrial societies of the world can't afford to do anything less than the GMP.

One reason people associate these kinds of ideas with the consciousness of a freier is that those who advocate for them in the public sphere tend to be defensive and appear to lack backbone. For example, most Democrats in Congress usually act as though they know the real way to defend the country is through the military, and they are hoping to do a little bit of generosity on the side to satisfy their religious or humanistic impulses. Even when the majority of Americans opposed the wars in Iraq and

Afghanistan, the Democrats refused to use their power over the budget to cut the funding for those wars.

Contrast that with people on the Right who, even when they were a minority in the Congress, managed to get their way on issues like cutting taxes for the wealthy or opposing environmental or immigration reform. They are willing to fight for what they believe in even if the perspective they are fighting to legitimate is temporarily unpopular. Democrats unintentionally convey the message that generosity or caring for the earth or for the powerless is a wimpy strategy. It is not. But those who want a world transformed need to assert the wisdom of the Strategy of Generosity just as powerfully as those on the political Right have asserted the wisdom of the Strategy of Domination.

How the GMP Campaign Supports Middle East Peace

Many people in the United States and Europe wonder what they can do to help bring peace to the Middle East. A too small number decide to volunteer on behalf of nonviolent demonstrations against the Occupation or to monitor human rights abuses on both sides of the struggle. Others organize dialogues between Jews, Christians, and Muslims both at home and in Israel/Palestine. Still others try to lobby Congress and show that there is a constituency for peace. Some push for a negotiated settlement. All of these are great and valuable activities.

But they also have a limitation: they end up getting framed either within a pragmatic discourse or as acts of moral witness. Though both are valuable, neither addresses the need for a transformation in mass consciousness. I believe a lasting peace will become possible only once people on all sides of the struggle in the Middle East are thinking about the Other in different terms.

You might object: "We didn't need to accomplish that after World War II. We changed the worldview of fascism from the top and didn't need to engage in consciousness-raising in the United States." This is quite true. If that kind of conquest were possible by the West over both Arabs and Jews, and if we wanted our troops to stay in the region for twenty or thirty years to re-educate people and jail those interested in perpetuating violent struggle, that way might work. But that is not going to happen, nor do I think it would be good for that to happen.

Moreover, it wasn't military conquest alone that changed the dynamics in Western Europe; it was also the original Marshall Plan introduced by the United States after World War II to provide funds to rebuild Europe. The plan was later extended to Japan. For the first time in recorded history, a victor rebuilt the society and the economy it had destroyed—and it worked! So the Strategy of Generosity was already tried once and proved to be viable.

One example of how this change can happen is the way that consciousness in the Jewish and Arab worlds has begun to change around sexism. The gains against sexism have gone far beyond what the realists of thirty years ago imagined was possible, thanks to feminists' aggressive challenge to the dominant paradigm. That is exactly what needs to happen now in regard to peace. We need to challenge the view that the only way to be "tough" is to be a militarist or to seek domination and control.

Precisely because it is about changing the dominant paradigm, we need to be on our guard against those who say, "We can get the GMP passed, but we need to cut out this utopian rhetoric." Our response: the new way of thinking is what the program is about, and it must be explicitly articulated at every stage in the struggle. And if passed, the GMP must explicitly embody this utopian vision in every dimension of its activities. Otherwise, it will end up as another useless aid program that helps some but discourages many more. The goal is not only to win; the goal is also to change the way people think. And if we do that, we will find that we have an amazing impact on the thinking of people in Israel/Palestine.

But, you might object: "This is a long-term goal for ten or twenty years from now. We need a solution right now."

I encourage you to go get that solution implemented right now or as soon as possible. Nothing in this book is meant to discourage you from seeking short-term remedies that satisfy all sides of this struggle. But I've been involved in this search for many decades, and the long run eventually becomes the "now." As far as I can see, the movements seeking peace and justice for Palestinians and security for Israel have failed in part because they didn't take time to consider a bigger picture involving changes of consciousness.

There is no reason you can't simultaneously volunteer on a short-term project in the next few years and insist that every such project teach people explicitly about the need for generosity, openhearted repentance, and acceptance of the legitimacy of both narratives. Moreover, we should all insist that some time in each demonstration and political meeting be devoted to learning the skills of a discourse of love and caring for anyone conceived of as the Other. If, for example, you are someone who believes BDS1 is a good strategy or someone whose primary focus is on educating Congress or building an effective counter-lobby to AIPAC, ask yourself how to get your movement to spend some of its time training one another to speak about generosity, openhearted repentance, acceptance of the legitimacy of both sides' narratives, and love and caring for the Other.

I urge members of the peace movements to organize their supporters in the West to advocate for the Global Marshall Plan, to teach people about the pathological fear of being a freier, and to learn how to honor the narratives of both sides. Projects with this kind of energy will likely go viral on the internet and in personal relationships; this will help make our peace movements actually feel peaceful rather than filled only with righteous indignation.

And let lobbyists, demonstrators, public assemblies, and conferences dedicate part of their time to the Strategy of Generosity as manifested through a GMP. Let those on all sides of the struggle in both Israeli and Palestinian camps begin to hear that the world is seeing those who resort to violence or oppression or occupation not as "strong" or "heroic" but as people who are suffering from PTSD and therefore need compassion and treatment rather than celebration and encouragement. Some of the swagger will then drain from their self-image, and their dedication to entrenching this conflict will diminish.

And then there is an even more direct way that the GMP is relevant. In light of the Arab Spring with all its strengths and some of its limitations, this may be a perfect moment to call on our elected leaders to try out the GMP strategy in the Middle East. Eliminating poverty and hopelessness in Egypt, Palestine, Israel, Jordan, and Lebanon could be an important contribution to encouraging the openheartedness that is so badly needed. Israel Lobby folk would jump at any opportunity to see more U.S. money go to Israel, even if it had to be used to end poverty (which is extreme in Israel). Liberals and progressives would support this as an opportunity to see an end to the conflict between Israel and Palestine. And a growing number of conservatives would throw in their support because they want the United States to bring the military home and stop putting troops in danger to resolve tribal feuds that are unlikely to impact the safety of Americans. All of these groups could be weaved together to support a Middle East-focused GMP.

It all seems so fanciful at a moment when congressional Republicans have convinced the country that what is really needed is to cut social programs and defund the government so that corporations and the rich will no longer face any constraints in their efforts to amass huge wealth in the hands of the few. At *Tikkun* we predicted all this from the third month of the Obama administration. We understood that the huge positive energy for fundamental change that brought Obama to office had raised hopes in people and opened them to the voice of the Left Hand of God that exists in almost everyone. When people start to move their consciousness toward hope, caring for others, generosity, and belief that there is a "we" that can together change things, we also experience intense anxiety and vulnerability. We don't want to believe that we have been snookered once again. The voice of the Right Hand of God is also there, warning us not to trust anyone, telling us that everyone is really selfish and out for themselves, and that nothing fundamental can ever change.

So when the Obama administration decided to use the moment that it inherited, one in which the capitalist system itself was begging for public funds to help the wealthy and largely ignore the plight of the unemployed and those losing their homes to rapacious mortgage companies, the bubble of hope started to fade. It faded as Obama escalated the war in Afghanistan. It faded as Obama refused to punish those involved with torture and violations of our domestic civil liberties and human rights. It faded as Obama abandoned his promise to fight for a public option in health care and instead backed a plan that forced people to buy private health insurance without any corresponding limits on the escalating costs generated by money-hungry private insurers and health profiteers. And it faded as Obama failed to push for any serious environmental or immigration reforms and then announced that he believed that the government should run its finances like a private family—and hence not create the kind of deficit spending that had worked to get the United States out of the Great Depression of the 1930s.

No wonder so many people felt like freiers. Instead of feeling outraged and betrayed, most of those who had allowed themselves to hope retreated into their private lives, hoping to get their own finances or jobs secured. They thereby created the space for the Right Hand of God strategists of domination to become the loudest voice in politics. The ultimate betrayal was not that Obama failed to convince Republican obstructionists or Democratic Party congressional leaders to enact his programs. Rather, it was his failure to affirm the values that people who responded to his message had believed he would articulate, and hence his failure to bring together a force that could ultimately change American politics to become a manifestation of caring and generosity.

Why talk about this in a book about Israel/Palestine? Because the hope in a Strategy of Generosity, the hope for openhearted reconciliation and lasting peace, are weakened when people despair about whether their highest vision is really possible or just a utopian pipe dream.

What I've learned about politics in my fifty years of involvement in it is this: those who tell you that politics is the art of the possible have forgotten a very important truth. *You never know what is possible until you commit your life energies to fighting for what is desirable.* So before you give up on this book and think that Rabbi Lerner is a naïve optimist, consider these facts:

- When Theodore Herzl published *The Jewish State* in 1897, there were few Jews on the planet who thought he was anything more than a naïve optimist if not a crackpot. Fifty years later, his saying "if the community wills it, it is not a legend" sounded like common sense.

- When Israeli peace activists met with PLO leaders in the 1980s, they were called traitors, and Israel promised never to speak to the PLO. Less than ten years later, Israeli leaders were in deep negotiations with the PLO.

- When a small group of feminists in the 1960s said they wanted not just equal pay for equal work, but an end to sexism and patriarchy, they were dismissed as fantasizers who simply did not realize that patriarchy had been around for 10,000 years. By the early decades of the twenty-first century, sexism and patriarchy (while far from being defeated) were being challenged in advanced industrial societies and even in many traditional and economically underdeveloped societies.

- When twenty years ago gays and lesbians moved beyond the demand to stop harassment of homosexuals and called for gay marriage, few in their community and fewer in the rest of American society thought that would be achievable in the next hundred years. Today, six U.S. states have legalized gay marriage.

- Whatever the limits of the Arab Spring of 2011 as it plays out over time, the idea that Tunisians, Egyptians, Syrians, and Libyans would rise up against their dictatorial regimes and against what appeared to be overwhelming military odds, risking death and torture to fight for their own liberation, would have been dismissed as utopian fantasizing just a few months before it actually happened.

After victories are won, or mass struggles are launched, the very "savvy" opinion shapers, political scientists, sociologists, economists, and television talking heads who once explained why these developments were impossible suddenly write and talk about why these victories were inevitable.

And so it will be when there is a triumph of the new ethos on this planet that I've been describing. So go on reading the rest of this book, allowing yourself to momentarily suspend all of the voices in your head (and in all of our heads, because we've all been conditioned to "be realistic" and dismiss transformative possibilities) that are screaming that none of this is possible.

Chapter Ten

EMBRACING THE LEFT HAND
OF GOD

IF WE LOOK CLOSELY AT THE DYNAMICS of the struggle underlying the politics of the contemporary world, we can see a contest between two spiritual worldviews that has been going on for thousands of years in the West: the struggle between a worldview of domination and a worldview of generosity, openheartedness, forgiveness, and love.

Understanding this struggle, which saturates the consciousness of almost everyone, is key to understanding not only Israel/Palestine, but also the politics of most of the world's advanced industrial countries and those in the underdeveloped world whose cultures have been penetrated by the culture of the West. These two conflicting worldviews stem from two different conceptions of the nature of human beings that have been in contention for thousands of years—conceptions that I call the Left Hand of God and the Right Hand of God.

Here is a quick summary of the dueling worldviews:

The Right Hand of God is a perspective of fear and domination. In this view, humans are thrown into the world alone. Narrowly self-interested others surround us and are waiting to manipulate, control, and dominate us to achieve their own goals of power, success, sexual conquest, and material wealth. Faced with such a world, the rational strategy for each of us is to maximize advantage by learning how to be effective in dominating, manipulating, and controlling others. In fact, the world around us judges us to be rational, efficient, productive, and savvy precisely to the extent that we excel at the skills of domination, manipulation, and control. In this worldview, to be rational is to maximize one's self-interest. And to achieve security, we must learn how to dominate others. This wisdom not only constitutes the shared wisdom of daily life but also serves as a foundational principle of the capitalist economy and of national strategies for "homeland security."

The Left Hand of God is a perspective of love and generosity. In this view, human beings do not come into the world alone but through a mother and father; our capacity to survive and thrive in the first years of our lives is dependent on "nurturing others" who have given us loving care without a reasonable expectation of a good return on their investments of time and emotional energy. This experience indelibly sticks in our minds and leads some contemporary theorists to argue that human beings are hardwired to be empathic, compassionate, and loving. To the extent that we've had this experience as children (and nearly everyone has had it to some extent), we begin to be moved by theories, often articulated through one religious and spiritual tradition or another, that the way to a good life is through building cooperative, caring, and loving relationships, first in personal life, but then also in our broader communities. In this view, "homeland security" can best be achieved through generosity and caring toward others—behavior that in many if not all situations will elicit a similar response.

Most people alive today have been exposed to both of these worldviews, and most are somewhere on the continuum between the worldview of fear and domination and the worldview of love and generosity. Where we are exactly at any given moment is a product of:

1. Our actual childhood experiences (How much loving did our parents communicate? Did the kids and teachers we encountered at school and in the rest of our lives communicate love to us too?)

2. Our adult life experiences (How much did we encounter people who treated us like embodiments of the sacred rather than instruments to fulfill their own needs, desires, and goals?)

3. Our society's predominant worldviews, religious systems, and ideologies (These are communicated through the media, the educational system, and the religious, spiritual, political, civic, and professional organizations to which we are exposed, not to mention the workplaces in which we spend much of our waking lives.)

4. The continuous moving of social energy toward fear or hope (When the societal energy moves toward fear, as it has in the past few decades, the worldview of fear sounds more profound and obvious, and its articulators sound smart and prophetic. When social energy moves toward hope and generosity, then those who articulate an ethos of generosity and openheartedness begin to sound more wise and prophetic.)

In class-dominated societies in which the wealthy and powerful shape the educational systems, the media, and much of what happens in the political arena, it is no surprise that the worldview of fear and domination becomes the most widely accepted perspective. Given that people spend all day in a world of work based on competition, they come to believe that the status quo is all that is possible in "the real world." They may hate this reality and seek solace by attaching themselves to a religious or spiritual community with a worldview of love and generosity, but in daily life most people today tend to have the skeptical or even cynical perspective generated by the worldview of fear and domination.

Often people are encouraged to displace the anger they feel at being in this kind of world onto some Other, who then becomes for them the symbolic representation of the hurts they feel but dare not attribute to the social and economic order in which they live—lest they be inclined to express their outrage against the powerful, who could punish them severely for having such disloyal thoughts. It's far easier, then, to simply believe that they are stuck in a world in which domination and power over others is the only possible reality and their best hope is to ally with the most powerful forces rather than resist those forces.

Nevertheless, the other voice is there, still part of our hardwiring and always ready to burst forth. That is why ruling elites invest so much money and energy in trying to reindoctrinate us. Once we believe the worldview of fear, the notion of trying to build a different kind of society seems utopian and childish, if not irresponsible. We base this on the theory that fighting for "the best" could be destructive in achieving "the good enough."

I want to also note here that whenever we talk about ruling elites, spiritual progressives want to stop the conversation long enough to remind ourselves that these people are also created in the image of God and that they are filled with the same needs as everyone else. While ruling elites may manipulate fear for the sake of strengthening their own power and increasing their wealth, it is also true, as my colleague Peter Gabel points out, that they act this way primarily because they are themselves caught in the same fear as everyone else. They do not believe in the possibility of a loving community of people and are certain that they will never find people whom they can really trust. They hence put their trust in money and power. When those who have money discover movements or communities that do provide some of this caring and mutual recognition, enough so that they can come to believe in the real possibility of a society based on love and generosity, they are often willing to give up part or all of their wealth to help sustain these communities and that dream.

In our own historical period, we've seen a resurgence of "domination as realism" appearing both in the foreign policy statements of politicians across the political spectrum and in various religious worldviews. This happened in some parts of Judaism in response to the trauma of the Holocaust. Angry and depressed about "the God that didn't save us in the Holocaust," too many Jews have embraced a false god, the god of power and financial security, which often translates into a quasi-religious belief that the Israeli army can defend Jews and that the American army can defend everyone else, including Israel, and that financial security is more important than a loving community. These beliefs then take on almost spiritual significance for some Jews, as they already have for tens of millions of right-wing Christians. Not all Jews and not all Christians have fallen into this trap, yet there is no way to deny that the struggle between the Right Hand of God and the Left Hand of God is a major part of the cultural, political, and religious reality of most religions in the contemporary world.

To the extent that Western societies have been increasingly tied to the dynamics of fear and increasingly adopt the logic of capitalism, people turn to contemporary religions in search of higher meaning and purpose. They seek a community in which the old-fashioned values of love, caring for others, solidarity, family, and community are esteemed. Religious communities become one of the last havens in a heartless world; they are a way of escaping and transcending the soullessness of the capitalist marketplace and implicitly criticizing its values. Unfortunately, people are often offered this kind of nurturing community at a price: the need to demean or exclude, from whatever salvation that religious community offers, the Others—those who are seen as "less than" because they are not part of the elect, the saved, the really valuable who are part of that special religious (or national) community.

And yet, the good news is that while the Right Hand of God predominates in some religious communities, including some Jewish communities, the past sixty years has also seen a growing challenge to the temptation to reject the Other and to dismiss the possibility of fundamental healing and transformation. Starting from a small group of people in the most privileged and powerful countries of the world, entrenched ideas and practices of racism, sexism, and homophobia have gone from being "just the way things are" to being put on the defensive within our societies' institutions, including religious institutions. Only a few decades ago, these elements of ordinary consciousness were so pervasive that anyone claiming that they could be overturned was dismissed as someone completely out of touch with reality.

So what makes such a shift possible? Let me describe some of the critical elements of the process, which may be helpful to new activists in Israel and in the United States.

Movements often begin with a small, ethically and psycho-spiritually awakened group. This group recognizes the problem and commits to changing society and individual behaviors in ways that might solve it. The group carefully studies the social, psychological, and ideological factors that have created or sustained the problem, and they develop a variety of strategies to tackle it.

This awakened group is usually attacked as elitist, judgmental, and out of touch. In fact, starting with Moses' fellow Israelites in the Bible, who denounced him as having made matters worse by telling the pharaoh to "let my people go," it is often the people who are most hurting who are also most angry at anyone who proposes a "solution"—particularly a solution that makes people feel momentarily uncomfortable with the way they have accommodated to their own situation and feelings of powerlessness.

The awakened group begins educational and consciousness-raising activities in the larger society, often facing ridicule or overt repression. The awakened group also helps create mass activities to draw in people who may not yet be ready to embrace all parts of the vision of social transformation. These activities spread a new understanding of some of the issues at stake and attract participation from many people who suspect that the vanguard group is onto something. Many who come are conflicted—they both want a change and feel pessimistic and unready for it internally. Those who are conflicted argue against the core vision of the awakened group.

New organizations begin to promote a shared vision of a healthier consciousness. Despite having previously been derided in the mass media and by political leaders, these organizations begin to be more proactive. Some of them bring their messages into their jobs. Others run for office, even though they are likely to be defeated at first, and use the democratic process as a way to spread their ideas. Still others begin to preach about these ideas in local churches, synagogues, mosques, and ashrams. While some lose their jobs for doing so, others find receptive audiences in their congregations. Eventually, they develop some social presence, emboldening those who wanted to believe in the new ideas but previously felt too scared. As the movement grows, more people who are not part of the movement begin to question their own thinking.

On the other hand, some of the movement's activists feel uncertain that the deepest goals of the movement can be reached. Fearing that the moment of growth will lead nowhere unless the movement becomes more "practical," they start to frame the issues very narrowly, seeking to translate the movement's central ideas into "winnable" demands within the current system. These new pragmatists often avoid highlighting the most transformative ideas of the movement's original vision. They develop legislative agendas that avoid incorporating elements seen as "too utopian" or "too idealistic."

Struggles break out within the movement about what is central and what is peripheral. Splits and divisiveness may occur, and if the movement itself is seen as a potentially serious threat to the existing social order, undercover agents may join the movement and encourage those splits, attack the most effective leaders or spread rumors and lies about them, and encourage people to act out their frustrations through actions that discredit the movement.

When conducted in a respectful way, these internal struggles can strengthen a movement. When conducted in a disrespectful way, they usually tear a movement apart. But if the more idealistic leaders are able to convince movement activists to stay with the deepest goals, there is a good chance that the movement will make a significant impact on mass consciousness.

If the movement's ideas make sense and correspond to most people's inner ethical intuitions; if a sizeable portion of the public can see past the movement's own distortions; and if the movement doesn't suffer too much violence or economic intimidation from those in power—then eventually the ideas become accepted as mainstream. At that point, at least some of the journalists, academics, and politicians who opposed the ideas at the beginning begin to talk as though these ideas are nothing new and everyone has always supported them. They say that the success of the movements that advocated these ideas can be explained by sociological or psychological factors that had always guaranteed such success. Frustrating as that often is for those who risked life, limb, job opportunities, and financial security or endangered their own close relationships for the sake of the cause, we should rejoice when previously "outrageous ideas" are talked about as ordinary and obvious.

That is precisely what will one day happen for those who are currently engaged in trying to build peace, reconciliation, and healing between Israel and Palestine. Those of us who are attempting to build a movement to reconcile hearts are motivated in large part by our concern to reduce the amount of suffering on both sides. We hence look at a twenty-to-thirty-year horizon rather than a fifty-to-sixty-year horizon within which reconciliation will take place.

As much as I wish to see the fulfillment of the prediction that "from out of Zion will come Torah, and the Word of the Lord from Jerusalem," I believe that the psychological and spiritual traumas of both Israelis and Palestinians make it harder for many of them to tap into the deepest ethical and spiritual intuition of the human race expressed most explicitly in the wise command of Torah: "Thou shalt love the stranger." The fear that leads so many religious Jews and Muslims away from their own historical attraction to the caring attributes of God—in addition to the deep cynicism held in secular Israeli and Palestinian circles about everything except the individualist global capitalist system—makes these countries less likely places for the worldview of generosity to first become public policy.

For this reason, healing and peace depend on the ascendency, within each religious and national grouping, of a worldview that unequivocally affirms the possibility of changing our world so that love, generosity, and compassion become the new common sense of all peoples.

The conflict in Israel/Palestine has put in sharp relief a larger struggle for the heart of Judaism, Islam, and Christianity. In my view, every major religious denomination or community is struggling over whether to align with the Left Hand of God or the Right Hand of God. Most people are capable of gravitating toward both of these conflicting perspectives. For example, those who are momentarily locked into the worldview of the Right Hand of God tend to be most responsive to the harsh, punitive, and judgmental parts of the Hebrew Bible, the New Testament, or the Koran—the parts that call for suspicion and the rejection of those who are not 100 percent committed to the path being advocated. Conversely, those who are attracted to the Left Hand of God are more responsive to the vision of God as compassionate and generous and to the teachings that manifest that love-oriented sensibility.

Both sensibilities are there in the holy texts of Jews, Christians, Muslims, Hindus, Buddhists, Jains, Sikhs, Bahai, Taoists, and most other of the world's religious communities—just as they are in the central texts of Marxism, contemporary psychology, feminism, etc. There is an obvious reason for this: both sensibilities exist in every human being. Those who are reporting how they heard God's voice or who are designing revolutionary secular transformations are naturally going to express themselves in these fundamental frameworks.

It is this inner struggle that manifests in how one interprets the struggle in Israel/Palestine and evaluates what interventions seem to make sense. The solutions proposed in this book will seem silly, naïve, or even ridiculous to those who are trapped in the worldview of fear but will seem hopeful to those who embrace the worldview of generosity and love. Most people, however, alternate between these two views; so at moments my interpretation of the conflict and my strategy to resolve it will have appeal and at other moments it will be summarily dismissed.

The religious and spiritual communities that do in fact embrace the Left Hand of God could stop being so modest about it and instead start to champion those ideas with a level of enthusiasm and commitment that has too often been expressed only by those who embrace the Right Hand of God. To do this, however, we need to rethink our own religious traditions and find a way to disassociate ourselves from the parts that have disempowered the Left Hand of God. I can illustrate that process by reflecting on the history of Judaism.

SETTLER JUDAISM AND POWER WORSHIP AFTER GOD'S "FAILURE"

The Jewish people faced many disappointments throughout our history to the extent that we believed in a "big man in heaven" version of God, who could and would intervene in history to save the righteous and condemn and defeat the forces of evil. The destruction of the first and second Temples in Jerusalem, and the subsequent exile from our land—not to mention the violence done to us by Christian communities that culminated in our expulsion from Spain and then in the pogroms in Europe—were major shocks to this perspective on God. The vastness of the Holocaust—its destruction of most of the ultra-Orthodox communities of Eastern Europe as well as the secular and assimilated communities of Jews in Western Europe—undermined any plausibility that the ancient understanding of God once had.

Zionism had been from the start a predominantly secular worldview: many Zionists thought Jews who embraced God and Judaism were suffering from a pathological powerlessness that led them to wait for God to lead them out of the oppressive and increasingly hate-filled reality of diaspora life. What was needed, these Zionists argued, was a new kind of Jew, a Jew who embraced power and acted from that power to save the Jewish people. And that could be accomplished only with a state of our own, an army that was powerful, and a rejection of the pitiful concern about "what will the *goyim* (non-Jewish nations of the world) think about us?" Jews must reenter history and become a nation like all other nations, using the tools of power that other nations use.

It was in this context that a new form of idolatry emerged and gradually became the dominant version of Judaism in the post-Holocaust age. This is what I call "Settler Judaism." There have been strands of the Right Hand of God in Judaism from the moment the Torah was written, but they were always balanced in the past by a strong commitment as well to the Left Hand of God. The most frequently repeated sentence on the most sacred day of the Jewish calendar, Yom Kippur, is the biblical quote affirming God's loving and forgiving consciousness: "*YHVH, YHVH, el rachum ve'chanun, erech apayim ve'rav chesed ve'emet*—YHVH, YHVH, enwombed and compassionate, patient, full of kindness and truth, bringing loving kindness to the many."

Moreover, to those of us who understand the frequent appearance of the Right Hand of God in Torah and subsequent parts of our tradition, the meaning of calling God a "Lord of Hosts" or a "Man of War" (*ish milchamah*) was to empower the powerless by assuring them that they were being cared for by a power greater than those who oppressed them.

Settler Judaism Grew to Dominate Zionism

Settler Judaism became the dominant ideology of religious Zionism in the years after the 1967 victory of Israel over Egypt, Syria, and Jordan. It found its first legitimization in the post-1948 prayer created by the Chief Rabbis of Israel, which is now said in all Orthodox synagogues and in some Conservative, Reform, and Reconstructionist synagogues throughout the world. The prayer begins, "Our Father in Heaven, Rock and Redeemer of Israel, bless the State of Israel, the first manifestation of the approach of our redemption." In a growing number of synagogues (including almost all Orthodox synagogues) this prayer is soon followed by another blessing for the IDF. Part of this prayer reads:

> May Hashem cause the enemies who rise up
> against us to be struck down. May the Holy One,
> Blessed is He, preserve and rescue our fighting
> men from every trouble and distress and from
> every plague and illness, and may He send
> blessing and success in their every endeavor....
> It is Hashem, your God, who goes with you to
> battle your enemies to save you.

Whereas the Bible is filled with prophetic energies that vigorously criticize the distortions of the kings and leaders of ancient Israel, here we have Judaism being appropriated to sanctify the enterprise of building the Jewish State and its military without the slightest recognition of the ease with which a state and a military can lose their way and serve interests that conflict with Jewish ideals. God is appropriated to serve national interests, thereby demeaning God and reducing the divine to narrow and self-interested national purposes.

Lest you wonder, while everyone prays for peace in the abstract, there is no widely accepted comparable prayer for the peace movement, for those who have risked their lives for the sake of maximizing love and compassion, or for those who have embraced the command to "love the stranger." Nor is there a prayer to protect those who seek peace from those in our community who use violence against them (for example, the murderer of Israeli Prime Minister Rabin). Nor is there any comparable Shabbat or holiday prayer in most branches of Judaism for the righteous of all other religions and nations who are seeking to build a world based on love and kindness. Nor is there a prayer for the well-being and health of the Palestinian people with whom Jews are sharing Palestine, much less a prayer for the success of their many peace activists. Some Jewish groups and synagogues are developing alternative prayers. Here's one that I've created:

> God of our ancestors and of our people, bless
> those people in every nation, ethnic group,
> religion, and race who are the peacemakers,
> the justice seekers, those who promote love and
> generosity, those who act in caring ways toward
> others, those who seek to end poverty and hunger
> and homelessness on this planet, those who
> welcome the undocumented immigrants and the
> refugees, those who heal the physical and psychic
> wounds of others, those who are the teachers
> and the nurturers of the young, those who are
> the caregivers of the aging and the sick, those
> who seek to increase respect, tolerance, and
> nonviolence, those who support the expansion
> of human rights not only for their own group
> but for those who have been labeled "enemies,"
> and those whose actions promote environmental
> sustainability and human dignity. We pray for
> an end to all wars and all forms of economic,
> social, and political oppression, for a triumph of
> love and caring for others to suffuse all peoples,
> and for a global recognition that our well-being
> depends on the well-being of all on this planet
> and on the well-being of the earth itself. We pray
> also for an end to the struggle between Israel
> and Palestine, for a healing of the physical and
> emotional wounds of the Jewish people and

the Palestinian people, wherever we and they
may be scattered. We pray that both Israel and
Palestine will become known among the nations
for their generosity and openhearted caring
for each other and for their ability to recognize
each other as sisters and brothers. Let love and
generosity prevail among all peoples and let us
as the human community repair all the damage
that has been done to our planet earth and live
in harmony with it from now on. Let our eyes
behold Your return to Zion in compassion, and
let the words of the prophets then be fulfilled
that from Zion will flow forth Torah, and the
word of the Lord from Jerusalem. Amen.

When Jews were among the most oppressed of peoples and
the vision of God as a powerful redeemer who would help destroy
all enemies gave comfort and hope to the powerless, the Right
Hand of God conception served a very positive function. Even in
the early days of Zionism, the empowerment being sought was
one of a minority population of Jews among a majority of sometimes hostile Arabs. Yet after the Holocaust, after God had not
reentered history and saved us from destruction, the survivors of
the concentration camps, their relatives, and fellow Jews fell into
a powerful disillusionment with "the God who failed" to save the
Jewish people. If the God of loving kindness was not present on
earth, then there was little to worship except power itself. And
so a strain of Judaism began to develop that lost its compassion
for anyone but fellow Jews and that increasingly substituted the
worship of power for service to God and humanity. More precisely, God was now seen as manifesting in the State of Israel
and its army and, for some American Jews, in the United States
and its army as well.

How could this happen? It required Post-Traumatic Stress Disorder, which manifests in the inability to recognize that Jews are no longer powerless and hunted by the forces of evil. Who could reasonably expect a quick adjustment or transformation of self-image? Yet, as I write this, some sixty-six years after the end of the Holocaust, there is little sign of Jews overcoming this self-perception. So it's time for us to develop a culture and an approach within Judaism to heal this deep national malady that has led so many Jews to reinvigorate a Right Hand of God approach to the world.

The Spiritual Crisis within Judaism

The persistence of a Right Hand of God conception at a moment when Jews have become powerful creates a real crisis for Judaism because in its name an idolatry is emerging. Many Jews feel that whatever is done by the State of Israel must be necessary for our very survival and is hence a religious command. The Talmudic rabbis taught that when the Torah, referring to God's commandments to the Israelites, says "and you shall live by them," this meant that you were not commanded to do anything that would end in their destruction as individuals or as a people (with the exception of three commands for which one's life should be risked, the rabbis added: not to murder, not to engage in sexual perversion, and not to commit idolatry).

So if the only way for Jews to survive is to have a powerful State of Israel, many Jews argue that this must be the precondition for engaging in any other aspect of Jewish religious life. Of course, one could accept all that and still argue, as some of us religious Jews do, that the State of Israel is taking actions that are actually imperiling rather than enhancing its own survival and the survival of the Jewish people. From that perspective, a precondition for engaging in any other aspect of Jewish religious life is to change this destructive behavior—else we violate the notion of "live by them."

This kind of Israel-worshiping Judaism also becomes increasingly alien to those younger Jews whose ethical perceptions lead them to see Israel as a bully using power without compassion. They see Judaism as increasingly defined by its adherence to a blind faith in the government of the State of Israel, no matter what that government is like or what principles it adopts. So it is destructive to Jewish continuity and hence a violation of "and live by them," since it is a path to destroying our people's future as Jews.

Too often I've encountered among the people at Orthodox synagogues where I sometimes *daven* (pray), and among people in Reform, Conservative, Reconstructionist, and even Renewal synagogues, a willingness to cast Palestinians in the role of the latest embodiment of (in the Passover Haggadah's language) "those who in every generation arise and seek to destroy us." It is not infrequent to hear references to them as Amalek, the tribe that attacked us in the desert and whose memory we are commanded to wipe out.

Many young Jews and most non-Jews do not even know that for many centuries Jewish religious leaders were among the most morally developed and sensitive people on earth, always extending principles of kindness and generosity. When these ancient rabbinical teachers came upon the Torah text that proclaims God to be "a merciful and compassionate God, long forbearing and abundant in loving kindness and truthfulness," they commented that "just as God is merciful and compassionate, so must you, the people of Israel, also be merciful and compassionate." Yet today many of the religious leaders of the Jewish people learn more from the harshness of the Books of Joshua and Samuel than from the universalism and kindness of the biblical books of Ruth and Jonah.

So complete and systematic has been this hijacking of Judaism by advocates of the Right Hand of God and so much is it now accompanied by religious triumphalism and demeaning of the Other (at first, primarily Arabs and Palestinians, then all non-Jews, then eventually even Jews who did not give blind loyalty to Settler Judaism) that most Israelis have come to think that "religious" and "politically right-wing" are virtually synonymous concepts. Indeed, in their voting patterns in both Israel and the United States, this seems to hold true for most (not all) Orthodox Jews. The majority of Orthodox Jews have frequently voted along with the small percentage of Wall Street Jews to support right-wing politicians, believing that their militarism will keep the United States militarily strong enough to help Israel fight off those who seek its destruction.

TORAH VALUES AND THE LEFT HAND OF GOD

Just a few lines after Judaism's famous injunction in Leviticus to "love your neighbor as yourself" comes an injunction whose essential message is repeated over and over again in Torah: "When a stranger resides with you in your land, you shall not wrong him. The stranger who resides with you shall be to you as of your citizens. You shall love him as yourself, for you were strangers in the land of Egypt" (Leviticus 19:33).

It is a wild distortion of Judaism to build a version of it that ignores the powerful ethical command articulated in that sentence. Yet Settler Judaism de facto ignores that command. So many times when I've engaged in conversations with Settler Judaism's proponents in the Jewish world, I'm told: "That idea is simply unrealistic and unworkable in the modern world."

What is most troubling about Settler Judaism are the arguments made from the basis of "what others do" and "realism."

One frequently hears the argument about Israel being judged by a higher standard. For example, torture that has been revealed in Syria, Iran, or China is used as an excuse; rightwingers argue that these other states are not being condemned, so Israel is being subjected to a double standard. Factually, they are incorrect since these other states are frequently criticized; our knowledge of torture and other antidemocratic behaviors in those societies helps account for the fact that there is little support in the United States for providing them with the kind of financial support that our government yearly doles out to Israel.

From a more Left Hand of God religious standpoint, this kind of argument is subversive in the extreme to the original conception of the Jewish people. Jews were never enjoined by our Torah to make a sociological study of the morality of other nations and then to conform to that morality. While it seems illegitimate for others to hold us to a higher standard than they hold themselves or the rest of the world, it is perfectly legitimate for us to hold ourselves to a standard that is not based on what everyone else is doing. That is precisely what having the Torah is about—having a special responsibility to bring to the world a way of living in accord with our understanding of God's revelation.

"Wait a second," someone may object, "That is utopian, because God's requirements as presented in the Torah are really impossible given the actualities of our real world. That's why the *halakhic* tradition has always had to make accommodations, which is what is needed today." This seems a perfectly legitimate counterargument to me, but it must be carefully scrutinized. "Ought" always implies "can," so Israelis cannot be under a moral obligation to do something they cannot do. But this is also a very slippery slope, because what one "can" do is not necessarily a fact about the world that is independent of one's beliefs about the world.

I remember how for many years some Israelis said that they wanted to negotiate peace but there was nobody in the Palestinian world with whom to negotiate. But when they decided to actually proceed, suddenly they managed to find somebody (the Palestinian Liberation Organization). What can be done is often a question of assessing whether certain risks or consequences are "acceptable," and that depends on one's moral worldview. From the standpoint of those of us who seek peace, asking the Jewish people to hold a state that claims to be the Jewish State to the highest ethical requirements of Torah is absolutely necessary for Israel's survival.

In short, if one argues that it is utopian to act in accord with moral ideals in a world in which those ideals are usually not acted upon, then one might as well reject the entire Torah. That way of thinking has substantively abandoned the God of Torah and the most central aspect of Jewish destiny: to be the people who testify to the possibility of a different logic in the world from the logic of cruelty and power. In fact, for those of us who take Torah seriously, the warnings to the Israelites that the land will literally vomit us out if we do not live in accord with God's moral order ("love the stranger," "pursue peace and chase after it," "justice, justice shalt thou pursue") are as applicable today as they were in the ancient world.

What is Meant by "Jewish State"

What makes the state Jewish if in maintaining itself it must abandon any serious commitment to the moral guidelines and sense of mission that have been the defining characteristics of Jewish life?

If by "Jewish state" you mean a place where lots of Jews live, then I'm in favor of there being such a state—but only if Jews are willing to live and be judged by the same moral standards that we should apply to the rest of the world. And if you say that for security reasons the Jews need such a state, but it won't be a state that can live according to the higher moral standards required by Torah, then I say let there be such a state, and let it be secure, because the Jewish people have suffered too much in history up to now to make their security depend on their morality.

But please, please, please, don't call it a Jewish state. Call it a state of many Jews, but don't allow Judaism to be identified with that state. Because doing so imperils the moral integrity of Judaism and the well-being of Jews around the world. And certainly don't argue that Jews have no right to criticize that state.

In short, the great danger to Judaism is its collapse into being a cheerleader for an existing reality. Judaism's contribution is precisely in its ability to provide a standard of criticism for existing reality—including, and particularly, Jewish reality. That is what Judaism did traditionally. Read the Prophets and you see that they were not primarily criticizing the non-Jewish states around them; they were criticizing the behavior of the Jewish people and the distortions that were becoming part of the practice of Judaism in their time. Today those prophetic voices are effectively silenced in the Jewish world.

I believe that the Jewish people have been so traumatized by the Holocaust that it may take yet more time for us to be ready to return to the norms of Torah. That compassionate attitude toward the Jews is important. But that is very different from saying, as Settler Judaism and many other contemporary forms of right-wing Jewish thought are doing, that Judaism's norms must be shifted according to the realities of the current State of Israel. You can hear this argument made by people in every branch of Judaism, including people who on every other issue remain strongly committed to Torah values and universal human rights values. But unfortunately, as the dichotomy between their liberal views on other issues and their views on Israel becomes more apparent, too many of them have moved to become more economically and politically conservative, more militaristic, and more drawn to a religion of power.

To reduce Judaism to a spiritual service station for a Jewish state is to reduce it to idolatry. Israeli philosopher Yeshayahu Leibowitz may exaggerate when he refers to this as a form of fascism, but his reminder to think of any national flag as nothing more than "a shmate [rag] on a stick" should be a useful corrective to those who wax eloquent about the religious meaning of Jewish nationalism.

The fundamental belief in Judaism is that the world can be transformed from that which is to that which ought to be. Over and over again, the Torah insists that Jews have no claim to the land of Israel if they don't live according to God's moral law. Jews will be exiled and the land will literally vomit them out if through immorality they pollute the land. What the Jewish people actually do or think they need to do for national survival can never be equated to what God wants, because God's requirements are never reducible to a sanctification of the actual.

Every attempt to reduce the tension between Judaism's utopian vision and an existing reality by changing Judaism is a betrayal of the God of the Bible and an emptying of the Shma of all its significance. Unfortunately, many of the forms of Judaism that have emerged today do not proclaim, "Hear, O Israel, the Force that makes possible transformation is also the Force that created and sustains the world, and that Force permeates all Being and makes for a fundamental unity in the universe." Instead they proclaim, "Hear, O Israel, the God of the Jews doesn't have power to change the world anymore, so whatever seems good for the Jews in the short run is what we will now call God's will."

I believe that this abandonment of hope in God is based on despair that God didn't act on our behalf. Thus, God is in no position to make prophetic demands on us anymore. Or, in a more polite way, they say that God has given us the responsibility to interpret the law; this has given us a new sense of dignity and adequacy so that we no longer have to respond to the old commands. On first hearing, it sounds progressive and empowering. However, this notion can have a very reactionary meaning if it frees us from all transcendent responsibility to transform the world and allows a democratic community of Israel to decide that it no longer needs to live in accordance with the moral vision of Torah.

A New Vision of Judaism: Love-Oriented and Emancipatory

Like most other religions, Judaism has had a variety of different ways of understanding God. Judaism has been remarkably tolerant of many of these differences as long as they were held by people who continued to observe the core practices and holidays of the Jewish path.

God did not abandon us. We as the human race failed to transcend the long history of negativity and cruelty that traps so many of us and leads us to act out in destructive and hurtful ways against other people. It is true that we must give up the vision of God as a big man in heaven who intervenes whenever He feels like it. That conception of God must be transcended now. Many Jews realized that after the destruction of the second Temple two thousand years ago, and they embraced a mystical-spiritual tradition that was in sharp contrast to the big-man-in-heaven vision. That tradition further developed in the Middle Ages and began to be called Kabbalah. It was embraced in part by Hasidism, and today it is being further developed by some of the great theologians of Judaism, Christianity, and the Sufi interpreters of Islam, sometimes with the aid of insights derived from Hindu and Buddhist mystics as well. But that is a subject for one of my next books. For our immediate purposes, this mystical tradition sees God working in partnership with human beings as one part of the evolution of the consciousness and goodness of the universe.

The lesson of the Holocaust is not that everything is permitted or that power is the only path to Jewish security or salvation. The lesson is that the healing of the world is desperately necessary and that we humans, created in God's image, ought to change our lives to give that focus a much higher priority. God's revelation to us through the Torah tradition, which evolves from generation to generation but never abandons its commitment to building a would of justice, fairness, compassion, love, and generosity in the here and now, far from being irrelevant or outdated, is all the more relevant and necessary.

We need an Emancipatory Judaism that emphasizes love for the Other and unambiguously embraces the Left Hand of God. Emancipatory Judaism:

- is about love not only of Jews but of everyone on the planet, seeing everyone as equally created in the image of God and equally deserving of the bounties of life as anyone else on the planet.

- emphasizes the task of saving the planet and its people from ecological catastrophe as the central religious duty of Jews and everyone else in the twenty-first century. That must minimally include cutting global carbon emissions to sustainable levels; stabilizing of the world population by 2040; eradicating poverty and providing adequate health and education for everyone on the planet; and restoring forest, soils, aquifers, and fisheries.

- recognizes that environmental sanity cannot be achieved without policies that embody genuine caring for the well-being of everyone on the planet and the end of the selfishness and materialism that has characterized the policies developed by governments who serve the rich.

- encourages a daily spiritual practice and inner transformation, so that we can each become a deeper embodiment of the values that we hold. It does so in a way that is compassionate, recognizes the limitations of each of us, and does not condition commitment to social change on our having become fully embodied and realized spiritual beings.

- reclaims the radicalism of demanding a sabbatical year once every seven years for everyone—the same year—and the cancellation of all debts on that sabbatical year.

- advocates the return every fifty years to the Jubilee year, during which the wealth and land of the earth would be redistributed so that everyone has an equal share.

- embraces the notion of vegetarianism to protect the animals and to preserve the earth, whose resources are strained by the raising of animals for human consumption.

- enthusiastically embraces a strict observance of the Sabbath, a day each week to stop exercising control over nature and focus instead on celebration, awe, wonder and radical amazement at the grandeur and mystery of the universe. This day also involves developing one's spiritual capacities and ceasing and desisting from all work, use of money, shopping, cooking, cleaning, or other ways of "getting things together" or "catching up with tasks."

- embraces the full range of Jewish religious law and practice to the extent that they are consistent with and encouraging of our human capacities to be loving, conscientious, free, creative, pleasure-oriented, mutually caring and responsible to each other, joyous, and awe-filled beings.

- seeks to replace patriarchal traditions and behavior as well as patriarchal views of God. It honors the Goddess, but does so in a generous and compassionate way that does not put down men but sees them as equal victims of the fear that drives many people to embrace the Right Hand of God.

- embraces equality for and full participation of gays, lesbians, bisexuals, and transgendered people, as well as of all marginalized groups including the disabled, the homeless, the unemployed, and the refugees of global capitalism.

- seeks to overcome ageism and to create traditions to pass on the wisdom of those who are aging to the next generations while also encouraging people of all ages to learn from the young.

- encourages spiritual and theological exploration and experimentation, openness to the wisdom of other traditions, psychological growth, and an atmosphere of tolerance and acceptance of those with whom we disagree, both in our own communities and in other communities. It also encourages a vigorous challenge to policies that do not respect the needs of all people on the planet or the survival needs of the planet itself. In particular, it welcomes new understandings of YHVH (loosely translated as God, but understood by many as "the transformative power of the universe toward goodness and love") that are consistent with the notion that God is All and, as the Torah says, "There is nothing else."

- emphasizes tikkun olam, the healing, repair and transformation of the world, as a sacred duty that goes beyond individual acts of *tzedakah* (charity/ righteousness) to a focus on transforming global economic, political, and social systems so that they nourish our capacities to be loving and caring human beings.

- holds the State of Israel to the highest moral and spiritual requirements and the requirements of an Emancipatory Judaism articulated here, to the extent that Israel continues to claim to be a Jewish state. It also holds the Jewish people and Israel, religious/Jewish state or not, to the same moral standards to which we seek to hold all people on the planet.

- places compassion, generosity, kindness, gentleness, forgiveness, awe, love, and wonder at the grandeur of the universe above all else. And unapologetically and vigorously seeks to make these values the New Bottom Line of all our economic, political, social, and religious institutions, as well as of our personal behavior.

WORLD TRANSFORMATION NEEDS EMANCIPATORY ISLAM AND CHRISTIANITY TOO

The tikkun olam that we need cannot be achieved without larger world transformation. The failure of the Stalinist fantasy of "socialism in one country" or of "socialism in one kibbutz" shows that no healing and transformation on the micro level is possible without a healing on the macro level as well.

It is delusional to imagine the fate of the Jewish people as somehow independent of the fate of the rest of the world. In this sense, Zionists who thought they could build a special solution to the Jewish problem were mistaken. The fate of the Jews of the entire world is inextricably linked to the fate of that world. And this is true for Palestinians, Arabs, and Muslims as well. There is no "private solution" for the Jewish people that isn't simultaneously a global solution for all peoples. There is no "private solution" for Palestinians, Arabs, and Muslims that isn't a global solution that serves the interests of all people in all religious, national, and ethnic groupings. So while an Emancipatory Judaism vigorously champions the multicultural vision that values, esteems, and seeks to preserve the particularities of each tradition, we must simultaneously realize that our fate is inextricably bound with the well-being of all other peoples and with the fate of the earth, and that hence being a good Jew must necessarily involve being a good citizen of the planet with all that that entails.

I am fully aligned with Chabad and other Hasidim in arguing that *Ahavat Yisrael* (caring for the Jewish people) is a very important part of my religious life. Where I differ from them is that I believe that the best way to care for the Jewish people in the twenty-first century is to care for the well-being of everyone else. Ahavat Yisrael mandates an end to the Occupation and genuine caring for the well-being of everyone with whom we share the planet. It is not only for reasons of self-interest that we should care for their well-being. It is because those of us rooted in a God-centered spirituality see these others as equally precious to God and equally valuable; their needs and their lives are as important as Jewish needs and Jewish lives. But it is also in our self-interest.

Those who hope to redeem religion in Jewish communities in the Disapora and/or in Israel must be engaged in trying to build a climate in which God's merciful presence is welcomed— manifesting in new cultural ideals of kindness, gentleness, and sweetness inside and out and replacing the "tzabra" cultural ideal of an Israeli as tough on the outside and sweet only on the inside. If existing religious communities are too afraid to embrace an emancipatory and love-oriented Judaism, then new religious institutions and a new religious movement must be built to fearlessly proclaim that God's presence in Zion is dependent on a community of those unafraid to embrace Israel/Palestine and to live a life that takes seriously "ve'ahavta la'ger," that you shall love the Other. It is time to put to rest the God who calls for the destruction of other people.

As I observed the tremendous response to my book *The Left Hand of God*, which was a national bestseller in 2006, and the range of people drawn to read *Tikkun* and to become members of the Network of Spiritual Progressives, I felt reaffirmed in the belief that the foundations for a love-oriented Christianity and Islam lie in their traditions as well. Those who respond to the love-oriented parts of their traditions have far more in common with those of us who wish to reclaim an Emancipatory Judaism than they have with the more domination-oriented adherents of their own religions. The love-oriented, emancipatory forces are there in Christianity and Islam, in Buddhism and Hinduism, in secular humanism, and even in those who are committed atheists. Our task is to overcome the triumphalist interpretations of these faiths that proclaim that their particular faith will ultimately be validated as "the one right path" and replace these mistakes with a genuine love for all people who are committed to a path of love, no matter how that gets framed in their tradition.

In seeking to build this alliance among the love-oriented secularists and people of religious faith, I do not want to confuse this with a rejection of all the features of the religious and cultural heritages of the human race. I totally reject the notion, espoused by some secularists, that the religions of the world need to be abandoned because every form of particularism contributes to the hatred and hurtful rivalry that has long divided the human race. In the case of most religions, ethnicities, and national identities, the hatred is rarely intrinsic to the essence of these particular identities. The embracing of love, generosity, and openheartedness can be accomplished without abandoning the particularities and specificities of each religious, ethnic, and national identity.

It is global capitalism that would benefit most from the elimination of these particular identities. It would be far easier to manipulate and control a global population whose historical roots had been undermined and who then had few cultural forms with which to resist the manipulations of advertising and corporate domination. Multicultural diversity can be encouraged at every level even as we transcend the elements of hatred, demeaning of the Other, and domination.

The spiritual progressives in Israeli, Western, and Muslim societies have the ability to launch a spiritual progressive campaign that could fundamentally alter the nature of American, Israeli, and Palestinian politics, if we can count on the support of secular progressives as well. However, this alliance will become possible only when the Left and secular progressives overcome their conscious and unconscious phobias of religion. They must stop conveying the message that they think religious or spiritual people are either intellectually retarded or psychologically handicapped and hence in need of the crutch of a big father figure in the sky.

Secular progressives need to stop identifying religion with the most extreme patriarchal, chauvinist, and repressive versions of religion and start opening their minds to the emancipatory aspirations and theologies that have already emerged in sections of the Jewish, Christian, Muslim, Hindu, and Buddhist traditions.

Whether or not the emancipatory and love-oriented versions of these religions become mainstream, there are already many individuals and groups, including churches, synagogues, and mosques, who embrace the "love first" ethos as central to their spiritual practice. If such people consciously commit themselves to working together, they can play an important role in bringing the Strategy of Generosity to the forefront in the politics of the West.

This is precisely what is needed in order to change the dynamics in Israel/Palestine to arrive at a true and lasting peace. Let's be partners, allies, and friends working together to achieve all this. And let's do it with a strong sense of humor (including the ability to laugh at oneself), playfulness, loving energy, and joyousness—all indispensible elements in keeping ourselves and one another adequately nurtured to sustain the difficult challenges we face. Without that humor and playfulness, social movements become dour and unattractive. Who (not I, for sure) wants to be part of a movement that cannot foster and encourage the joyousness, humor, and erotic energies that sustain human life?

And let's keep at the front of our consciousness the need for compassion for Israelis and Palestinians, for Jews and Muslims, and for all the world's peoples. The prophetic voice of chastisement is important. But it must also be tempered by a deep compassion for the suffering that so many people have faced throughout the past thousands of years. We can only hope to transcend the distortions in ourselves and each other that the social, economic, political, and psychological legacy of the past has embedded in us all if only we are able to put a loving, caring, generous, forgiving, and compassionate attitude at the very fore-front of our consciousness. That is why I have named this book *Embracing Israel/Palestine*. Without our ability and willingness to embrace the broken parts of all of us on the planet, there is little hope of achieving the tikkun olam that we so badly need.

Let me end by blessing you to be able to take the ideas in this book and use them to bring more love, kindness, generosity, caring, social justice, peace, and environmental sanity into the world. May you be blessed to be even more of an embodiment of your own highest ideals. May you be blessed with the recognition that even though we may not finish the task, we are not free to desist from trying. And may you be blessed with a deep sense of meaning for your life and personal fulfillment as you join me and others in the task of healing and transforming our world.

QUESTIONS AND ANSWERS

BELOW YOU WILL FIND THE QUESTIONS I am most often asked, both by those who identify themselves as pro-Israel and those who identify themselves as pro-Palestine. Many of these questions don't have a simple answer.

My answers are useful only if they are used in a respectful manner, showing as much compassion and care for the people with whom we disagree as we wish they would show toward their presumed antagonists. No amount of intelligence or quick answers can replace the power of an underlying humility, a recognition that we may be wrong, a willingness to learn from others even when their perspectives differ from our own, and a generosity of spirit in the way we approach others even if they do not treat us with a similar generosity of spirit.

Yet humility should not translate into timidity. Our goal, after all, is to stop the endless killings, terrorism, torture, house demolitions, and occupation while simultaneously providing security and justice for Israel and the Palestinian people. It is perfectly appropriate to approach this task with moral intensity, dedication, and commitment to avoid getting bogged down in a sea of moral relativism, even while attempting to remain open to other perspectives and retaining a powerful recognition of our own fallibility.

I've found in my work as a psychologist and rabbi that meditation, prayer, and other techniques for developing an inner spiritual life can contribute to maintaining a balanced perspective, can help us get back on track when we've gotten so powerfully moved by a particular perspective that we momentarily lose sight of the fundamental humanity and goodness of those with whom we disagree, and can help us remain committed to seemingly overwhelming goals that might otherwise leave us in despair.

Even better, we can meditate, pray, or engage in other techniques of spiritual centering with people who share our worldview and are equally committed to the healing and transformation of the planet. Here, as elsewhere, a loving heart needs companions, colleagues, and comrades—in short, a community of people who are both loving on a personal level and committed to building the social, political, and economic arrangements that will foster a world based on love, generosity, and kindness.

1. *Hasn't Israel used its overwhelming power advantage and the camouflage of a "peace process" to conduct a de facto conquest and absorption of the West Bank? What actions can you name that Israel has taken to show it is really prepared to make peace with Palestine?*

Yes, since the assassination of Yitzhak Rabin by a right-wing Jewish religious fanatic, the government of Israel has shown little willingness to take the steps necessary to achieve peace with the Palestinians and continues to absorb the West Bank by building settlements. Yet there are many in Israel who hope to replace the current government with a government more interested in reaching a substantive compromise that would work for both Israel and Palestine.

On the other hand, it would help greatly if the Palestinians would insist that Hamas give up its stated ultimate goal of eliminating Israel altogether and would accept Israel as an "affirmative action state" for Jews and seek to make the West Bank and Gaza an "affirmative action state" for Palestinians.

2. *Don't the Palestinians really want to destroy the State of Israel? Aren't they just using the camouflage of a "peace process" to build up their military strength until they get the chance to do this?*

There are now, and will continue to be long after any peace accord is reached, a significant minority of people in each community that aspires to see the full elimination of the other side. But maximalist fantasies have typically yielded to new realities in the Middle East. If the majority of Palestinians and Israelis are living in their own secure states with democratic and human-rights-observing governments and with economies providing a decent standard of living for everyone, those troubling aspirations to destroy the Other will become more like the Jewish prayer books' call for the restoration of animal sacrifices on the grounds of the Jews' ancient Temple—not yet given up, but nevertheless not likely to be made the cornerstone of any but a small and manageable fringe.

3. *Israelis are acting like Nazis, so how can Palestinians be expected to think that peace with them will ever be possible? And why do Jews think they have the right to tell others to not make Nazi comparisons?*

Although the policies of recent Israeli governments have been oppressive to the Palestinian people, the Nazi analogy is false and misleading.

The Nazis were engaged in systematic genocide of all of the Jews that they could find. They even deflected men and material away from the Russian front during World War II so that they could be more effective in killing as many Jews as possible. There is nothing even vaguely comparable going on in the West Bank and Gaza or in Israel itself. There is no systematic attempt to murder every Palestinian. There are no gas chambers. There are no roundups of Palestinians who are then systematically murdered by the Israelis. People who say that Israel is acting like the Nazis simply know nothing about who the Nazis were and what they did, or know nothing about what Israel is doing. Or else they blindly hate the Jewish people and are attempting to spread their hate to others.

At the same time, there are some uncanny similarities in the hateful stereotyping and demeaning discourse that Jews suffered from some sections of German society in the period 1933–1939 and the discourse that Palestinians are now suffering from some sections of Israeli society, particularly in the settlements. There are some Israelis who would like to see the entire Palestinian people "transferred" (ethnically cleansing Israel).

4. *Is a political settlement really possible? Won't these people always be hating each other and fighting?*

A political settlement really is not possible without a spiritual and psychological transformation as well. Until both sides can embrace the Left Hand of God (the compassionate values articulated in every religion as opposed to the more militaristic and domination-focused values that also exist in almost every religion) and treat each other with a spirit of generosity and open-heartedness, there will be some on both sides who nurture their own hatreds and desire for revenge. This kind of change of heart is unlikely as long as both sides are caught in a cycle of mutual trauma, with Israelis occupying the West Bank and Gaza and Palestinians murdering Israeli civilians in terror attacks.

However, Jews and Arabs have often lived in peace in the past, and they can live in peace together in the future. There is nothing inevitable about this conflict persisting. There were people who made the same argument about France and Germany after World War II, since these two countries had engaged in three major wars against each other and had murdered a far greater percentage of each other's populations than Israel and Palestine have now. Yet changed circumstances have created a reality in which these two former bitter enemies now cooperate and are strategically and economically aligned.

The changes at the heart level must begin with Israeli repentance. Each side has done terrible and unjustifiable acts toward the other, and both sides must repent and atone. But given the vast asymmetry of power between the two sides at this historical moment, it must be the more powerful Israel that takes the strongest first steps toward repentance and atonement.

5. *Won't any peace negotiation fail because the Palestinians will insist on "the Right of Return," a right that if granted would mean in effect the end of the Jewish State?*

There is no possibility that Israelis would agree to a Right of Return in the context of Israeli insecurities and fears. The way that the Right of Return is sometimes articulated by Palestinians and some of their supporters, Israelis could envision 4 to 6 million Arabs claiming to be refugees or descendants of refugees arriving in Israel in the next five years, demanding their rights and a return of their land and homes. For Israelis, the Right of Return is simply a code word for ending the Jewish state, and faced with that possibility, the majority of Israelis would rather fight endlessly. So as long as the Right of Return is articulated as a symbolic "right" that Palestinians insist upon, rather than a political goal to be achieved in partial ways consistent with what is actually possible, it becomes a major stumbling block to peace.

Yet I also recognize that there is no possibility of creating lasting peace without healing the wound caused by the expulsion of Palestinians in 1948. In my proposal for two states at peace (see Chapter Eight), I call for compensation for refugees at a level adequate to provide a life for Palestinians comparable in quality and material comfort to those with a median income in Israel. I envision this as part of the process of creating an economically viable Palestinian state.

Eventually, however, there must also be a way for at least some significant number of Palestinians to return to the places of their birth in Israel and a public acknowledgement by Israelis of their part (only their part, not the total responsibility) in creating the tragedy of the Palestinian refugees. That's why I've proposed that as part of the peace agreement Israel should allow a return of 20,000 Palestinians a year for the next thirty years.

6. *Shouldn't any peace agreement insist on the return of Israeli settlers in Palestine to the pre-1967 borders of Israel? Otherwise, won't the whole region become awash in Balkan-style ethnic violence?*

There is no compelling reason that a peace agreement must include the dismantling of all Jewish settlements in the West Bank and the forcible transfer of all settlers back to the pre-1967 borders of Israel. Just as there are Palestinian Arabs living as citizens of the State of Israel, so Jews should be allowed to remain in the settlements as citizens of the State of Palestine. Just as Palestinian citizens of Israel are under the full jurisdiction of the laws and courts of Israel, so those Jews who elect to remain in Palestine would have to become citizens of the State of Palestine and live in accord with its laws. There might be legal proceedings against settlers who build settlements on the land of others and legal demands for compensation to those Palestinians whose lands were taken illegally or under cover of the Israeli occupation authorities.

There certainly ought to be (in both Israel and Palestine) laws prohibiting discrimination in housing and hiring, so that the homes left by Israelis being resettled in Israel would be available for purchase by Palestinian Arabs and not just by Jews, and so the settlements would be quickly integrated. It would have to be made 100 percent clear to the Jewish settlers that they could expect no intervention on their behalf by the State of Israel, just as Palestinians living in Israel could expect no intervention on their behalf by the State of Palestine. Jews who agree to live as law-abiding citizens of the State of Palestine should be allowed to do so but should face legal punishments should they engage in acts aimed at destroying the Palestinian state or inciting violence.

7. *You are using Western concepts and experiences and applying them to the Arab and Muslim world, which has different cultural assumptions and a different psychology than you and other naïve liberals have. Don't the continuing brutal acts of Palestinian violence against Israelis show that they are morally underdeveloped as a people?*

Any generalizations about a people or a religious community should be treated with deep suspicion—particularly by those of us who are Jews and who have been the subject of a long line of cultural calumnies. We have been accused of being materialistic, greedy, selfish, vulgar, too emotional, too rational, communistic, capitalistic, naturally inclined to crime, naturally inclined to self-righteousness, stiff-necked, more interested in justice than in love, etc.

It has been typically true that Western societies use the notion of cultural differences to assign to "native peoples" various forms of pathology that they see as intrinsic to these peoples' "nature"— which then provides a justification for Western colonial expansion, domination, and "reeducation" of the native populations.

This tendency has gained particular ferocity whenever the other population has resisted domination in some way. The very acts of resistance are used as further proof of the demented and distorted consciousness of the natives. So it comes as no surprise that in the period after Arab states started to use their control of oil as a counterforce to Western colonial expansion, hatred of Arabs and Muslims became prevalent in Western societies.

In this context, it is most reasonable to be very suspicious of any generalization made about Arabs or Muslims or the societies they have created. Of course, there will always be people like those in Al-Qaeda who do indeed want the destruction of Western influence in their world and who are willing to use terror and violence. However, these people do not represent Arabs or Muslims any more than Timothy McVeigh, the bomber of the Federal Building in Oklahoma City, represented the American people or all Christians, or the rabbis who issued a statement in 2011 forbidding Israeli Jews to rent apartments to any non-Jew represent "the Jews."

The Talmud was very wise when it cautioned, "Don't judge your fellow until you stand in his place."

8. *Isn't it clear by now that the democratic tradition in Israel is a vanishing Western European import and that Israel is returning to the repressive theocratic tradition of the shtetl? With efforts to criminalize free speech in the BDS debate and the discrimination against Palestinian Israelis, aren't you falling for the AIPAC propaganda that Israel is the "only democracy in the Middle East?"*

It's true that there are many troubling undemocratic developments in Israel, particularly in the sphere of freedom of speech. Yet as long as Palestinian Israelis maintain the same rights as Jewish Israelis to vote, organize their own political parties, publish their own newspapers, and create public nonviolent demonstrations, Israel will continue to be seen as a democratic society. Palestinian Israelis still have had much more freedom of political expression in Israel than in any other Arab countries—that is, at least until the democratic movements of the 2011 Arab Spring yield real democracies. At the moment of writing this, we don't yet know what kind of governments will come from the Arab Spring revolts.

If you read the Israeli press, the debate in Israel is far freer than it is in the United States. And if you study the Talmud or Jewish commentaries on the Torah, you find a plethora of voices, and most feel perfectly comfortable in challenging each other quite strongly rather than piously submitting to authority or tradition.

On the other hand, I question the right of Israel to claim itself a democracy as long as it continues to rule over a million and a half Palestinians in the West Bank while denying them equal voting rights within Israel. As long as the Occupation continues, Palestinians have every right to demand "one person, one vote" in Israeli elections.

9. *Isn't it time to make Israel a binational state of all its current inhabitants rather than a state with a special set of advantages for Jews? After all, if Israel was created as an affirmative action state in response to the oppression of the past, the reality that it sought to repair has now been repaired. Jews are no longer living in fear; instead they are powerful forces in Western societies. And Israel itself is one of the strongest military powers in the world.*

As Michael Walzer pointed out in *Tikkun* magazine, there is nothing inherently undemocratic about a state identifying with the history, culture, and philosophy of a given people or religion. This is a kind of "soft" nationalist identity, as long as it gives equal political rights to all of its citizens. The United States, for example, makes Christmas a national holiday, closes all government functions and offices, just as it requires its office holders to put their hand on a bible as they swear to uphold the laws of the land.

I strongly support getting Jewish religious practices and coercive institutions separated from the state power of Israel. That separation is Judaism's only chance to survive in an Israel where, at the moment, many secular Israelis feel more anger at the manipulations and power over them by the Orthodox than they do about almost any other issue facing their country. As a result, many have become alienated from Judaism. On the other hand, I'd be delighted if the loving energy of what I've described above as Emancipatory Judaism became the ethos and flavor of Israeli culture.

Most Jews believe that there is still a need for a Jewish state. Jews have gone through other periods in which they seemed to be secure economically and politically—for example, in Spain in the two centuries before Jews were legally expelled in 1492, or in Weimar Germany before Hitler came to power. Many Jews remember that these periods of security were followed by periods of persecution, and they are no longer willing to live in a world where they can find no refuge if this should happen again. Israel was created in part because of this historical memory, reinforced by the horrible genocide of Jews in the twentieth century. To expect Jews to give up the one place in the world that is theirs is to ask more than is humanly possible at this historical moment.

10. *Isn't it a simple fact that Zionists came to Palestine and took the land of another people?*

Most Jews coming to Palestine in the last 120 years came as refugees escaping oppression in Europe, the Muslim states of North Africa and Asia, and most recently communist and then post-communist Russia. Until 1948, the Palestinian leadership did everything it could to keep them from coming. This meant preventing Jews who were trying to escape the Holocaust from entering a land where they might find safety. This was morally tragic behavior, made no less morally tragic by the fact that most other peoples acted in exactly the same way or that much of the world today still closes its doors and shuts its ears to the cries of despair of refugees seeking asylum.

The creation of the State of Israel was the first instance of affirmative action or restorative justice practiced on an international scale. It set the precedent for all future affirmative action programs. Most instances of affirmative action have the same downside: they disadvantage, at least temporarily, some other group of people who are not themselves directly the perpetrators of the wrong for which affirmative action is the solution. But there is nothing fundamentally unjust about the attempt to create a state for which the primary goal is to rectify past injustices.

On the other hand, there are great dangers to this affirmative action approach, particularly when you create an entire state with a military that intends to use its power to rectify past errors and is willing to do so by disadvantaging others. How do you create checks and balances so that the state doesn't overstep its affirmative action mandate and begin to oppress or unnecessarily disadvantage other people? This is part of the problem faced by Palestinian citizens of Israel—they often don't get equal access to the benefits available to Jews (e.g., in housing and employment). Israeli Jews use a clever ruse to cover this racism—they offer the benefits to people who served in the Army, which de facto turns out to be almost all Jewish Israelis and almost no Arab Israelis. Moreover, for many decades, Palestinian Israeli towns and the

Palestinian sections of Jerusalem have received less in the way of state subsidies than have those living in primarily Jewish sections of Israel. So we need to be very careful to work to remedy the injustices caused by our attempts to remedy past injustices.

11. *It is people like you who thought peaceful resistance could stop Hitler—and look what happened. Don't you know that the Arabs want to drive Jews into the Sea? You are naïve if you think you can stop these Nazis with compassion and nonviolence.*

Seeing the world as though Hitler were still here and ready to hurt us is a trauma from which the Jewish people need help to recover. On the factual level, the claim is absurd. Hitler was the head of one of the most powerful economic and military forces in the world, capable of conquering other major powers. The Palestinians are a tiny people without an army, and though the surrounding Arab states are very large in number, they also have no serious military capacity to challenge the power of Israel. Israel is one of the most powerful military forces in the world.

It is not the Palestinians who occupy Tel Aviv and Haifa but the Israelis who occupy the West Bank and Gaza. Moreover, many military authorities in Israel have long argued that a Palestinian state, even one with arms, would be no serious threat militarily to Israel. However, the continued Occupation does present a serious threat because it demoralizes the Israeli people and its army and weakens its ties with potential allies around the world.

Arab states do not seek the destruction of all Jews as Hitler did. The reality is that there are Jews who continue to live in Baghdad, Damascus, and Cairo. In the past forty years, although there have at times been outbursts of anti-Semitism that should not be tolerated, Arab countries do not have a policy of systematically exterminating Jews or putting them into concentration camps. To the extent that Jews prove loyal to the regimes in which they live, they have been allowed to continue to do business and live in peace. Believe it or not, this is news to many Jews who have been taught that there is no difference between the Arabs and the Nazis. But there is.

Don't get me wrong—few existing Arab countries are models of human-rights-respecting societies, and I wouldn't feel safe living in most of them, neither as a Jew nor as a politically progressive-thinking individual. But that's different from claiming an analogy with Hitler, who sought the destruction of Jews based on their racial origins, not on the basis of their politics. It's easy to hear this as an "apology" for those states—but that is not what I intend. Even after the Arab Spring, most Arab states are oppressive dictatorships. If I were living there, I'd be part of a revolutionary movement seeking (in nonviolent ways) to overthrow them. In fact, were Israel to change its policies in the directions I've been suggesting in this book, that overthrow of oppressive Arab regimes would become easier and less easily diverted into anti-Semitism, which certainly does exist in many Arab states.

However, it is naive to believe that a Jewish state can exist among 100 million Arabs in a constant state of war, be perceived as oppressive to nearby Arabs, and hope to continue to exist this way for the next several centuries. Only an Israel that has manifested a whole new attitude can possibly hope to provide for its own safety. The naïveté of relying on power is far greater than the supposed naïveté of relying on good relations, kindness and generosity.

As to the uselessness of nonviolence against Hitler: nonviolence against Hitler once he took office in 1933 was unlikely to have been effective. But nonviolence by German spiritual progressives in the period 1924–1932 might have been very effective if combined with a discourse of caring and generosity toward the

German people. Far fewer might have voted for Hitler in 1933 had they fully understood how far away he was from the principles of Christianity or of common humanity. Unfortunately, Christian institutions were still very enmeshed in their anti-Semitism, and that made it impossible to build an interfaith spiritual progressive strategy. The secular socialists and communists spent more of their energy attacking each other (sometimes physically) than they did developing strategies to articulate and respond to the suffering of the German people imposed on them by the Allied victors of the First World War. The growth of fascism in the 1920s cannot be separated from the context, and nonviolence is effective only if it is coupled with a moral or spiritual vision that is articulated in a way that ordinary people can understand.

12. *What about the threat from Iran?*

Iran, a non-Arab but Muslim state, has had some of its leadership call for an end to Israel. But it then backed off and said that it only meant ending the Zionist regime in Israel; it denied proposing to use a nuclear capacity (not yet developed in a way that could militarily threaten Israel) to perpetrate a genocide against the Jewish people. Nevertheless, the language they did use was suggestive of genocide, and when coupled with this same leadership's denial of the Holocaust, it reasonably causes great fear in Israel, the Jewish people, and most people in the world.

The solution to this is not to try the futile acts of bombing or invading Iran but rather to make it harder for Iranians to believe that Israel, either of its own volition or as a surrogate for the United States' imperial ambitions to control all the remaining oil supplies of the world, is a threat to them or to the Palestinian people. So, here is the way to deal with Iran: End the Occupation of the West Bank and Gaza in a spirit of generosity. Embrace the humanity of the Palestinian people. And use the terms for an agreement that I proposed in Chapter Eight. Then, let the United States take the lead in launching a Global Marshall Plan along the lines articulated at www.spiritualprogressives.org/GMP. With those two steps, the United States and Israel would do far more to eliminate the "Iranian threat" than it could possibly do through any imaginable military interventions short of the immoral and potentially world-destructive strategy of using nuclear weapons to destroy the Iranian military capacity.

13. *Isn't it time for Israel and the Jews to put the Holocaust in the past and get over it? Every time it is invoked by an Israeli politician, it is used to justify outrageous crimes against the Palestinians.*

There are two sides to an answer. One side is that yes, the relationship to the Holocaust must change over time. (Avram Burg, the son of Holocaust survivors, has called for a national healing of memory in his recent book, *The Holocaust Is Over; We Must Rise From Its Ashes.)* The other side of the answer is that the Holocaust was a catastrophe that we must never "get over"; we should maintain its importance by changing how we treat the marginalized people in all nations. The call for "Never Again" must never be forgotten, and it must apply to all marginalized or oppressed people on the planet.

Asking Jews to "get over" the Holocaust and the 2,000 years of anti-Semitism is like asking African Americans to "get over" their experience of slavery and racism even though they still live in a racist society.

14. *If Palestinians don't want to destroy Israel, where are the voices of moderate Palestinians—and why don't we ever hear them?*

Palestinians who are moderate and nonviolent are trying to make their voices heard. You don't hear them for the same reason that most Americans don't hear the voices of the many American Jews who opposed Ariel Sharon and Benjamin Netanyahu's policies. The official media of the American Jewish community ignores these voices. Mainstream media tend to either ignore these voices or to relegate them to the back pages, where they are rarely noticed. We have created a space on our website where we publish some of the many voices of Palestinian, Arab, and Muslim moderates at www.tikkun.org.

15. *Aren't you aware of the vicious anti-Semitism in Arab countries, and aren't you afraid that you may unwittingly be generating anti-Semitism by your criticisms of Israeli policies?*

For Jews who have suffered abuse and hatred for so long, the notion that there could be such a thing as legitimate anger at Jews for policies that we support seems incomprehensible. Isn't all anger at Jews simply irrational anti-Semitism? No. It's not anti-Semitic to be angry at those Jews who support Israeli policies that are oppressive.

It is anti-Semitic when the anger gets directed at *all* Jews, or gets articulated in anti-Jewish language, because not all Jews do support the policies of Occupation or oppression of Palestinians. When non-Jews are told by the American Jewish establishment that it is anti-Semitic to criticize Israel, they may be effectively silenced. But at some point in the future, when American global interests may not seem so well served by the current state of Israel, the media and American political leaders may not be so willing to support Israel or the American Jewish establishment. At that point, there is likely to be an explosion of anger against Israel and Jews by many people who have been silenced today and who unconsciously resent that fact.

Of course, there are some anti-Semites who will use anything to advance their own hateful agendas. This is all the more reason we need to carefully distinguish between legitimate criticisms of the State of Israel and illegitimate criticisms of the entire Jewish people. Moreover, we need to insist that the criticisms of Israel be proportional to its crimes (not, for example, making it seem as if they rival the far worse crimes being perpetrated by many other nation states), that they be balanced (acknowledging and giving appropriate energy to criticism of the crimes of some of those who speak on behalf of the Palestinian movement and the crimes of Arab states), and that they be accompanied by the kind of compassionate understanding with which we should view all of human activity at this moment in the evolution of consciousness.

The most effective generator of anti-Semitism in the world today, creating a legacy that may lead to global hatred of Jews, is the State of Israel and its policies toward Palestinians. Anyone who is truly fearful of the growth of anti-Semitism should dedicate his or her energies to changing Israeli policies in the ways described in this book.

16. *How can we possibly ask Israel or the United States to negotiate with a Palestinian government that has Hamas as part of it, knowing that Hamas is so clearly dedicated to the destruction of the State of Israel? Any agreement that it signs is meant only to give it time to develop the strength and capacities to eventually achieve that goal.*

This same kind of objection was raised against the United States negotiating with Russia, when it was the Soviet Union and its leaders embraced doctrines calling for the violent overthrow of the capitalist world. This objection was raised again against negotiating with the North Vietnamese and their National

Liberation Front in South Vietnam. We eventually recognized that, if we want to end wars and struggles, we need to negotiate with our enemies, not just with our friends. Indeed, any agreement reached with the more friendly elements in the Palestinian world won't be worth much unless it was agreed to by those who otherwise might be most likely to undermine those agreements.

Moreover, Hamas is, like most religious fundamental movements, a complex reality. Hamas has attracted many of its adherents not because it advocates the destruction of Israel, but because of its daily activities in Gaza and the West Bank. It is involved in providing social services that are not otherwise available to the Palestinian people. When a Palestinian state with adequate financial support comes into existence and begins to function, it will be able to provide many of these same services. Hamas's attractiveness may correspondingly decline to the extent that the government of such a state is perceived as democratic, respectful of human rights, and genuinely interested in serving the interests of the Palestinian people and not just of its economic and political elites.

However, I don't expect a total decline in Hamas as long as the global ethos of materialism and selfishness embedded in capitalist globalization continues to colonize the world and shape daily life through its media and global corporations. To resist this ethos of selfishness and materialism, people turn to distorted, fundamentalist forms of Islam, Christianity, Judaism, or Hinduism. Such people rely on their own form of selfishness—namely, that the salvation and generosity that their faith offers is only for those who are part of the particular fundamentalist community, however it defines and shapes itself.

Until emancipatory and love-oriented forms of these various religions emerge, people will be attracted to organizations like Hamas. But that attraction is not primarily based on hatred toward Israel. Israeli policies that embrace Palestine and implement the peace agreement as I've proposed in this book will be able to weaken the previous memories of a hateful Israel and create the conditions for an inner transformation in Hamas.

In the meantime, Israel should negotiate with a Palestinian government that includes Hamas, but only for the sake of achieving an agreement that will be carefully monitored and strongly supported by international forces called upon to supervise the implementation of this agreement as proposed in Chapter Eight. Verification and strong safeguards should be built into the implementation phases of this agreement.

17. *The Palestinians rejected a good deal offered to them in 1947 by the United Nations, which mandated the partitioning of the land into an Israel smaller than the 1967 borders and a Palestine that included the Golan Heights, the Sinai, and the entire river Jordan. Instead of accepting this deal, the Palestinians chose a belligerent path that has led to the many wars between Israel and the surrounding Arab states. By making that choice in 1947, didn't the Palestinians lose all legitimacy to complain about what has happened since?*

Many Palestinians question whether the United Nations had the right to make the decision to split up the land into Israel and Palestine in 1947. The United Nations, they say, was only ratifying a previous division of the Middle East by colonial powers after the First World War. After all, why should the United Nations, the organization of the military victors after World War II, have the right to make this decision on behalf of the world's people?

Israelis who argue that the 1947 partition plan was legitimate and that Palestinians had a moral obligation to accept the division of their land ordained by the United Nations are usually inconsistent when it comes to their own obligation to live by subsequent resolutions of the United Nations. Those resolutions have called upon Israel to withdraw from the West Bank and Gaza and have condemned Israeli violence and human rights violations. Either the UN has the moral authority to determine national boundaries or it doesn't.

In fact, the unelected Palestinian leaders' rejection of the 1947 UN partition was a serious ethical and political mistake for which the entire Palestinian people have been paying for a long time. Though some Palestinians point to writings by Zionist leaders that suggest that Israel might have sought to expand anyway (Israel has never been willing to define what its boundaries are), the political reality is that Israel would have had a much tougher time justifying war against Palestinians and surrounding Arab states if the Palestinian people and the Arab states had embraced the boundaries of 1947 and welcomed the new state into existence.

Most Palestinians living in refugee camps in some of the worst circumstances of any human beings on the planet were born in those refugee camps or were under the age of fifteen when the 1947 partition plan was rejected. They have no moral culpability for the actions of those who took that decision in 1947, however disastrous it proved to be. There is no reason the decisions taken by a previous generation should legitimate the suffering of future generations of Palestinians, nor any reason the Palestinian people should accept arrangements with regard to their own national self-determination that are less than those of other national groups on the planet. In fact, the Torah explicitly forbids punishing children for the sins of their parents.

18. *If you are right, why aren't the Israeli peace parties calling for this kind of heart-oriented approach or symbolic gestures of atonement?*

First, the peace forces in Israel (and many of their supposedly sophisticated followers in the United States) believe that it
would sound unrealistic, foolish, or utopian to talk as though the
Palestinian people were really human beings who could respond
to a serious change of heart on our parts. No one in Israel is prepared to be seen as a freier. Instead of risking being thought too
soft, the Israeli Labor Party continually uses a language that suggests that they too would be "tough" with the Palestinians, whom
they too consider a menace. They thereby strengthen the general
level of fear and distrust in Israeli society of the Palestinian people, rather than laying the foundation for future reconciliation.

That demeaning message of fundamental distrust of the entire Palestinian people, conveyed explicitly by the Right and implicitly by some among the peace forces, leads most of the electorate to feel that both the Left and the Right distrust Palestinians.
Voters think: "So then who is best equipped to deal with people
we can't trust? Probably the Right." By failing to build an alternative discourse to the Right, the Left in Israel guarantees
that the Right will always win—by either winning an election
with their own right-wing parties or in effect by getting the Left
and peace forces to select as their candidates people who will be
tough and hard-nosed with the Palestinians.

The Israeli peace forces would be far more effective if they
were willing to lose an election or two (which they are going to
do anyway) by taking an explicitly humane attitude toward the
Palestinian people, challenging the prevailing chauvinism and
anti-Arab sentiments, and educating Israelis about the importance of a reconciliation of the heart with the Palestinian people.
This would also give Palestinians some reason to hope that they
are going to face something besides endless Occupation.

Spirit matters. It matters that you treat people as though they
are embodiments of the sacred and not just instruments for your
own ends.

19. *Isn't your language of compassion really a moral dodge? You're evading the reality of real power imbalances. Your attempt to develop a discourse of compassion covers up the fact that one people is dislocating another people and expropriating its land through force and violence.*

The discourse of compassion and transcending blame will be difficult for those people who can get motivated to do political work only when they have a simplistic picture of the world that includes totally good guys and totally bad guys. For them, the complex picture being drawn here will be disappointing and will be dismissed as "too" something, whether that is "too pro-Arab" (as seen by the Israel-is-always-right crowd) or "too pro-Israel" as seen by the "Israel-is-fundamentally-evil" crowd.

This is not to deny that there are power imbalances. For that reason, even with the compassionate analysis we advocate, we still support making demands on the Israeli government to take the first step and end the Occupation immediately. But we also know that it is only when the Israeli people feel safe that they will mobilize on a mass scale to support peace. For that reason, as well as for ethical and spiritual reasons, we urge an immediate end by Palestinians of all acts of terror at the same time that we advocate an end to the Occupation.

It is a mistake to talk of one side as having all the power. The Palestinian people do not have the power to overthrow Israeli rule, but they do have the (self-defeating) power to keep Israelis scared. And as long as Israelis are scared, they are more likely to fight to the death rather than put themselves into a position of vulnerability. And it is a mistake to underestimate the power of nonviolence to transform the political situation dramatically. (For more on this, read Jonathan Schell's *The Unconquerable Planet.*)

20. *Compassion is one thing, but why are you setting your call for compassion in the context of spirituality and God-language? Isn't religion the whole problem in this conflict?*

Don't let my religious language freak you out. None of my argument depends on being religious. You don't have to believe in God to be a decent person. Nor is everyone who believes in God a fanatic.

The Israeli-Palestinian conflict is often defined through right-wing interpretations of religion. Neither Islam nor Judaism, however, belongs to those who hate the Other. The God-language of Judaism, Christianity, and Islam has its share of mean-spirited and sometimes violent rhetoric, but it also frequently stresses the path of love and generosity. Both a discourse of domination and a discourse of love are there, because most human beings have some of both inside us.

I believe that all religious, secular, or even militantly atheistic communities still have to deal with the internalized voices of fear that lead to a strategy of domination and power over others. Hopefully they will subordinate them to the voices of hope, caring, and generosity that have been suppressed. As a Jew, I think this is particularly urgent for Judaism, but as my colleagues in the Network of Spiritual Progressives assure me, this is just as important a struggle inside Christianity, Islam, Hinduism, Buddhism, and almost every nationalist or ethnic community as well. I've concluded that to secure the Jewish future, the Jews must become known as a force of idealism, generosity, and love, not a voice of selfishness, racism, tribalism, violence, and fear. As Rabbi Hillel said, if not now, when?

21. *How do you manage to keep your hope when the obstacles are so great?*

It is true that this is not an easy moment or an easy position. There are people who say that the Tikkun community's perspective is nothing but a carefully construed pro-Israel perspective, and there are people who say that the Tikkun perspective is nothing but a carefully construed pro-Palestine perspective. I get hate mail from both sides, although the death threats come mostly from fellow Jews who say that I am betraying the Jewish people, that I am a traitor "worse than Hitler," and many other hurtful and hateful things.

I sustain a commitment to that healing process by strengthening my own inner spiritual practice of Judaism, but I know that there are many other equally valid spiritual paths. I'm often nurtured by the teachings of people in the Network of Spiritual Progressives whose primary spiritual source is in Christianity, Sufism, Islam, Buddhism, Hinduism, or other spiritual paths.

Yet I must admit that I get special nourishment from Judaism. For me, the nourishment I get from observing Shabbat, doing the commandments (the *mitzvot*), following the path of Jewish tradition, and doing that with a community of fellow Jews who have joined Beyt Tikkun Synagogue-Without-Walls in Berkeley is deeply sustaining. Studying Torah and Prophets, and all the elaborations, debates, Midrash, and spiritual meanderings of our people through the past three thousand years provides me with a source of inspiration. Ultimately, it is my own personal connection to God, the Goddess, Spirit, YHVH, the Power of Healing and Transformation (or however else you wish to name it, including Krishna, Allah, the Cosmic Christ, etc.), knowing how that energy has manifested throughout history, and witnessing it manifesting in many loving beings that continues to provide me with a foundation for hope.

The practice of tikkun is about healing and transforming our consciousness to the point where we can all recognize that there is enough and that we can share the world's bounties with generosity, ecological sensitivity, great joyfulness, and unlimited love. This should become the aim and major focus of every individual, every profession and vocation, every charitable foundation, every political party, every religion, and every university. There are many areas where that healing energy is needed—and one is the pains and fears of Jews, Arabs, Israelis, and Palestinians. The way to start is with an attitude of compassion for all of them.

Our world can be healed. When we overcome all the cynical realism taught us by the shapers of public opinion, when we allow ourselves to be compassionate toward each other, when we refuse to allow the powerful to define for us the limits of the possible, when we learn to support one another in a spirit of generosity, we can build a world that corresponds to our highest ideals. Many blessings will come to you if you dedicate your life to building a world of peace, justice, generosity, and love.

Let's do it together!

22. *Don't the Arab Spring and the UN vote for a Palestinian state change everything?*

It is too early to see if the Arab Spring produces genuinely free and human-rights-respecting societies or just other forms of repressive societies. I hope it will produce the former. But even democratic Arab societies can succumb to hatred of Israel and even hatred of all Jews, unless Israel begins to systematically embrace a policy of generosity and caring for the well-being of its own domestic Palestinian population and the well-being of the Arab world. Hatred of all Jews is never excusable, but it may soon prevail unless the self-proclaimed Jewish State either becomes an embodiment of the pursuit of justice, peace, and withdrawal or it stops calling itself a Jewish State and instead identifies itself as a secular humanist state that happens to have a lot of

Jews living there. Anger against Jews will be based increasingly on the memory of Israel's insensitive treatment of Palestinians plus its alignment politically with the American Empire.

UN recognition of Palestine will temporarily harden the perception Israelis have of being alone in the world and hence will momentarily give strength to the Israeli Right, but over time it may help more Israelis come to realize that the Occupation is against Israeli self-interest. It will also strengthen Palestinian self-respect as Palestinians see that they have the support of much of the world's population. It may also give Palestinians a greater chance of using UN committees to challenge various aspects of the Occupation. But the bottom line is this: until the Occupation ends, not much is going to change in Israel/Palestine, and that is not likely to happen solely on the basis of a UN resolution. What is needed is the kind of transformation of consciousness that I've described in this book. That can only happen if you, I, and many others become the agents of that change.

—Rabbi Michael Lerner
rabbilerner@tikkun.org

Appendix

RESOURCES FOR PEACE

GETTING INVOLVED

1. NETWORK OF SPIRITUAL PROGRESSIVES (NSP) & TIKKUN

A central task facing us today is the spiritual healing of the planet, a healing that requires a fundamental transformation of our economic and political lives, as well as the development of strong inner lives. The problem of healing Israel/Palestine cannot be fully separated from the task of healing the entire world.

None of us can do this by ourselves. I've been working with thousands of people in an international organization called the Tikkun Community/Network of Spiritual Progressives (NSP). Although this is in effect one big network, we often refer to it as the Tikkun Community when dealing with Israel/Palestine, and the Network of Spiritual Progressives when dealing with everything else, largely because so many non-Jews feel uncomfortable expressing any opinions on Israel/Palestine, lest they be labeled in one way or another. Over the past years, I've at times been blessed with co-leadership from Susannah Heschel, Cornel West, and Benedictine Sister Joan Chittister.

The Tikkun Community and the Network of Spiritual Progressives (NSP) are developing strategies for social healing and transformation that can address these issues. Our network includes religious leaders, philanthropists, psychotherapists, community and/or union organizers, environmentalists, students, techies, entertainers, comic strip designers, filmmakers, musicians, lawyers, nurses, physicians, atheists, evangelicals, secular activists who identify as "spiritual but not religious," authors of fiction and poetry, artists, high school teachers, college professors, government employees, political leaders, and healers of every sort who are committed to this vision.

Some members of this network share their ideas through *Tikkun* magazine (www.tikkun.org). If you join the NSP, you get a free subscription to *Tikkun* online and a subscription to the print version for an extra $10 per year. Others have created local Tikkun Community and NSP chapters. Yet others connect through regional seminars and international conferences that NSP and Tikkun periodically organize. Over the years, tens of thousands of people have joined, and we hope to extend this network to provide powerful avenues of support to those who are involved in social change work—not only activism focused on Israel/Palestine but also work on democracy and human rights, the environment, poverty, social justice, peace and nonviolence, and the treatment of others as embodiments of the sacred. We want to help make it possible for a lifetime commitment to social change work to be sustained.

If you want to learn more about the full scope of our project or (hopefully) join us, visit www.tikkun.org and also www.spiritualprogressives.org. You can email us at magazine@tikkun.org or email Rabbi Lerner personally at rabbilerner@tikkun.org. Tax deductible contributions can be made to *Tikkun* at: 2342 Shattuck Ave, Box 1200, Berkeley, CA 94704. We only survive through the generous donations of people who want to see our perspective get more traction in the world, and we badly need and deeply appreciate that support.

2. J STREET

J Street identifies itself as "the political home of pro-Israel, pro-peace Americans." It is the most media savvy and inside-the-Beltway of the U.S.-based, pro-Middle-East-peace organizations, and it targets the political center of the Jewish community. In its own words: "The organization gives political voice to mainstream American Jews and other supporters of Israel who, informed by their Jewish values, believe that a two-state solution to the Israeli-Palestinian conflict is essential to Israel's survival as the national home of the Jewish people and as a vibrant democracy. J Street's mission is two-fold: first, to advocate for urgent American diplomatic leadership to achieve a two-state solution and a broader regional, comprehensive peace and, second, to ensure a broad debate on Israel and the Middle East in national politics and the American Jewish community."

J Street can be reached at info@jstreet.org. Its website is www.jstreet.org.

3. JEWISH VOICES FOR PEACE (JVP)

Jewish Voices for Peace is a grassroots organization that articulates a pro-peace perspective that particularly appeals to left-wing activists. In its own words, it "conducts global campaigns to defend and free Israeli and Palestinian human rights activists, fights McCarthyite censorship of debate and misuses of the charge of anti-Semitism, especially in the Jewish community, supports the growth of the Boycott, Divestment, and Sanctions movement through divestment from companies that profit from the Occupation, and works in coalition with others including Arab, Muslim, Palestinian, and Christian groups to fight bigotry and end the Occupation."

Jewish Voice for Peace can be reached at info@jewishvoice-forpeace.org. Its website is www.jewishvoiceforpeace.org.

4. Churches for Middle East Peace (CMEP)

CMEP is a coalition of 24 national church denominations in Catholic, Orthodox and Protestant traditions. In its own words: "CMEP believes that the policy perspectives and experience in the Middle East of our member churches and organizations should be better known and directly influence U.S. foreign policy. Our work is based on the understanding that sound and balanced U.S. policy is crucial to achieving and maintaining just and stable relationships in the Middle East. Besides sharing information with the various denominations, CMEP's major activity is to bring representatives of the various denominations to a yearly conference and lobbying activity in Washington, D.C."

CMEP can be reached at ellen@smep.org. Its website is www. CMEP.org.

5. Christian Peacemaker Teams (CPT)

Christian Peacemaker Teams is "a living answer to the question: 'What would Christians do if they devoted the same discipline and self-sacrifice to nonviolent peacemaking that armies devote to war?' CPT partners with nonviolent peacemaking groups around the world and sends teams of Christians to participate in nonviolent activism and to serve as witnesses in situations where violence regularly occurs." CPT's team in Hebron has often protected Palestinian children from violent assaults by Israeli settlers and challenged the indifference of the IDF to these and other assaults on Palestinians. Yet CPT also rejects teachings of hatred against Israelis.

CPT can be reached at peacemakers@cpt.org (in the United States) or at canada@cpt.org (in Canada). Its website is: www.cpt.org.

6. Holy Land Trust

When Israel expelled Palestinian teacher of nonviolence Mubarak Awad, his role was taken up by Sami Awad who established nonviolence trainings in Bethlehem in an institution called Holy Land Trust. Its programs include training Palestinian leadership in nonviolence, sponsoring encounters with the Palestinian people for Israelis and others visiting from around the world, and running a Palestinian news service called PNN Holy Land Trust. It provides an alternative, nonviolent model for how to resist the Occupation.

Holy Land Trust can be reached at palestine@holylandtrust.org. Its website is www.holylandtrust.org.

7. Rabbis for Human Rights (RHR)

Under the courageous leadership of Rabbi Arik Ascherman, RHR has championed the cause of the poor in Israel, supported the rights of Israel's minorities and Palestinians, worked to stop the abuse of foreign workers, endeavored to guarantee the upkeep of Israel's public health care system, promoted the equal status of women, helped Ethiopian Jews, battled trafficking in women, and more. It's the only rabbinic organization in Israel to include Orthodox, Conservative, Reform, Reconstructionist, and Renewal rabbis working together to support Judaism's traditional teachings on human rights, and to bring them into the real world by demonstrating against human rights violations.

RHR also takes action in Israel and Palestine to reach out to Palestinians. Whether in challenging the IDF's treatment of Bedouins, in planting olive trees in Palestine that were uprooted by Israeli settlers, protecting homes from demolition, or protecting Palestinian civilians from assault, Rabbi Ascherman and RHR in Israel play an important role in promoting the vision of religious Judaism as committed to the humanity of all peoples. In the United States, Rabbis for Human Rights provides a forum for rabbis who wish to challenge American human rights violations, including torture, using the Jewish religious tradition and texts as the jumping off point for such critiques.

Rabbis for Human Rights can be reached at info@rhr.israel. net. Its website is www.rhr.org.il.

8. PEACE NOW—SHALOM ACHSHAV

Peace Now is the Israeli peace group most able to mobilize large numbers of people for demonstrations in Tel Aviv against the Occupation. It played a very important role in the 1980s and 1990s in creating mobilizations that demonstrated popular support for peace. In the twenty-first century, it has been less successful in bringing hundreds of thousands of people to demonstrations, largely as a result of the reaction of Israelis to the Second Intifada. Peace Now's "Settlement Watch" program provides up-to-date exposure to the expansion of West Bank settlements and to settler violations of Israeli law and human rights. Its affiliate Americans for Peace Now works primarily to raise funds for the Israeli branch and to bring some Israeli speakers to Jewish communities in the United States.

Peace Now can be reached at yarivop@peacenow.org.il (in Israel) or apndc@peacenow.org (in the United States). Its website is www.peacenow.org.il.

9. Gush Shalom

The primary aim of Gush Shalom is to influence Israeli public opinion and lead it toward peace and reconciliation with the Palestinian people. Its leader Uri Avnery regularly writes analyses printed in *Tikkun* and in *Ha'aretz* and other Israeli newspapers. Gush Shalom publishes a weekly ad in *Ha'aretz* exposing the fallacies underlying Israeli militarism and racism toward Palestinians. Its perspective is very close to that expressed in this book. Although small, it plays a major role in shaping progressive, peace-oriented consciousness in Israel.

Gush Shalom can be reached at info@gush-shalom.org. Its website is www.gushshalom.org.

10. The Israeli Committee Against House Demolitions (ICAHD)

ICAHD is a nonviolent, direct-action organization established in 1997 to resist Israeli demolition of Palestinian houses—24,000 have been demolished at the time of this writing. In its own words: "As we gained knowledge of the brutalities of the Occupation, we expanded our resistance activities to other areas—land expropriation, settlement expansion, by-pass road construction, policies of 'closure' and 'separation,' the wholesale uprooting of fruit and olive trees, the Separation Barrier/Wall, the siege of Gaza....We engage in a vigorous campaign of international advocacy to end the Occupation altogether and to achieve a just peace between Israelis and Palestinians."

ICAHD can be reached at info@icahd.org. Its website is www.ichahd.org.

11. The Islamic Society of North America (ISNA)

The ISNA places great emphasis on strengthening interfaith relationships and has helped break down barriers of misunderstanding, form genuine partnerships of faith and ethics, and establish a platform to advocate social justice issues for the common good.

ISNA has made significant progress in advancing relations between Muslim and Jewish communities in particular by promoting a nationwide series of local Muslim-Jewish interfaith dialogues. These dialogues aim to promote mutual respect, understanding, and communication and to build the capacity to achieve peace and social justice on a global scale. Together the organizations created a methodology and a handbook that provides a roadmap for groups to engage with one another and explore the commonalities in their spirituality and practice. The handbook, called Children of Abraham, includes the topic of Israel/Palestine and is available for free online. ISNA is also a member of the National Interreligious Initiative for Peace in the Middle East (NILI), which advocates for a two-state solution in Israel/Palestine.

ISNA can be reached at isnaioica@gmail.com. Its website is www.isna.net/interfaith.

Recommended Reading

Dr. Izzeldin Abuyelaish, *I Shall Not Hate*
Sami Adwan, Dan Bar-on, & Eyal Naveh, *Side by Side*
Uri Avnery, *Israel's Vicious Circle: Ten Years of Writings on Israel and Palestine*
Nigel Barber, *Kindness in a Cruel World*
Omar Barghouti, *BDS: Boycott, Divestment, Sanctions: The Global Struggle for Palestinian Rights*
Zygmunt Bauman, *Modernity and the Holocaust*
Jeremy Ben Ami, *A New Voice for Israel*
Meron Benvenisti, *Sacred Landscapes*
Daniel Berrigan, *Essential Writings*
David Biale, *Power and Powerlessness in Jewish History*
Azmi Bishara, *The Arabs in Israel*
Ian J. Bickerton, *The Arab-Israeli Conflict: A History*
Daniel Boyarin, *Unheroic Conduct: The Rise of Heterosexuality and the Invention of the Jewish Man*
Michael Brenner, *A Short History of the Jews*
Lester R. Brown, *World on the Edge*
Jimmy Carter, *Our Endangered Values*
I.W. Charny, *Fascism & Democracy in the Human Mind*
Kim Chernin, *Everywhere a Guest, Nowhere at Home: A New Vision of Israel and Palestine*
Amir S. Cheshin, Bill Hutman & Avi Melamed, *Separate and Unequal: The Inside Story of Israeli Rule in East Jerusalem*
Hillel Cohen, *Good Arabs*
Rich Cohen, *Israel Is Real*
Stanley Cohen, *States of Denial: Knowing About Atrocities and Suffering*
Stephen P. Cohen, *Beyond America's Grasp: A Century of Failed Diplomacy in the Middle East*

The Dalai Lama, *Little Book of Inner Peace*
Abba Eban, *Abba Eban: An Autobiography*
Robert Eisen, *The Peace and Violence of Judaism*
Sidra Ezrahi, *Booking Passage: Exile and Homecoming in the Modern Jewish Imagination*
Samih K. Farsoun, *Palestine and the Palestinians*
Tarek Fatah, *The Jew Is Not My Enemy: Unveiling the Myths that Fuel Muslim Anti-Semitism*
Richard Forer, *Breakthrough*
Chaim Gans, *A Just Zionism*
A. Ghanem, *The Palestinian-Arab Minority in Israel 1948-2000*
Martin Gilbert, *In Ishmael's House: A History of Jews in Muslim Lands*
Daniel Gordis, *Saving Israel: How the Jewish People Can Win a War That May Never End*
Neve Gordon, *Israel's Occupation*
Ilan Gur-Ze'ev, *Destroying the Other's Collective Memory*
Yoram Hazoni, *The Jewish State: The Struggle for Israel's Soul*
Michael Henderson, *No Enemy to Conquer: Forgiveness in an Unforgiving World*
Tamar S. Hermann, *The Israeli Peace Movement: A Shattered Dream*
Abraham Joshua Heschel, *Who Is Man?*
Hanan Hever, *Producing the Modern Hebrew Canon*
Arthur Hertzberg, *The Zionist Idea*
Brad Hirschfield, *You Don't Have to Be Wrong for Me To Be Right*
Adam Horowitz, Lizzy Ratner & Philip Weiss (editors), *The Goldstone Report: The Legacy of the Landmark Investigation of the Gaza Conflict*
Jill Jacobs, *There Shall Be No Needy: Pursuing Social Justice Through Jewish Law and Tradition*
Jill Jacobs, *Where Justice Dwells: A Hands-On Guide to Doing Social Justice in Your Jewish Community*

Victor Kattan, *From Existence to Conquest*

Maxine Kaufman-Lacusta, *Refusing to be Enemies: Palestinia and Israeli Nonviolent Resistance to the Israeli Occupation*

Rahsid Khalidi, *Palestinian Identity: The Construction of Modern National Consciousness*

Baruch Kimmerling, *The Invention and Decline of Israeliness*

Baruch Kimmerling, *Politicide: Ariel Sharon's War Against the Palestinians*

Irwin Kula, *Yearnings: Embracing the Sacred Messiness of Life*

Michael Lerner, *The Socialism of Fools: Anti-Semitism on the Left*

Michael Lerner, *Jewish Renewal*

Michael Lerner, *Spirit Matters: Global Healing and the Wisdom of the Soul*

Michael Lerner, *The Left Hand of God*

Mark LeVine, *Overthrowing Geography: Jaffa, Tel Aviv, and the Struggle for Palestine, 1880-1948*

Mark LeVine, *Impossible Peace: Israel/Palestine Since 1989*

Arno J. Mayer, *Plowshares into Swords: From Zionism to Israel*

Benny Morris, *The Birth of the Palestinian Refugee Problem, 1947-1949*

Alfred A. Knopf, *Righteous Victims*

Efraim Nimmi (editor), *The Challenge of Post-Zionism: Alternatives to Israeli Fundamentalist Politics*

Sari Nusseibeh, *What Is a Palestinian State Worth?*

Am Oved, *Immigrants, Settlers, Natives: The Israeli State and Society Between Cultural Pluralism and Cultural Wars*

Ilan Pappé, *The Forgotten Palestinians: A History of Palestinians in Israel*

Ami Pedahzur & Arie Perliger, *Jewish Terrorism in Israel*

Uri Ram, *Israeli Society: Critical Perspectives* (in Hebrew)

Michael Riordon, *Our Way to Fight: Israeli and Palestinian Activists for Peace*

Eugene Rogan, *The Arabs: A History*

Eugene L. Rogan and Avi Shlaim (editors), *The War for Palestine*

Sara Roy, *Hamas and Civil Society: Engaging the Islamist Social Sector*

Jonathan Sacks, *To Heal a Fractured World: The Ethics of Responsibility*

Edward Said, *Culture and Imperialism*

Shlomo Sand, *The Invention of the Jewish People*

Gershon Shafir, *Land, Labor and the Origins of the Israel-Palestinian Conflict 1882-1914*

Avi Shlaim, *The Politics of Partition*

Avi Shlaim, *The Iron Wall: Israel and the Arab World*

Donald Shriver, *An Ethic for Enemies*

Lawrence Silberstein (editor), *Postzionism: A Reader*

Zeev Sternhell, *The Founding Myths of Israel: Nationalism, Socialism and the Making of the Jewish State*

Gadi Taub, *The Settlers and the Struggle over the Meaning of Zionism*

Michael Walzer, Menachem Lorberbaum, Noam J. Zohar (editors), *The Jewish Political Tradition*

Idith Zertal & Akiva Eldar, *Lords of the Land: The War for Israel's Settlements in the Occupied Territories, 1967-2007*

Yael Zerubavel, *Recovered Roots: Collective Memory and the Making of Israeli National Tradition*

Steven J. Zipperstein, *Elusive Prophet: Ahad Ha'am and the Origins of Zionism*

Index